Learning to Change

Learning to Change

Teaching Beyond Subjects and Standards

Andy Hargreaves

Lorna Earl

Shawn Moore

Susan Manning

 JOSSEY-BASS
A Wiley Company
San Francisco

Jossey-Bass books and products are available through most bookstores. To contact Jossey-Bass directly, call (888) 378-2537, fax to (800) 605-2665, or visit our website at www.josseybass.com.

Substantial discounts on bulk quantities of Jossey-Bass books are available to corporations, professional associations, and other organizations. For details and discount information, contact the special sales department at Jossey-Bass.

TCF Manufactured in the United States of America on Lyons Falls Turin Book. This paper is acid-free and 100 percent totally chlorine-free.

Library of Congress Cataloging-in-Publication Data

Learning to change : teaching beyond subjects and standards / Andy Hargreaves . . . [et al.]. — 1st ed.
        p. cm. — (The Jossey-Bass education series)
Includes bibliographical references and index.
    ISBN 0-7879-5027-0 (alk. paper)
    1. School improvement programs—Ontario—Case studies.   2. Curriculum change—Ontario—Case studies.   3. Middle school teaching—Ontario—Case studies.   I. Hargreaves, Andy.   II. Series.
    LB2822.84.C2 L42 2001
    373.19'09713—dc21   00-011524

FIRST EDITION
HB Printing   10 9 8 7 6 5 4 3 2 1

The Jossey-Bass Education Series

Contents

Preface

This book looks through teachers' eyes at what we call the new orthodoxy of educational reform and at how well it meets the complex and diverse learning needs of adolescents today. The book scrutinizes this new orthodoxy and draws on original research to get behind, go beside, and move beyond it in an effort to understand what powerful teaching and learning look like as cognitively deep, emotionally engaged, and socially rich practices. It steps into the world of exemplary teachers who work with young adolescents to see how they engage with the new educational orthodoxy; interpret, adapt, and move beyond it to make it come alive for their students; and question, challenge, and struggle with the more disturbing and impractical parts of the orthodoxy. This book also reveals how bringing this new and complex world of teaching and learning into being requires enormous dedication, demands hard intellectual work, draws deeply on reserves of emotional energy, and consumes immense amounts of time among even the very best teachers.

For the past ten years, we have each been involved in many studies of educational change, as teachers everywhere have been bombarded with demands and plans to "fix" education (Fullan & Hargreaves, 1992, 1996; Earl & LeMahieu, 1997; Hargreaves & Fullan, 1998; Hargreaves, 1997b; Hargreaves & Evans, 1997; Hargreaves, Lieberman, Fullan, & Hopkins, 1998; Bascia & Hargreaves, 2000). We have spent hundreds of engrossing hours in classrooms and staff rooms, in formal interviews and casual conversations, talking with and listening to teachers of all kinds as they engage with educational change. In the opening years of a new century, the changes seem like no others in their substance or their scope.

A new orthodoxy of schooling appears to be emerging in many parts of the world, especially in the predominantly Anglophone nations. In this orthodoxy, learning is based on prescribed standards (especially in literacy, numeracy, and science) that almost all students are expected to achieve. These standards are linked to centralized textbooks and redesigned assessments and are enforced through systems of accountability and monitoring that reward successful schools and provide support or threaten closure to those that persistently fall short.

Alongside this movement of standards-based reform is growing concern worldwide about the apparent disengagement of many young adolescents from their schooling and about the risks they increasingly encounter in their lives: drugs, family abuse or neglect, bullying, violence, suicide, alienation, consumerism, and loss of purpose and direction. The approaches that educators have devised to meet the needs of young adolescents today are sometimes in tune with the modern standards movement—in raising expectations for learning or putting consistent emphasis on getting all students to succeed. Sometimes, however, they appear to be at odds with subject-based standards—for instance, focusing on curriculum integration as a way of making learning more relevant to the different and diverse lives that young people now lead. Standards-based reform therefore appears to have an ambivalent relationship to the kinds of schooling and teaching that work best for young adolescents, especially those who are most at risk.

Over the years, much of our writing and research keeps returning to this particular group: the ones in the middle—both young adolescents and their teachers. Our own collaborative research began with this group, and we have since observed and studied them through several waves of reform as governments have changed and policies have shifted. Indeed, we are continuing to follow the paths of transition and reform in the classes of these students and their teachers (Hargreaves, 1986; Hargreaves, Leithwood, Gérin-Lajoie, Cousins, & Thiessen, 1993; Hargreaves, Earl, & Ryan, 1996; Earl & LeMahieu, 1997; Earl & Lee, 1998; Earl & Katz, 2000).

Teachers of young adolescents do demanding, difficult, and educationally vital work. Their work and experience also open a window into the larger system. Like other teachers, especially their colleagues in the secondary years, they must respond with urgency to the new orthodoxy of standards-based reform. At the same time, dealing with the demanding learning needs, complex social worlds, and socially toxic environments (Garbarino, 1995) of young adolescents calls for great flexibility in the curriculum so that it engages young adolescents, has meaning for them, connects with their lives, and is grounded in relationships between teachers and students in which each knows the other well. This can create problems for the standards monolith:

- Whereas standards push the curriculum toward detailed central prescription, the needs of today's diverse adolescents call for the flexibility of broader guiding frameworks.
- Whereas standards tend to emphasize common, subject-specialist knowledge, the needs of young adolescents push teachers toward a more contextualized, integrated curriculum that engages learning with young people's lives.
- Whereas standards tend to be externally imposed on teachers and students, the varying and pressing needs of young adolescents push the best teachers toward involving students in defining, interpreting, and being more involved in setting and reaching high standards of learning themselves.

This book therefore addresses some of the key issues at stake in the new orthodoxy of standards-based reform through the eyes and experiences of some of the best teachers of adolescents. In doing so, it also gets behind, moves beside, and pushes beyond the standards orthodoxy.

The study that forms the basis for this book began as a snapshot of how teachers in the middle years of grades 7 and 8 were understanding, implementing, and coping with a new curriculum policy that embraced many of the principles of standards-based reform. Yet this curriculum approached standards more openly and broadly (as outcomes) than many other current versions, so as to allow and encourage greater responsiveness among teachers to the needs of adolescents. Our conversations with these teachers have extended beyond the first two years of the project, which we report in this book. We have now been following their experiences of and responses to successive waves of reform for more than five years. We thank these teachers enormously for allowing us to glimpse their world, its frustrations and successes, and to try and represent it to a wider audience.

Organization of the Book

The book is organized into eight chapters. Chapter One, the Introduction, sets out the framework and the central arguments for the chapters that follow. It also describes the study of twenty-nine teachers on which this book is based.

Part One comprises three chapters framed by the major reform initiatives being faced by the teachers in this study, as by many of their colleagues elsewhere. Chapter Two focuses on standards and outcomes, Chapter Three investigates new developments in classroom assessment, and Chapter Four describes the teachers' experiences with curriculum integration. In each case we offer a conceptual lens for investigating the reform and show how the teachers in this study were coming to understand it, interpret it, and integrate it into their practice.

The four chapters that make up Part Two describe what it takes to achieve deep and abiding changes in schools. Chapters Five and Six respectively address the intellectual and emotional work that teachers have to do when they are engaged in change efforts. In Chapter Seven we explore the kinds of conditions that support and sustain teachers in the midst of change. Finally, in Chapter Eight we summarize what we learned about how these dedicated teachers have gone about learning to change, and we offer suggestions for others based on what we have learned.

Acknowledgments

Embarking on a study that includes interviews and observations and that takes place in sixteen schools in four school districts is taxing at the best of times. We could not have done it without the research officers and graduate students with whom we work at the International Centre for Educational Change at the Ontario Institute for Studies in Education, University of Toronto. Shawn Moore and Susan Manning have made the most extensive written contributions to this book, and we are accordingly pleased to include their names as authors. Michele Schmidt, Steven Katz, Clay Lafleur, Rouleen Wignall, and Debra Wilson conducted many interviews and analyzed the data along with us, in meeting after meeting. Leo

Santos, as always, is the magician who turned our bad keyboard skills and chicken scratching into something legible, even elegant.

Our partners, Pauline Hargreaves and Bob Thede, have continued to provide immense intellectual and emotional support to us as we have each closeted ourselves away week upon week, month upon month, to pull together the manuscript for this book. As ever, we are enormously grateful for their love and patience.

Toronto, Ontario, Canada   ANDY HARGREAVES
November 2000   LORNA EARL

The Authors

ANDY HARGREAVES is professor of education in the Department of Theory and Policy Studies and codirector of the International Centre for Educational Change at the Ontario Institute for Studies in Education of the University of Toronto. He is editor in chief of the *Journal of Educational Change* and the author and editor of many books in the field of educational change, including *Schooling for Change,* with Lorna Earl and James Ryan (1996); *Changing Teachers, Changing Times* (1994); *The Sharp Edge of Educational Change,* edited with Nina Bascia (2000); and *What's Worth Fighting for Out There?* with Michael Fullan (1998).

LORNA EARL is associate professor in the Department of Theory and Policy Studies and codirector of the International Centre for Educational Change at the Ontario Institute for Studies in Education of the University of Toronto. Her research focuses on large-scale educational reform, with particular attention to the role that assessment plays in school improvement. As an applied researcher and evaluator, her primary interest is the wise application of research, assessment, and evaluation knowledge to the realities of schools and classrooms. Recent publications include *Schooling for Change,* with Andy Hargreaves and James Ryan (1997); *Assessment and Accountability in Education: Improvement or Surveillance* (1999); *Developing Indicators: The Call for Accountability* (1999); *Education for the Middle Years: The Paradox of Hope* (1999); and *The Evaluation of the Manitoba School Improvement Program* (1998).

SHAWN MOORE is a senior research officer at the Ontario Institute for Studies in Education of the University of Toronto. He works in the International Centre for Educational Change. Currently he is involved in two longitudinal research projects that examine how teachers frame their practice and relationships, the impact of secondary school reform on teachers' lives, the relationship of school improvement to mandated educational reforms, and the processes of change over time through teachers' eyes in different secondary school contexts.

SUSAN MANNING is a project manager in student and community services with the Toronto District School Board. She was formerly research manager with the Scarborough Board of Education. Her areas of interest include organizational behavior and development and school effectiveness and improvement initiatives.

Chapter One

Introduction
The New Educational Orthodoxy

A new, official orthodoxy of educational reform is rapidly being established in many parts of the world. This is occurring primarily in predominantly Anglo-Saxon countries, but through international funding organizations such as the World Bank and the global distribution of policy strategies, elements of the orthodoxy are increasingly being exported to many parts of the less-developed world as well. The new orthodoxy has the following major components:

- *High standards of learning,* which all students (excluding only those with the most severe mental dysfunctions) are expected to achieve (Tucker & Codding, 1998, 1999)
- *Deeper learning,* which moves beyond mere memorization of content to emphasize conceptual understanding, problem solving, and knowledge application, which are essential for successful participation in the new knowledge economy or knowledge society (Schlechty, 1990)
- *Centralized curriculum,* which eliminates the chaos of high school course options and ensures a common and consistent commitment to and coverage of what students should know and be able to do and which attains the high standards that are necessary in today's society
- *Literacy and numeracy,* and to a lesser extent science, which are prime targets for reform and for attaining significantly higher learning standards (Hill & Crévola, 1999)

- *Indicators and rubrics* of student achievement and curriculum planning, which enable teachers and others to be clear when standards have been achieved (or not)
- *Aligned assessments,* which are tightly linked to the prescribed curriculum, learning standards, and indicators, ensuring that teachers keep their eyes on the prize of high learning standards for all
- *Consequential accountability,* where overall school performance in terms of standard raising is closely tied to processes of accreditation, inspection, and the relationship of funding to levels of success (and failure)

This new orthodoxy consists of some fundamental and commendable shifts in educational thinking about the most specific details of classroom learning and the broadest design features of educational administration. It emphasizes high standards for almost all students, not just a few, and it drives teachers and their schools to combine excellence with equity throughout their work with students from many different backgrounds. It moves the priority in the curriculum from the convenience and conventions of what teachers teach to the quality and character of what students are expected to learn. It addresses the kinds of applied and problem-based learning that are more appropriate to an electronic, informational society than a mechanical, industrial one. By making many assessments more performance based than pencil and paper based, it tries to ensure that assessment is used as a tail to wag the new curriculum dog. Last, but not least, a national or statewide curriculum tries to ensure that irrespective of the school, its locality, its teachers, or its leadership, all students will be pushed to meet the same high standards. No one will be allowed to fall through the cracks.

In principle, these educational developments promise significant progress in educational reform in terms of improving quality and standards of learning and opportunity for all kinds of students. However, the new educational orthodoxy also misses some important dimensions of learning and teaching, and it carries within its reform package some disturbing components that threaten to undermine its more positive educational goals.

Questioning the Orthodoxy: The Karaoke Curriculum

It is hard to question the concerted push for higher standards. Who could possibly be opposed to standards-based reform? To pronounce against standards seems tantamount to being in favor of sin. Yet there are differences between supporting the *principle* of high and inclusive educational standards and the particular *programs* of reform in which those principles are often embedded.

In reality, the new orthodoxy of educational reform represents what we call a "karaoke curriculum." The literal meaning of the Japanese word *karaoke* is "empty box." This is precisely what the new curriculum orthodoxy is—an empty box. Behind the broad advocacy for high standards, deeper learning, and more rigorous assessment, all kinds of meanings and interpretations are possible. The devil, as they say, is in the details, and the details of the particular approaches being taken to standards-based reform in many places are indeed devilish.

The Hurried Curriculum

In his writing on the postmodern family, David Elkind (1989, 1997) has described children in contemporary society as being increasingly pushed to do more and more things earlier and faster: to engage in dating earlier; to be sexually aware earlier; to learn many things sooner; to sign on to more and more organized clubs, teams, and activities; and generally to experience a hurried, accelerated, overscheduled childhood. Moving curriculum content to earlier and earlier grades, he argues, is part of this problem and robs young people of important aspects of their childhood: to engage in innocent wonder, to play alone and with others in unstructured environments, to pursue learning that follows their own interests and curiosity, and so forth.

Writing in England after more than a decade of standards-based reform, Dadds (forthcoming) criticizes what she calls "the hurry-along curriculum," in which coverage becomes more important than learning. This curriculum, she argues, leads teachers to push children through material without developing their understanding, it contracts the vital period of "wait-time" that good teachers allow children before they answer teachers' questions (Gutierrez, 2000), it eliminates any space for the student's voice in the learning process (Rudduck, Day, & Wallace, 1997), and it inhibits the development of the very lifelong learning skills that standards-based reform is supposed to promote.

The Clinical Curriculum

The common, standards-based curriculum is often, in practice, a clinical and conventional curriculum in which literacy, numeracy, and science are accorded supreme importance. Indeed, in key texts in the area, Tucker and Codding (1998, 1999) argue that these should be the fundamental areas of standards setting. The arts and social sciences, they say, should become areas to which students' fundamental learnings are then applied. This, of course, arbitrarily designates science skills as fundamental and arts skills as "applied," when the converse—in terms of artistic skills of invention and creativity, perhaps—is equally plausible. Hill and Crévola (1999) similarly argue for primacy to be given to literacy in the primary and elementary curriculum and advocate for other "clutter" (such as arts) to be removed from or reduced in the curriculum to make space for it.

In England and Wales, this familiar refrain preceded the introduction of its National Curriculum in 1988. In an earlier book, we documented how much of the derided "clutter" that made way for the staple diet of National Curriculum subjects was emotional, social, or critical in nature, such as political education, peace studies, personal and social education, and the arts—the very stuff of democratic schooling that develops critical and expressive minds (Hargreaves, Earl, & Ryan, 1996). Peculiarly, and perplexingly, the foundation subjects of this new National Curriculum were almost an exact replica of the secondary school curriculum first designated by law in 1907, when the policy intention had been to define a university-qualifying curriculum that excluded technical subjects that were more amenable and relevant to working-class students (Goodson, 1988).

In the United States, specification of the new learning standards has fallen very much under the purview of the national subject associations, reviving and perpetuating their influence over the school curriculum and what counts as knowledge within it. Crowded content and a brisk pace of movement through the various standards leave little space or incentive for teachers to connect learning to students' interests (Rudduck, 1991), to contextualize it and give it relevance in relation to their diverse lives (Tharp, Dalton, & Yamauchi, 1994), or to create programs of integrated and interdisciplinary study that make such deep contextualization possible. Yet Tucker and Codding (1999) dismiss the "interdisciplinary" curriculum in just one passing set of sneering quotation marks. Moreover, the overwhelmingly cognitive and clinical focus of most sets of learning standards pushes concerns for emotional learning and personal development to the periphery of teachers' classroom concerns. Yet it is precisely these kinds of curriculum experiences that are emotionally engaging for students and contextualized in their lives and are especially valuable for improving learning among minority and disadvantaged students. These students' experiences of learning and of life in their families, cultures, and communities are definitely nonstandard in nature (Cummins, 1998; Nieto, 1998). The powerful progress that can be made by basing a science curriculum for children of Mexican immigrant farmworkers around their own cultural knowledge base of agriculture, for example, finds no space within an overly standardized curriculum (Stoddart, 1999). Excessively standardized curricula connect poorly with culturally diverse societies. They do not recognize that especially in these contexts, learning is a social practice, not just an intellectual one (Lave & Wenger, 1991).

In general, high-fat rather than "light" standards frameworks place too much emphasis on what Sergiovanni (2000), after Habermas (1972), calls the *systemsworld* of knowledge, cognition, technical skills, and systems. By comparison, not enough importance is accorded to the *lifeworld* of morals, values, emotional learning, and social experience. In today's complex informational society, we will be poorer democracies and weaker economies if we cannot educate students for the artistic, critical, and social-scientific lifeworld as much as for the literate, numerate, and natural-scientific systemsworld.

Standardization and Deprofessionalization

However well founded new sets of learning standards might be, teachers become dispirited and lose their effectiveness if they feel they have no voice in the development of the standards and if standards are prescribed so tightly that they leave no real scope for teacher discretion in how they are implemented and interpreted in their own classes. So far, however, the growing evidence suggests a yawning chasm between the confidence and even grandiosity with which policymakers prescribe their master plans of standards and the confusion and disillusionment among classroom teachers who have to implement them.

In England, Marion Dadds (forthcoming) retells one teacher's perception of herself as nothing but a worker bee after teaching for more than a decade within an overly standardized system:

> They tell us to go and be busy over there, so we all swarm over there and get busy. Then they change their minds and say, "No, over there!" So we all swarm over there and get busy again in a different way. And then it's "over here," then over somewhere else. And we all keep on swarming as they point fingers in new directions. Every few years, they come to watch you to see if you're swarming properly.

In England and Wales, more than a decade of detailed curriculum prescription has left many teachers feeling deprofessionalized (Nias, 1991), less confident (Helsby, 1999), cynically compliant (Woods, Jeffrey, Troman, & Boyle, 1997), and increasingly stressed (Troman & Woods, 2000)—to the point that there is now a severe crisis of recruitment into teaching (Dean, June 30, 2000) and that sons and daughters of teachers express little interest in joining the profession (Hargreaves & Evans, 1997).

Similar teacher recruitment crises also afflict the United States, especially in urban areas (Darling-Hammond, 1997). A public (and classroom) image of teaching as highly stressed, overloaded, and increasingly subject to external regulation and control does nothing to help. Writing in a book about standards, Los Angeles teacher Myranda Marsh (1999, p. 192) fires a warning shot across the bows of her more strident academic and policymaking peers when she observes that "if reform of any kind is to succeed, teachers must believe that they will have a meaningful voice in decisions and will not become the lone scapegoats of a failure to reach goals."

Teachers, Marsh notes, resent being labeled as "resisters" simply because they adopt realistically cautious attitudes to reform. "Resistance to standards," she says, "is not rooted in a desire to avoid accountability but rather in a fear of being out of the discussion of what constitutes success" (pp. 194). As a complement to standards, Marsh and others (Lieberman & McLaughlin, 2000) propose placing a focus on processes of teacher inquiry (especially around the meaning of performance data) and on building professional communities of practice where teachers experience the time, encouragement, and standards-based urgency of working on standards and reform together. This is an appealing combination. However, in order to link learning standards to such professional standards of collegiality and inquiry in teaching, the learning standards themselves need to leave sufficient scope for professional judgment and involvement. Moreover, sufficient levels of support and funding for teacher inquiry and collegial discussion to take place in school time are crucial. Although there are promising results in special initiatives and pilot programs that combine standards-based reform with processes of teacher inquiry, there are few signs that regular, across-the-board levels of support for such forms of improved professionalism in teaching are imminently forthcoming elsewhere.

Contradictory Contexts

Standards-based reform has not been and is not being implemented in contexts that are neutral. For one thing, levels of taxation support for public education, like public welfare and other areas of public life, remain pitifully low in many nations (Hargreaves, 2000). In his brilliant trilogy on the network society, Castells (1996, 1997, 1998) produced data to show that the state of California spends more on its prisons than its schools. The public schools in some urban areas like those in Los Angeles have been almost totally evacuated by the white population. When one of us worked with a large group of Los Angeles urban principals recently, two-thirds of them stated that on the basis of their experience of overregulation and poor support, they would not become a principal if given the choice again.

The increasingly widespread contexts for standards-based reform are, in practice, ones of decreased resources and support for public education along with the development of quasi-market systems of school-by-school competition for students or resources, or both (Whitty, Power, & Halpin, 1998). In New Zealand, for example, the evidence is that years of such reforms have not narrowed the learning gap between advantaged and disadvantaged students (Wylie, 1997). In Australia, broad-based systems of support for disadvantaged schools, including assistance for schools to work with families and with students who have multiple problems, have been replaced by reform measures specifically targeted at improving literacy—as if instructional standards are unaffected by these far-reaching contextual factors (Thomson, 1999).

Meanwhile, Kentucky's much-vaunted standards-based reforms were, after a period of early success, soon stifled by excessive central control, diverted by the competing imperatives of standardized testing, and quashed by shifts of political control and focus (Whitford, 2000).

In England, the *Times Educational Supplement* regularly reports increasing rates of exclusion and suspension from school (disproportionately of working-class and cultural minority students) as schools struggle to keep their performance records rising. Moreover, increased adolescent alienation from the early years of a content-driven secondary system with its hurried curriculum is widely reported across the quasi-market systems of the Anglophone nations (Cumming, 1996). In our current projects, we are starting to see emerging evidence of this in the context of imposed standards-based reforms in Ontario, Canada, alongside reduced resources, poorer professional development support, and less time for teachers to work with colleagues or meet with students outside their classes.

Summary

The questions that need to be raised about standards-based reform are not so much ones concerning its basic and often admirable principles: to focus on learning that benefits all students and link this to clear indicators of progress in assessment and accountability systems. The questions, rather, concern the number and range of the standards; how slanted or not they are toward utilitarian subject areas; whether they arbitrarily privilege some kinds of learning over others; and whether, as a result of all these influences, standards enhance or inhibit the prospects for deep, engaging learning among poor, disadvantaged, and minority students in particular. Standards-based reform also needs to be questioned when it is associated with lowered resources and levels of support for public education, quasi-market systems of policy that provide no evidence of narrowing the learning gap, and deprofessionalizing processes of implementation that undermine the most powerful resources we have in schools: their teachers.

Beyond Standards

How is it possible to meet the ambitions of standards-based reform without getting bogged down in its frequent, practical problems of overstandardization, underresourcing, deprofessionalization, and curricular narrowness? How can we move beyond the difficulties and drawbacks of standards programs to embrace and realize the virtues of the best standards principles?

To explore these questions and move beyond standards as they are often currently interpreted, we can learn a lot from examining reform efforts that in many places immediately preceded the "standards stampede" (Sergiovanni, 2000), that still persist as the major educational change initiatives elsewhere, and to which a number of nations, such as England and Australia, appear to be returning after years of standards fatigue. These alternative reform efforts define and interpret standards more broadly as outcomes; they include and value a wider range of the curriculum; they support curriculum integration and not just subject specialization; and they leave greater scope for teachers to exercise professional judgment and discretion. To return to this moment before standards were narrowed, tightened, made more specific and prolific, and imposed more forcefully is to recapture the principles of standards at a time and in a place where teachers were able to commit to them, make sense of them, and bring them to fruition themselves. By examining this crucial moment, we hope to rekindle debates not only about what was worth fighting for in education before subject-specific standards, but also about what continues to be worth fighting for besides and beyond those standards.

The time and place we use for our inquiry is Ontario, Canada, in the mid-1990s. Before the election of an ultraconservative government, wide-ranging educational reform efforts in grades 7 through 9 emphasized basing the curriculum around broadly defined common learning outcomes, encouraging moves toward greater curriculum integration, implementing mandatory detracking (destreaming), and developing a related set of performance-based assessments (Ontario Ministry of Education and Training, 1995). All of these measures were designed to create a high-quality and inclusive educational system that would retain and engage young adolescents of all backgrounds in the educational process.

Ontario's curriculum policy comprised three closely interrelated components:

• *Outcomes*. The curriculum policy specified ten very broad "Essential Outcomes," organized into four broad program areas: the arts; language; mathematics, science, and technology; and self and society. Within each of these areas, outcomes were specified as knowledge, skills, and values that students were expected to have developed at the end of grades 3, 6, and 9. There were no prescriptive guidelines for teaching and learning or curriculum delivery and no required resources. Teachers were expected to review the outcomes and plan learning activities that would enable students to achieve the outcomes.

• *Integrated curriculum*. The curriculum policy promoted integrated learning through grouping subjects into four broad program areas and explicitly encouraging teachers to make connections using four approaches to curriculum integration: parallel content across subjects, content connections across similar subjects, concept connections across several subjects, and full-scale cross-curricular connections. It mapped out the broad possibilities for integration yet provided little specific direction or incentive for teachers to overcome their reticence about integration.

• *Assessment*. The assessment role of teachers was reinforced in the curriculum. They were expected to assess progress toward the outcomes by developing curriculum, planning rubrics, identifying indicators of reaching the outcomes, developing appropriate modifications for individual students, assessing both the process and product of learning, encouraging self-assessment, and using frequent and varied assessments. In addition, teachers were responsible for communicating the assessment changes to the parents of their students.

At the time of the study, schools in Ontario had historically experienced high status, and there had traditionally been a high commitment to public education from governments, taxpayers, and parents alike. For years, teachers had been well educated and well paid. The public seemed happy with the education their children received (Livingstone, Hart, & Davie, 1998). Curriculum policy was formulated centrally by the Ministry of Education, with widespread input from educators around the province. These general guidelines were sent to schools and districts for implementation. Large school districts then wrote "second-generation" documents that translated the policy into more specific guidelines designed to suit the local district. Teachers had varying levels of support and training, depending on the resources that were available in their district for in-service training or consulting support. Assessment was exclusively in the purview of the classroom teacher. There was no province-wide program of assessment beyond sample assessments designed for curriculum review.

The Study

Our study focuses on twenty-nine teachers who were teaching in grades 7 and 8 within the context of this curriculum reform. The teachers were selected from four large school districts (over fifty thousand students each) with the assistance of the Learning Consortium, a partnership for teacher development established between the Ontario Institute for Studies in Education at the University of Toronto and the four districts. Each of these districts is urban, and two of them are extremely multicultural in their student populations. The purpose of our study was to examine the understandings that teachers developed of the changes embedded in the new curriculum policy; to determine how and to what extent teachers were able to integrate the changes into their practice;

to identify what conditions, supports, and processes were necessary for them to do so; and to understand their experiences of the changes involved.

The teachers in our sample had been identified by administrators in their districts as actively engaged in efforts to incorporate the curricular changes into their practices. Two teachers in each of the schools in each of the districts were asked to allow us to visit their classrooms and interview them about their experiences as they attempted to respond to the curriculum mandates. All but three agreed to participate in the study.

The teachers were interviewed for one to two hours about their personal understanding of existing policies on curriculum integration, common learning outcomes, and assessment reform; where they had acquired this understanding; how they integrated the changes into their practices; what these practices looked like; what successes and difficulties they had encountered during their process of implementation; what professional development they had been offered or had sought out to support that implementation; and how well they felt their colleagues and their principal supported their efforts at change. More generally, we asked the teachers about their longer-term record of investment in change and about the relationship between their professional commitments and their wider life commitments and obligations. Three of the teachers allowed us to observe in their classrooms and participated in several additional interviews to give us deeper insights into their work and their experiences of educational change.

Our sample is not, of course, representative of all seventh- and eighth-grade teachers. The teachers in the study were identified precisely because they were seen to have serious and sustained commitments to implementing transition-years changes. As such, the study offers significant insights into the experiences of highly committed teachers. However, if change creates difficulties for these teachers or for the relationships that are at the heart of their work, it is likely that these difficulties will be even greater for teachers who are less open to or enthusiastic about the changes described here or indeed about educational change in general.

Our purpose, then, is to understand how change-oriented teachers make sense of required, complex educational changes, how they bring them to life or make them real in their classes, what helps or hinders them, and what the process of change requires and demands of them.

Although reformers typically act as if change is simple for teachers—a matter of ingesting and complying with new requirements—the change situations that teachers face are highly complex. The teachers we studied were not just trying to implement single innovations, one at a time. They were facing multiple and multifaceted changes to their practice in curriculum integration, common learning outcomes, and alternative systems of assessment and reporting. Moreover, this set of changes could not be addressed in isolation from all the other aspects of their work in their schools. Some of the schools were also involved in developing cooperative learning strategies. Most were starting to come to grips with using computers and other new technologies. Building relationships with parents and establishing mandated parent councils was a parallel priority. Several of the schools' principals had just changed or were about to do so, leading to shifts in the style of leadership and in the focus for change efforts in these schools. In a deepening crisis of economic retrenchment, resources were rapidly dwindling (and continue to do so at the time of writing). There was talk, and sometimes more than talk, of class sizes increasing, courses being cut, and teachers being transferred or losing their jobs. The support of district consultants to assist teachers with change was disappearing, and professional development days had been reduced.

Through the eyes and the experience of teachers, we create and recreate a picture of how some of our best teachers make sense of and often struggle with the hard intellectual and emotional work of undertaking complex sets of educational reforms such as the ones described in this book. We portray what the emerging orthodoxy of educational change—based on what is to be learned, not what is to be taught—looks like in the finely grained texture of their classrooms. We draw on these teachers' experiences to go behind, beside, and beyond standards and examine what the new orthodoxy of educational change looks like when it includes and supports teachers and is not simply foisted on them. We show how teachers struggle to connect curriculum and assessment reforms to the diverse lives of their students, develop high-quality integrated programs that engage with the lives and learning of all their students, and search for ways to involve students and parents more fully in the learning and assessment process.

We show how, with proper support and sufficient discretion, teachers can take great strides in making the karaoke curriculum, or new orthodoxy of educational change, work for their students—making classroom learning come alive for them. We also show where clearer definitions of outcomes of the kind incorporated into subsequent standards efforts are sorely needed, where the numbers of outcomes (like present numbers of standards) can proliferate to excess, where support can be inadequate, and where the pace of change can run too fast, even for the best teachers.

Our book, in this sense, gets inside the complexities of educational change today, as teachers experience it within the new educational orthodoxy. It will take us inside, behind, and beyond standards. Acknowledging what complex educational reform means to teachers and really asks of them is neither a cynical quest nor a celebratory one. Our findings are far from being a catalogue of tragedies—of waning enthusiasm, fading hopes, or good intentions gone awry. Nor do they portray our teachers as incurable optimists who are totally unfazed by problems or setbacks that come their way. But they do open a window into the realities and not just the rhetoric of the new educational change orthodoxy at the beginning of the century. They make the karaoke curriculum sing!

Part One

The Substance of Change

Chapter Two

Standards and Outcomes

Defining student learning standards, outcomes, or targets has become a major feature of educational policy initiatives in many countries as a way to focus on what students should learn, not what content teachers should teach (Spady, 1994; King & Evans, 1991; Grundy & Bonser, 1997). The standards and outcomes agenda shifts the focus of teaching away from objectives for teaching to desired changes in students' learning (King & Evans, 1991). This orientation to education has been growing over the past half-century. In the 1980s and early 1990s, outcomes-based education became a popular movement in many places. From the late 1990s, standards-based reform has supplanted its outcomes-driven predecessor.

In a curriculum defined by standards or outcomes, high expectations (or ends) are set for all students, with time and teaching methods being variable, left to teachers' discretion (Spady & Marshall, 1991). An outcomes- or standards-based approach defines the curriculum in terms of what students demonstrate successfully at the end of their schooling, not just the end of the week or year (Spady, 1994). The more broadly defined outcomes-driven curriculum establishes the ends of education, but leaves methods (and often considerable choices over content) in the hands of teachers themselves. Its standard-based successor is typically more specific than this in its content prescriptions and performance demands.

The outcomes curriculum emerged and flourished in the United States in the early 1990s (Spady, 1994) but could also be found in places such as Australia (Grundy & Bonser, 1997; Brady, 1996) and Canada (Hargreaves & Moore, 2000). From the beginning, it was fraught with controversy. Its tendency to define desired student learning in rather broad terms and ways that often challenged traditional subject-based categories of curriculum content led to challenges from a number of groups, including the religious right (Zlatos, 1993).

Outcomes that challenge conventional subject categories and contents are perplexing to the public, a challenge to many teachers' existing assumptions (Pliska & McQuaide, 1994), and politically controversial. When they require the extensive involvement of teachers working together to interpret and implement them in their own schools and classrooms, they are also costly in terms of investment in professional development and scheduled time for teachers to plan and meet together.

Common learning outcomes, as they have often been defined, challenge deep-seated traditions of secondary school subject specialization that privilege narrow forms of knowledge and intelligence at which only socially advantaged students with the requisite cultural capital are most likely to succeed (D. Hargreaves, 1982; Hargreaves, Earl, & Ryan, 1996). They possess great potential to disestablish the academic, subject-based curriculum of secondary schooling, which continues to be one of the greatest sources of educational and social inequality. Not surprisingly, therefore, outcomes-based education has frequently been attacked and dismantled by political and religious conservatives. In our own province of Ontario in Canada, for example, the Conservative government abolished equity-oriented common learning outcomes (along with the integrated curriculum and detracking) that we describe in this chapter and replaced it with a standards-based, subject-bound curriculum that is centrally prescribed, closely linked to province-wide testing, and associated with parallel measures that reduce time and external support for teachers to improve their work in the classroom (Hargreaves, 1998c). In the United States, the outcomes-based education movement has been successfully swept away by the fundamentalist religious right as the devil incarnate because of its challenge to creationist and patriarchal values (Zlatos, 1993)—its replacement being a more precise and detailed list of standards in conventional content areas. In England and Wales, where there were strong grassroots movements in the mid-1980s to define the curriculum through broad areas of experience, defined in cross-curricular terms, the

Conservative government responded not with an outcomes-based approach but with detailed targets and standards defined in exclusively subject-based terms (Hargreaves, 1989).

Increasingly, there is a tendency to replace the discourse and practice of broad learning outcomes with specific standards or targets as the driving force of educational reform (Tucker & Codding, 1998; Hill & Crévola, 1999). Outcomes and standards are alike in the priority they assign to making desired student learnings the basis for curriculum planning, in getting more and more students to achieve these desired learnings, and in ensuring that learning standards, curriculum programs, assessment formats, and teaching decisions become more tightly aligned and consistent over time.

Outcomes and standards tend to differ in three ways. First are the *kinds of ends* that are desired in terms of student learning. Standards tend to embody more specific, content-based ends, in traditional academic disciplines rather than the broader, cross-curricular, and often more socially and intellectually critical ends defined in outcomes programs. In the United States, for example, the national subject associations have been strongly involved in, committed to, and influential in the development of standards.

They tend to differ as well in the *level of detail* in terms of which they are prescribed by policy. Outcomes tend to be broader, leaving more room for school-level interpretation. Standards tend to be more content specific, more detailed, and more tightly aligned with required assessment formats.

Finally, standards and outcomes differ in the degree of *teacher discretion* they afford in planning, preparation, and curriculum judgment. Standards typically define the process as well as the ends of learning in guidelines for teachers, and outcomes are stated in more general terms that give teachers more latitude in and responsibility for specifying the means.

Educational reformers increasingly have sidestepped the political furor associated with outcomes and embraced the standards-based approach as a way of bringing education into line and transforming it. Standards-based reform embodies the belief that education has been mediocre and undemanding and that much more intellectually challenging instruction is needed (Cohen, 1995). In bellicose language, Hill and Crévola (1999) refer to a

worldwide "assault on low standards" (p. 119) involving "zero tolerance of educational failure" (p. 119) in pursuit of the belief that
"the war on low standards can be won" (p. 121).

Advocates of standards-based reform argue that standards in education have been too low and that there has been no consistency
from district to district, or even from classroom to classroom, in what,
how, and how well students should learn. Debates have raged even
on the floor of the U.S. Senate about the content of standards. Nevertheless, many jurisdictions are continuing on the standards path as
a vehicle for deciding the important content and concepts for students to learn. Standards are seen as defining clear (and high) expectations for all students. Their proponents see them as a way to
address issues of equity as well as excellence in education.

Critics of standards-based reform argue that although it might
have raised measured standards of student performance in countries such as New Zealand and England, where they have now been
in existence for many years, such large-scale reform has produced
little or no evidence (beyond pilot projects) of narrowing the learning gap between advantaged and less advantaged students (Wylie,
1997). Moreover, these measured standards of performance, they
argue, constitute mainly narrow, subject-based, cognitive forms of
learning rather than the broader kinds of learning needed for civic
participation and sophisticated "knowledge-work" (dealing with
images, symbols, ideas, and communication) in today's informational society.

One of the most telling criticisms of detailed, standards-oriented
reforms (or those that possess similar characteristics and are labeled
as outcomes based) is that they reduce the curriculum, and curriculum planning, to narrowly technical and rational processes, losing much of what should be powerful and engaging in learning
and teaching. Hill and Crévola (1999, p. 131) perhaps exemplify
this problem when they argue that literacy standards help schools
reassess priorities and trim back the overcrowded curriculum,
which they describe as including "areas such as the visual and performing arts, languages other than English, information and other
technologies, and health and physical education."

At least two kinds of standards are commonly specified as being
integral components of the standards-based reform movement—
ones concerned with content and performance:

Content standards define the "what" and "when" of the curriculum: what is to be taught and in what order. Content standards provide a map of the curriculum that can be used to ensure important content is being covered.

Performance standards attempt to define what level students will progress and by which grade. Performance standards form the basis of longer term goals for school systems and of shorter term targets for individual schools and for individual students [Hill & Crévola, 1999, p. 125].

In response to this sort of stance, Sergiovanni (2000) takes umbrage at what he calls the "standards stampede" (p. 76) and argues that excessive preoccupation with the technical world of standards is squeezing the "lifeworld"—and, one might even add, lifeblood—out of education. He worries that "if we continue with this one-best-way solution, with standardized standards and assessment," then we "compromise the lifeworlds of parents, teachers, students and local communities" (Sergiovanni, 2000, p. 75):

> Instead of standards and accountability being derived from the needs, purposes, and interests of parents, teachers, and students in each school, the standards and accountability systems determine what the needs, purposes and interests are and script the behavior of teachers and students accordingly. [However], when the lifeworld [of culture, meaning, and significance in education] dominates, testing reflects local passions, needs, values, and beliefs. Standards remain rigorous and true but are not standardized [p. 88].

Perhaps one of the greatest difficulties with standards and the associated assessment of them is that although they may make sense subject by subject, collectively they can become overwhelming and confusing. While each subject discipline develops its own rigorous, detailed set of standards, people rarely take responsibility for examining their cumulative impact or their consistency. This job is left to the teacher. In Ontario, for example, outcome-based standards in *The Common Curriculum: Policies and Outcomes, Grades 1–9* (Ontario Ministry of Education and Training, 1995) were a bewildering maze of integrated curriculum goals, stages of student proficiency, cross-referenced to "essential" and "specific" outcomes for grades 3, 6, and 9. In England, the profusion of standards and targets that comprise its National Curriculum became so excessive and impossible to implement faithfully that a government committee— the Dearing Committee—had to be established to find ways of cutting back the overgrown garden of curriculum and assessment targets. California educator Cris Gutierrez (2000) develops the most practically compelling critique of the excesses of the standards movement in a review of Michael Fullan's *Change Forces: The Sequel* (1999). Her salutary response is worth quoting at length:

> Currently, conditions demand teachers to do more and more things to get the young to know more and more "stuff," contained in too many "high standards." . . . While "high standards" are essential, no curriculum should be determined by externally imposed standards amounting to more than 50% of a teacher's responsibility if the students are to be supported and challenged as learners within a particular context of community, place and time. Yet, today's conditions demand that one does too much at a faster and faster pace, which leads to doing little or less overall, incurring unnecessary stress. For example, studying the Bill of Rights . . . becomes a trivial pursuit that has little meaning in the lives of the students today except one more thing to know for an exam or one more project to accomplish. . . .
>
> Moving too fast, with more and more to do, compels teaching and learning to be an accumulation. Students begin to feel that there is no time to enjoy what they are doing, let alone figure out what their knowledge can mean in their own lives, except to get ahead, into college. Assembling things to do and know is not inquiry. Investigation means delving deeply into resources to question, explore and experience so one can assimilate, make meaning and internalize.
>
> Every hour a teacher sets up a class to engage in quality inquiry involves considerable preparation to integrate resources and instructional strategies suitable for the diverse personalities or intellectual dimensions of a certain class. A teacher also spends more hours responding to student work. For children to read, write, discuss, gather data, recollect information, probe ideas, make observations, weigh facts, communicate, calculate, collaborate, express themselves, share conclusions, critically think, problem solve, make

meaning and so on, as well as build deep understanding and community, takes real time.

While the rate of change may be fast these days, the majority of learning cannot afford to be. Accomplished teachers know how to enrich experiences and support youth by varying and managing pace.

Using time carefully, even slowing things down appropriately, keeps the pace in learning reasonable for each student and group [pp. 219–224].

In the face of these needs and demands, Gutierrez says, standards taken to excess are unachievable, unsustainable, and not even desirable: "Standards . . . meant to clarify academic goals and unify our efforts to achieve them . . . have turned into hurdles, which use industrial accounting systems, namely standardized tests as single measures of success" (p. 223). In trying to race over this dense collection of higher and higher hurdles, teachers and students alike "burn out; quit; hold back; barely try; or make heroic personal sacrifices that may well be rewarded or celebrated but are not the bases of a sustainable system of education or healthy models for our young" (p. 223).

Eisner (1995) points out that a common further problem with standards for all is their failure to recognize differences among students. Writing in the context of England, Goodson (1999) has described how the rightful concern with standards has drifted instead into an obsession with standardization that "unpicks" rather than enhances teachers' professionalism, turning teachers into "technical deliverer[s] of guidelines and schemes devised elsewhere."

Summing up the criticisms of standards-based reform, Smyth and Dow (1998) argue that learning standards (which they actually call outcomes) contain a kind of technical rationality that routinizes, deskills, and deprofessionalizes teachers, whose work is increasingly controlled by outsiders who measure and audit their competence and performance in ever-increasing detail. They conclude that a standards-based curriculum

is predicated on the *delimitation of curriculum* content and on the *deskilling of teachers*. Schools are required to adopt clearly defined and commonly identified norms and goals formulated at a distance from schools and classrooms, designed to produce a set of commonly agreed-upon standards and competencies. The distance of most teachers and all students from the process of determination of these norms and goals increases the likelihood of the separation of educational means from ends, conception from implementation, and fosters a deskilled and instrumentalist approach to teaching, in which teaching is described and understood largely in terms of facts, sequences, techniques and skills. Values, ethics and morals have little currency in this scenario [p. 297].

By comparison, learning outcomes tend to be broader and less exclusively subject based, leaving more space and responsibility for teachers' professional discretion and involvement. In Grundy and Bonser's (1997) study of how teachers interpreted and implemented Student Outcome Statements in Western Australia, for example, teachers mentioned the importance of "goal setting," "clarifying uncertainty," "changing their teaching practice," and "speaking to their kids in outcomes language." Working together on outcomes, teachers developed stronger collegial and collaborative understanding about the meaning and application of outcomes statements.

Our own study provides an opportunity to delve into these debates and differences. It goes behind, beside, and beyond rhetorical debates about outcomes and standards to examine their practical implementation among a group of teachers. It explores the insider world of interpreting and implementing broad outcomes and translating them into classroom practice. It also offers a counterpoint—a critical voice for reflecting on the value and dangers of more specific, detailed, content-based standards.

We will see that while high and clearly stated expectations seem manifestly desirable, there is profound disagreement about what those expectations should be—whether they should be regarded as mandates or guidelines, whether they should be defined in very specific or in more general terms, how they should be measured and assessed, whether they should apply to all students equally or exclude some, and what sanctions should be applied to students and teachers who fail to meet them (Zlatos, 1993). The experiences of the teachers we studied echo these points of tension and controversy. We look at two aspects of teachers' experience of learning outcomes: how they understood and defined them and how and with whom they planned and developed them.

Understanding Outcomes

Outcomes themselves can be something of an empty box for teachers. They are rarely self-evident in their written form and demand a great deal of interpretation by the teacher. Teachers in our study in some cases found outcomes too vague, and in other cases too numerous and cumbersome. They often had difficulty measuring outcomes or modifying them for students with learning disabilities.

Vague Outcomes

Translating multilayered, abstract outcomes into concrete curriculum units and student learning activities is not easy for teachers. Those in our study were at different stages in being able to see how learning outcomes fit into their programs. We asked all teachers to describe a unit from their program. Those in the earlier stages of understanding were aware of the outcomes that their units addressed, but only in very general ways:

> Right now we're doing a multimedia unit. We're looking at advertising and how images are used to communicate messages and to convince the public to buy. I haven't taken the time to actually look at the outcomes from the unit and compare them to the outcomes.

> I find the music outcomes here are not very concrete. I feel I could always say they're almost intrinsic. They're actually difficult to judge. Do the children love music? They just say, yes, they do—even if they don't really. Our children haven't had much music until now, so I'm using grade 3, 4 outcomes for grade 7, 8.

> One thing I could have done better is design my outcomes. I know what my outcomes are, but as a new teacher, sometimes it's hard for me to put them into words and into writing. Next year, if I do this unit again, I will do a better job of coming up with specific outcomes.

Teachers at this early stage of understanding often wanted more specific details in terms of unit design and teaching materials, to see just how the outcomes fit. As one teacher said:

> The documents we have from the district are excellent. The binders and the things that the district provided really do have a

lot in them. I just feel that we are lacking in more concrete ideas—for example, if the geography department could say, "When you're teaching human geography and are doing indigenous people, these are the two best videos. Here are excellent books." I'd like something specific. I may not agree with them, but at least it's a starting point rather than me having to do the making of the things.

These teachers wanted clear structures, more detail, things to fall back on. One explained that

because I'm a newer teacher, I might be a little more obsessed with the outcomes and knowing what they are than my colleagues who have been teaching longer. Maybe they feel more confident that they know what they want their students to learn. I think that I like to have outcomes stated so that I know. When I have developed more specific plans, I generally feel more confident. Also, I have to get to higher-level thinking in my outcomes for my students. I'm not there yet in everything that I do.

Other teachers' thinking about and experimentation with the curriculum framework had progressed much further in the detailed, nitty-gritty of planning curriculum units and classroom activities in relation to learning outcomes. In some cases, these teachers' approaches to curriculum planning were very sophisticated even before the advent of outcomes. The learning outcomes framework helped them clarify and advance this process even further:

We go back and look at our units from the last few years, sit down, and determine what the kids need. Then we design activities for what the kids need during the year. At the end of every unit, we had a big application activity, like a convention or a debate. It was an application of all the skills that the kids learned. Actually, when we wrote up our report cards on the old system, the first statement was "what we did this term." For example, kids were involved in an inventing process. Then they had to do a presentation of their invention. We had three areas for evaluation—language, writing, and independent group work—and we commented on whether the student was exceptional or needs improvement. Now with the outcomes, it really simplified it even more for us. It is sort of where we were going. It's been wonderful.

Some teachers described curriculum units they had taught and designed in great detail. They itemized the many aspects of knowledge they wanted their students to acquire. One teacher described a unit he had taught on solutions for children whose laboratory skills were weak and whose laboratory experience was limited. The unit involved teaching them

> everything from very simple things like filtering a solution and then judging whether you can filter a solution and take things out. If they are very bright, I'll do a little presentation on bonding, so that some of the kids will understand about molecules and why they unite and how they form this bond and what it means. The group process accounts for part of their mark, and by the end of the unit, they'll be designing the experiments, carrying them out, evaluating the experiment's design, and making changes to it, so if they were to do it again, they know what they would do differently. They are learning a lot of skills in terms of operating a triple beam balance, operating a microscope, each of them preparing slides, each of them being responsible for writing down the group's observations.

Although he did not describe his unit in the technical language of outcomes, this teacher clearly identified many different types of knowledge, skills, and values that he wanted his students to learn. He detailed how he expected his students to become proficient in the scientific method: designing an experiment, carrying it out, evaluating the experiment's design, and making appropriate modifications to it. By employing a collaborative learning approach, this complex unit also integrated social skills in group work with reasoning skills in scientific procedures and language skills in reporting results.

For teachers who were experienced at and interested in investing their imagination in curriculum planning for their own classes, broad and even vaguely defined outcomes were not an obstacle but an opportunity. However, considering the number and complexity of learning outcomes across four program areas involving knowledge, skill, and value dimensions, it is hardly surprising that many teachers found it hard to design outcomes for and within their integrated curriculum units. Beginning teachers in particular felt less comfortable with outcomes and how they fit into their units. Yet even experienced teachers had problems

understanding the outcomes because of their abstraction or ambiguity. Even finding time to read and understand the policy and
to integrate outcomes into their programs of teaching and learning was a challenge.

Cumbersome Outcomes

At their best, outcomes provide a structure that helps teachers to
clarify and sharpen their curriculum intentions—to think about
what students will learn before considering what they, as teachers,
will teach. Outcomes can help teachers evaluate students' achievement and select appropriate content, methods, resources, and organizational procedures more effectively (Brady, 1996). In practice,
though, some teachers felt overwhelmed with mastering the number and complexity of outcomes when they also had many other
priorities. Schools do not stand still while teachers work their way
through new curriculum initiatives. If the innovation is conceptually complex, being able to dedicate the proper time to figuring it
out can prove immensely difficult. One teacher proclaimed:

> I don't want to take on any more initiatives. There's just too much
> going on right now. I've let some things go that we had taken as ini-
> tiatives. It was getting so overwhelming that I decided that some
> things had to go.

Another teacher who was passionately committed to the idea
of teaching outcomes said she thought it was

> an excellent concept. We can do the backward mapping and start
> telling the fifth and sixth graders to start working toward those sev-
> enth- and eighth-grade outcomes. And that is what we are doing.
> So they are ready for tenth grade and up. And they are ready for
> the workforce, or university, or whatever else. It is an excellent idea.

But, she added, "to sit down and formulate those outcomes
and all the indicators—and there would be several for one outcome in all the different subject areas—is a mammoth job."
Part of the problem of mastering the outcomes, making sense
of them, and seeing how they worked in teachers' own practice was
that they were not stated sufficiently clearly in the relevant policy

documents. Many teachers found the language in which outcomes were written to be opaque and cumbersome. This made them anxious about just what the policy was saying, what was expected of them and their students, and how outcomes applied specifically to their teaching:

> It's unbelievable. It's overwhelming is what it is. You look at this policy binder from the school district and you think, "I will never ever possibly be able to understand this, let alone implement it."

> Just reading the outcomes, I had a lot of trouble understanding how they all fit together. At in-service, they laid everything out. It's taken several years to get to the point where I understand how they fit together. Initially, it looked as if they were all different documents. It was a little mind boggling. I tend to get very frustrated with that kind of thing. I like to know exactly what is wanted of me. I will do it, but it has to be specific. It was very frustrating. I still don't find the outcomes really that helpful as they are written. "Teacherese" is really strong in some of them. Just say it in plain English so everyone can understand it: the kids, the parents, the teachers.

The cumulative effect of interpreting and implementing learning outcomes or standards, as well as monitoring if they have been met by every student, can be one where teachers feel overloaded and pulled in too many directions, so they lose rather than gain focus and become exhausted in their efforts to cope. This is an ever-present, lurking danger in every program of standards or outcomes; we will return to it at the end of this chapter.

Measuring Outcomes

If you cannot specify outcomes clearly, you cannot measure them properly either. Not surprisingly, the teachers in our study often had great difficulty knowing how to measure the outcomes. They raised many questions about how indicators of achieving the learning outcomes could be developed into reliable tools for measuring them. "The hardest part," said one teacher, "is how to assess these outcomes. I think that's where I see a lot of teachers struggling." One exasperated teacher complained:

What is an "exceeds outcome," for example, in reading in a grade 7 class? What is it? No one has really told us. For example, if your outcome was—and these are from the list that they gave us—"reads widely and diversely," well, what does "exceeds" mean? Does that mean that they read twenty books a term? forty books a term? No one is really clear. When you begin to look at outcomes critically, if you want me to evaluate that skill, what does it really mean? I don't see the ministry giving us that! I don't see the district giving us that!

Modifying Outcomes

Nowhere else are the issues of clarity, definition, and measurement brought into sharper relief than in working out how outcomes apply to the whole range of students. Is everyone meant to achieve the outcomes, or should outcomes be modified for students with learning difficulties? In this terrain, defining outcomes clearly is not just a technical issue; it is also a fundamental issue of equity and social justice—where equity and excellence, standards and compassion start to rub against one another. Most teachers in our project taught in diverse classrooms characterized by a wide range of student backgrounds, capabilities, and aptitudes. Knowing how to plan in relation to outcomes and design units that would reach all students was especially challenging for them.

Some teachers reported that modified programs enhanced students' sense of achievement, self-esteem, and motivation. Adjusting outcomes to different student abilities enriched the learning in their classrooms and helped them raise their expectations for lower achievers.

> To me the concept of outcomes means results that I want specific students to have. With mainstreamed kids in my classroom, outcomes are not going to fit my whole class. I need specific outcomes for specific students.

> My classroom is richer than it was a few years ago. The kids are doing so many more things. The program is so much more open-ended, so the kids who are gifted can just go with it. My colleague and I work together because of our special education background. We have the special education kids in our classroom. We design our program so that it encompasses them as well as the gifted kids.

Yet program modification is not a panacea for setting standards in diverse classrooms. As it solves some problems, it introduces others. Teachers modified their programs for their at-risk students so that they would not fall further behind academically. However, the effort of making so many finely tuned adjustments for individual students who were struggling could strain the teacher's ability to manage all these variations and meet the needs of the whole class, as the following teachers' remarks indicate:

> Another obstacle would be the range of abilities. I had a grade 8 student last year who couldn't read or write. He was in my class full time. That's an obstacle because I feel obligated to program for that kid, and that's another demand on the teacher. And the way that special education is going, the reality is that there are not going to be many closed classrooms. That is a strain on teachers.

> I'd like to concentrate on the average child. I think the average child is getting lost in all of this. I think we're concentrating on those who need individual support, and the kids who need to be challenged are getting challenged. I'm a little concerned about the gray kids, as I call them, because I want to make sure that they are getting an equal shake in all of this. I'm not quite sure how we fit them into all of this.

In addition, program modification created serious reporting problems for the teachers in our study, as well as raising their concerns about student performance and achievement over the long term—for example:

> In the back of my mind I think, "What if they don't meet the outcomes? What happens to them?" The outcomes make sense, and we want to have people who are very functional in today's society— people who are very computer literate, can write, and so on. But what if they don't? Who knows what is going to happen? I can tell you right now that seven or eight of the kids in my classroom will not meet the full extent of the outcomes for grade 7, and I am probably underestimating. They are good students, and they are trying very, very hard, but they won't meet them. Do we keep them back until they meet the outcomes?

My mom and I talk about that a lot. She has special education kids, and a couple of hers will never meet the outcomes. She can't fail them because it is not their fault if they have a learning disability. In the meantime, however, the government is saying: "Sorry you didn't pass grade 7." I don't know if we are setting them up for a whole group of kids who are just going to leave school.

Another teacher observed in relation to some of her students with learning disabilities:

When you modify for these children so that they are successful and you have watered down the program to the extent that these children are on paper a success, and they go off to high school and these modifications aren't met, you've watered it down to the extent that it's not a true outcome.

For teachers, the prospect of some students' failing to meet the outcomes was compelling and emotionally troubling. Indeed, most were not only in a quandary about how to measure achievement of outcomes accurately and reliably, they were also deeply worried that some of their less able students might not be able to achieve the learning outcomes at all. Modified programs raised a disturbing dilemma. On the one hand, modifying outcomes solved the problem of students' being labeled as failures—at least in the short term. But it threw up other problems, such as misinterpretation of what modified grades really meant and false expectations in the minds of students, parents, and future employers. The expectation that all students should achieve certain levels of knowledge, skills, and values by particular grades places great pressures on teachers who work with a wide range of student academic abilities, learning styles, and rates of intellectual and emotional development. Policy-makers and administrators assert that everyone should achieve the standards, and teachers are made to feel that no one should fail. But when the outcomes are modified to avoid failure, standards seem to lose their meaning. This excruciating dilemma is not of teachers' making. It has its roots in policy itself, and it is there especially that the problem must be confronted.

Planning for Outcomes

Planning a curriculum around standards or outcomes to be achieved, rather than content to be covered, is difficult at the best of times. When the relevant policy documents are vague, excessively complex, or unreasonably ambitious, the task of planning outcomes is more demanding still.

The teachers in this project found planning their units in terms of outcomes to be extremely challenging. Some of the policy's directives for program planning and development were truly formidable. Consider, for example, the directive that "all aspects of program planning, including decisions concerning teaching and assessment strategies, must focus on helping students attain the outcomes. . . . As a general rule, learning activities, themes, and units of study should contribute to the achievement of appropriate combinations of outcomes." According to the written policy, teachers were expected to follow basic steps in program planning:

1. Review expected outcomes and standards of the program.
2. Assess student needs, interests, abilities, and learning styles using records of students' achievement, students' portfolios, teachers' comments, and discussions with students and parents.
3. Consult with other staff (for example, guidance, special education).
4. Select appropriate content and resources. and develop appropriate teaching and assessment methods.
5. Discuss outcomes and assessment methods with students and their parents.
6. Discuss ways of avoiding potential difficulties with each student.
7. Advise parents on how to help their children.
8. Plan their assessment, evaluation, and reporting strategies.

How did teachers deal with these planning demands? What did planning for outcomes look like in practice? Who was involved in the planning process, and what did their involvement look like? What does planning for outcomes demand of teachers, what supports do they need to plan effectively, and what obstacles get in their way?

Rationalities of Planning

Planning is often presented as a quintessentially linear, rational process in which clear goal setting and careful judgments about how to achieve those goals and to know when they have been achieved, are paramount. On paper, outcomes-based education or standards-based reform lends itself perfectly to this conception of planning. Learning standards or outcomes are determined first; then, through a process of backward mapping, indicators of what would count as achievements of those outcomes are established, followed by identification of curriculum materials and teaching strategies that will help students achieve these indicators of successful learning. Among the teachers in our sample, however, only three stated they planned in this textbook fashion, beginning with the outcomes, then mapping backward from them. Others talked about experiencing their planning as a reverse process—for example:

> I struggle with outcomes in the sense that I know that I still have to go through that process. I tend to do things in reverse. I do the global plan. I'm sure that I work backward that way.

Many teachers experienced the planning steps outlined in the curriculum as mechanistic and contrived, as this one did:

> As a staff, we tried to write a conflict theme for a unit. But because there are twenty-three of us, in groups of three, we chose the outcomes from the report card that we had selected as a school. Then we tried to develop activities to go with each of those outcomes on the theme of conflict. It turned out we had a very, very disjointed unit.

Teachers did not simply lift outcomes from the curriculum policy document without critical reflection. They worked diligently, individually and together, to make sense of the outcomes in relation to the realities they encountered in the everyday lives of their students. This process of critical reflection involved a great deal of intellectual work as they struggled to understand how outcomes fit conceptually into their program:

I am a little concerned about what is the knowledge base of my unit on the family. The only emphasis is on the skills. If students know how to find the information when they need it, they can. But what about the general knowledge? Are they going to get that? Are the ninth- and tenth-grade teachers assuming that the kids have a good base of Canadian history and geography? That's why I felt personally obligated to go back to those guides and make sure I tried to incorporate them into the Family, Conflict and Change unit. The next unit we do is Mysteries and Wonders of the World. I'm looking specifically at the integrated studies—history and geography. I'm not worried about the skills. I'm more worried about the content.

Teachers also needed to experience an emotional resonance with the outcomes. They were not planning outcomes clinically for hypothetical students in a purely rational way. Planning was rooted in understandings of their own students that were emotional as well as cognitive in nature. For this reason, many teachers leaned toward using an inside-out (classroom-based) strategy for planning outcomes because the backward-mapping, outside-in approach seemed counterintuitive or unnatural, as the following teachers noted:

I hate those ready-made kits that people buy—those integrated kits—because they don't take into account the kids in the classroom, and that's what the teacher has to do.

I try to do at least one concept attainment lesson a month. I did one just a couple of days ago on mass media. We pulled outcomes right from the document. To be honest, I found this kind of artificial. I was really trying to make circles fit into squares. At least that is how I felt.

For these teachers, there was a discordance between planning outcomes on the basis of linear rationality (objective and calculative) and planning outcomes on the basis of experiential rationality (subjective and intuitive). This tension between different rationalities of planning was pervasive. How most teachers actually planned and used outcomes was closely linked to their emotional connections with their students and their feelings as a teacher. Most teachers felt more comfortable starting with their knowledge about how their students learned, what motivated them, and their unique learning needs and styles. As one teacher said:

> The best lesson I learned in teaching was to be myself, and the stronger I got with being myself, the more communication occurred between the children and me and the more learning occurred. The more I imposed superstructures that were not me, and the kids knew I was doing this, the lessons didn't function as well.

Teachers' approaches to planning were grounded in their intuitive judgments about what worked in their classrooms and their feelings about and understandings of their students' needs. Some writers have argued that standards-based and outcomes based approaches deemphasize emotional aspects of teaching and learning relationships (Zlatos, 1993). This is a crucial point because our data show that in many instances, the language of outcomes left teachers feeling alienated from the curriculum planning process. Teachers felt constrained when trying to apply scientific planning procedures that began with outcomes detached from their actual experience. In practice, outcomes were shaped to a significant degree by teachers' ability to connect them with their teaching experience. Planning worked best when it moved inside out from teachers' practice and experience and their connections to students, not outside in from abstract statements.

Planning with Colleagues

Teachers planned individually, but they also collaborated with colleagues around outcomes within and outside the regular school day. They valued opportunities to share ideas and perceptions with their colleagues helped to bring clarity to the policy. It provided a context as well for exploring ideas about how to apply outcomes in their units, evaluate their students' achievement, and establish continuity in planning. Professional collaboration can be an exceptionally important asset to the curriculum planning process, giving it clarity, consistency, and momentum, as many of our teachers testified.

Planning collaboratively helped teachers gain an intellectual understanding of what learning outcomes meant as they discussed the policy with colleagues and designed outcomes-oriented units together. Working closely with colleagues also increased teachers' self-confidence in using and assessing outcomes. Collaborative planning was a powerful emotional and intellectual process that created learning opportunities for teachers and their students:

> My colleague and I were doing a lot of work designing integrated units of study, which had very specific knowledge, skills, and attitudes but also very concrete learning outcomes that could be evaluated. We were getting into the debate of how to evaluate outcomes and develop them, how to articulate them, and then how to get kids involved in that process as well. Then we began looking at portfolios. That was probably the most enriching experience that I had.

> What makes all the difference for me is working with one other person. It's time-consuming at the start, but once you persevere and get through it, the benefits are fabulous. I have more confidence in my programming. I'll stand up for what our programming is. I'm doing a better job teaching. The kids are learning more and being more creative. We have a long way to go, but really collaborating was the dynamic thing that put everything together for me. It's been personally and professionally transforming. Nothing else has had as much impact as collaboration. It's interesting because for years, we have expected kids to collaborate, and we haven't as teachers.

Sometimes the professional collaboration in which teachers engaged was structured into specific team tasks and ways of working together. Teamwork has many of the advantages of informal types of collaboration such as mutual support, but roles and responsibilities are defined more formally. Teachers saw great value in this sort of collaborative activity. They preferred working together through the uncertainties of curriculum planning rather than having to make presentations to and feel exposed and not completely knowledgeable in formal staff meetings.

> The most useful staff development that I have had was where we have been allotted time as teams, even a half-day, to do planning and try to sift through this information in a more relaxed atmosphere where you're not going to stand up in front of your whole

staff of thirty-eight people and say, "What is a rubric?" I don't feel uncomfortable with my team saying, "I don't have a clue."

Some wanted more teamwork. We don't have enough time to do team-building techniques, where you have the trust built in and you know you can really work with one another. That's all I really want: time to work through some of these things as a group and time to connect more with the ninth graders. That would be my one request.

Despite the widely acknowledged benefits of teacher collaboration and teamwork (Fullan & Hargreaves, 1996; Little, 1993; Nias, Southworth, & Yeomans, 1989), it is not enough merely to assert their importance to teachers and then expect widespread adoption. Teachers know and recognize the benefits of collaboration and teamwork well enough. They also know that meaningful collaboration is easier said than done and that simply mandating teacher collaboration can be counterproductive (Hargreaves, 1994). Our data suggest that collaborative planning (formal and informal) has intellectual and emotional benefits for teachers who are implementing outcomes. Faced with complex outcomes, the opportunity to share ideas and concerns with colleagues and to figure out together what these new frameworks and standards meant was a highly valued part of the planning process (Grundy & Bonser, 1997). But collaboration takes time, effort, commitment, resources, sensitivity, and skill. It does not come about by moral injunction. As one teacher remarked:

We do a lot of collaboration outside regular school time and coming in on holidays. This gives us time in class, and we make sure that we touch base with each other and the program and the kids. It helps us keep track of the kids as well as the program. The kids obviously are our biggest concern. If a kid is falling behind or having difficulty or acting strangely, then we can talk about this. And for the entire school, right from kindergarten to grade 8, every teacher has a mutual prep partner twice a week. But the biggest change for me has been actually working with my colleague, collaborating with her.

As we argue more fully in Chapter Seven, a continuing challenge for schools and policymakers is to create structures of time and space where collaboration is an integral part of planning outcome-based or standards-based programs and not simply peripheral to or an ad hoc feature of the teacher's day. Effective collaborative planning of outcomes cannot be left to chance and teacher initiative cannot be regarded as an expendable frill by budget-conscious reformers. It must be supported by new forms of school organization and professional development where teachers can learn new skills that help them plan and work in teams effectively.

Involving Students

Curriculum planning should encompass students and parents, as well as teachers. After all, they are the consumers of what is eventually planned. Yet students are often the last to be informed about educational innovations (Rudduck, Day, & Wallace, 1997) and even less likely to be involved in developing and implementing them. In this sense, an especially important aspect of planning for many teachers in our project was student involvement. As one teacher said, planning for outcomes "has to be in conjunction with the kids. I don't think you can remove yourself totally from the kids."

Most teachers thought carefully about the impact of curriculum reform on their students and their teaching. They were determined to make outcomes meaningful for and learning relevant to the lives of their students. For many teachers, one essential way to do this was to share the learning outcomes openly and explicitly with them:

> I told the students what the outcomes were, so the students were aware of them. The students knew how they were going to be evaluated. I knew what I was going to evaluate, and that would make a more effective lesson.

Some teachers went further and involved students in the planning process. This made the daily teaching and learning relationships into a starting point for their work with the outcomes. Teachers were able to test what the outcomes meant and how they worked practically in their classrooms by involving their students in planning them. One teacher described how this worked:

> The kids and I go to the wall where the outcomes are written once in a while in our classroom and say, "Here's what we are doing right

now. It fits here." They can see the connection with outcomes very quickly, and that's fine. The kids are happy with it.

Why teachers taught things and what students were meant to learn was described clearly and acknowledged openly between them. Teachers engaged in dialogue with their students to help them make sense of the learning outcomes and develop plans for evaluating the results of their learning together—for example:

> The outcomes are okay with me because I need that to make me focus more specifically on what I want to accomplish. I more often and more clearly tell the kids. I didn't always do that. Now I tell them what we are supposed to accomplish in the classroom. I put down our objectives or our goals at the start. Then, with my own class, I will have them process at the end: "Did we accomplish that?" "Where did I mess up?" "Where did you mess up?"

Teachers also reported that by sharing learning outcomes with their students, the students started to take a lot more responsibility for their own learning. Taking responsibility in this way was actually an essential outcome of the curriculum itself. This outcome entailed using the skills of learning how to learn more effectively by having students set goals for their learning, make realistic plans, and keep track of and evaluate their progress. It also required students to clarify their ideas by reflecting on their own thinking and the responses of others. Teachers were urged to organize their program areas so that students would learn to become independent learners. In an intriguingly recursive sense, this outcome was also a prerequisite for how students should be involved in planning it.

This process of planning outcomes with students was vigorous, dynamic, and emotionally engaged. It was an inside-out process that grew from teachers' relationships with their students and the practical ideas they could generate together. The reflections of one teacher reveal how and why this planning process worked backward to the official, outside-in logic:

> From those brainstorms with my students and from what interests they've expressed, we go to the learning outcomes—the big, awesome binder—and figure out what kind of skills could fit into this. We probably work backward because I know you're supposed to

start with the outcomes. We work with their interests, then to the outcomes. Then we develop a menu of activities that we feel would be valuable.

Consulting with their students was an integral part of many teachers' process of implementing learning outcomes in reverse. Teachers started with their students' understandings and interests and considered materials, activities, methods, and classroom approaches that would keep their students engaged and motivated. Talking to students about outcomes was one successful way that teachers helped keep learning meaningful for them. Planning around outcomes with students made learning less of a secret to them and shifted the power dynamics of the classroom. It is not just what teachers plan, but how they plan and with whom they plan that is the key issue.

Involving Parents

In addition to advocating student involvement in planning how to achieve common learning outcomes, the curriculum asked teachers to discuss guidelines with parents and advise parents on how they could help their children achieve the outcomes. This policy directive is consistent with studies in many countries that attest to the importance of parent involvement in bringing about student success and school improvement (McGilp & Michael, 1994; Muller & Kerbow, 1993; Dauber & Epstein, 1993; Epstein, 1988).

Some of the teachers in our study clearly regarded communication with parents as an important part of their approach to planning and developing learning outcomes within their programs—for example:

> We actually wanted to give the kids the outcomes yesterday and send them home in a newsletter tomorrow. That way they can be posted on the wall or the parents can have them on the fridge and the kids have them in their notebook.

> I think the parents have to be educated also about outcomes-based education. It has to be explained to them what we are looking for and what we expect. When we go through this with the parents, we

try to use some of the terminology, and some of the words with them. When I sent letters home explaining what I was doing about student-generated interviews, I did an explanation about outcomes to the parents. They still were a little fuzzy on it. But once they came in and heard the kids talking about it, and then talked to me afterward about it and went through the report card, it was a lot clearer.

Teachers talked about the need to communicate with parents so that they would become more knowledgeable about learning outcomes and their implications for teaching and learning in their children's schools. In some cases, this entailed using written materials prepared by the school district to help parents understand the new outcomes. Other teachers reported that developing their own materials for parents was not only valuable for parents, but it also helped them as teachers to come to grips with the learning outcomes:

> The other thing that I think really helped us as a grade team a lot, which we did at the outset, was to prepare a grade 8 package for parents. In that, we had to sit down and think together as a group and pick out the learning outcomes. We used the suggested format to inform parents and also to articulate for ourselves on paper what we hoped to accomplish. We were proud of that. It was well received by parents.

Teachers also found that involving parents more directly in classroom activities provided ideal opportunities for deepening the dialogue about students' learning and outcomes:

> We are going to bring in parents and see what they can contribute to our unit on flight. We have a partnership with a computer person. He's going to come in to talk to the kids about computers, and we hope to visit his workplace. A second parent does presentations on Canadian history to the kids. A third parent, the mother of one of the kids in my class, speaks Cantonese and works with my English as a Second Language kids. Her husband is also into computers, and we are going to make a partnership with him and his company. This is very valuable experience, and I mentioned this to a lot of the parents on the interviews. I have five or six more parents lined up who want to come in and talk about their jobs. One

parent operates a heavy equipment company. It fits right in with what we were doing on bridges and the math project on building. I can see this happening more and more in the future.

Yet partnerships with parents carry threats as well as promises for teachers. As their understanding of outcomes-based practices increases, parents are in a better position to make critical judgments about the quality of teaching and learning. Effective communication with parents about outcomes-based policies and programs implies greater accountability for teachers as well:

> Parents, especially in our community, are becoming aware and very well educated about these new things. They want to know, and they want to be a part of this. I think that this is a good thing. But if they have a list of outcomes, they want to know by the end of third grade why there is no check mark beside a designated outcome for their child. They ask, "What did you as the teacher do to get my child there?" I would like to see practical strategies for delivering assessments and evaluations to parents.

These teachers, like many of their colleagues elsewhere, were sometimes rather selective about the kinds of parent involvement they seemed prepared to accept and cultivate. Some were concerned that real shifts in power from the school to the parents might undermine their autonomy as professionals (see Hargreaves, 2000):

> I hate that parents are going to take more initiative and have little parenting groups that are going to start telling me to how to teach based on what their hours of work are. I don't think they are in the system. I don't think they understand the system and how it's changed.

Vincent (1996) found that teachers who seek parental involvement mainly want this to take the shape of parents' being supporters (for example, by fundraising or setting good homework habits) or learning about their work (about new programs or even, through helping out in classes, about how difficult teachers' work actually is). They are less prepared to view parents as more equal partners in a two-way dialogue about teaching and learning. Involving parents in (and not just informing them about) common learning standards or outcomes creates opportunities to develop a deeper dialogue between parents and teachers about teaching and learning than is often the case.

Phrases referring to parental involvement or to treating parents as partners are becoming clichés of educational reform. Whether parental involvement actually means giving parents more real power is another question. For such partnerships to be meaningful, they must move beyond fundraising, compliance with homework and discipline policies, and general supportiveness to the core of teaching and learning as it affects parents' own children (Hargreaves & Fullan, 1998). Such partnerships imply giving parents more power to influence such areas as school curriculum and their own children's achievement. Communicating about learning standards and outcomes offers excellent opportunities to deepen the partnership between home and school. Strong partnerships, however, are not only based on communicating information in one direction. Teachers must learn from parents just as parents learn from them. In Chapter Three, we examine two-way systems of reporting, such as student-led parent interviews, that were emerging in some of our schools. But many more of these genuinely reciprocal partnerships still need to be developed. In this respect, the dialogue about learning outcomes has only just begun.

Implications

Clearly defined learning standards or outcomes can transform how teachers think about curriculum, teaching, and learning, steering them into considering not just what they will teach but precisely what their students will learn and what they as teachers will need to do to ensure that such learning is achieved. Our evidence is that this framework of teaching and learning caused teachers who were prepared to think seriously about outcomes to look at their work differently and more deeply than before.

Our findings confirm the promise that common learning standards or outcomes can turn teachers' attention even more clearly to what exactly their students can and will learn. Where the standards or outcomes are in tune with constructivist as well as contextualized principles of teaching and learning and where they reach out to defining sophisticated standards of learning and thinking as worthwhile educational goals (instead of sticking only with clear and specific but low-level forms of learning), then their promise for raising educational standards is greater still.

The challenge that broadly defined common learning outcomes (rather than subject-specific standards) poses for existing forms of school knowledge, subject specialist hierarchies, and the more advantaged students who prosper from them imbues it with considerable potential for educational and social transformation. We have seen that there are risks of excessive vagueness on the one hand and technical-rational prescription on the other, but these run in tension with the movement's potential rather than fatally undermining it. However, even teachers like those we studied, who were genuinely excited about the outcomes or standards concepts and enjoyed using them with students and colleagues to redesign their teaching, found that implementing them and making them real and meaningful in their classrooms were extremely challenging.

Some teachers believed the outcomes were too vague. They were hard to define and harder still to measure. It took energy, inventiveness, and a great deal of trial and error to convert these outcomes into real units of work that would make sense in the practical world of the classroom. Perhaps this struggle is inevitable. Perhaps the demanding intellectual work it requires is a necessary part of learning. But plainer language (rather than "educationese"), sample units of work, and strategies of teaching that can help students achieve the outcomes or standards might help teachers think their way through how to connect broadly stated outcomes to specific moments of teaching and learning. In responding to the problem of vagueness, the temptation that policymakers and administrators too often find hard to resist (in some of the present standards movement, for example) is narrowing and simplifying what students will learn into forms that are more easily measured and stated, instead of simplifying how we describe what students will learn.

Another solution to the problem of meaning or vagueness is to specify or script outcomes and standards with increasing precision in policy writing in an effort to make them teacher-proof. This does reduce ambiguity, but at the expense of restricting teachers' ownership of and identification with the standards and outcomes process, leading to negative emotional reactions among teachers. As we argued earlier, this problem has been most spectacularly evident in teachers' reactions to the National Curriculum in England and Wales (Helsby, 1999). Producing tighter, more detailed written specifications for standards and outcomes can also spread teachers too thin across a bewildering multitude of outcomes and standards, exposing them to multiple and contradictory purposes. This is the encroaching and destructive logic of the technical-rational and administratively obsessive system of curriculum design that many have criticized (Smyth & Dow, 1998; Helsby & Saunders, 1993). We are not suggesting that standards or outcomes should not be clear, but they should resonate with teachers' purposes and leave space for, indeed demand responsibility from them to exercise professional discretion on making standards or outcomes judgments.

In our own study, it was not only the outcomes themselves but particularly the process by which teachers felt they had to plan for them that could seem like a straitjacket. The kind of expected curriculum planning that often accompanies standards-driven, outcomes-based, or target-oriented education is one that involves outside-in, backward mapping from standards to indicators, to materials and methods, in a linear, rational way. Yet the forms of rationality embedded in policy documents, administrative planning processes, and approved implementation procedures are sharply at odds with the inside-out forms of rationality through which many teachers seem to plan in practice. In this inside-out approach to planning, teachers are influenced by and take into account their own considerable practical knowledge; their emotional and intellectual experiences of teaching; the ebb and flow of their relationships with students, colleagues, and parents; and the uncertainties that pervade the context of their teaching in a world buffeted by the storms of change.

Although rational planning, strategic planning, development planning, and the like continue to be widely practiced, their usefulness in contexts of complexity, uncertainty, and emotionality has been strongly questioned and increasingly discredited (Mintzberg, 1994; Wallace, 1991; Fullan, 1999). As Giles (1997) puts it, "The inherently bureaucratic and hierarchical characteristics of the formal rational planning paradigm restrict spontaneity and creativity" (p. 36).

When teachers tried to plan for their outcomes in clinical and exclusively rational ways, they quickly became confused and frustrated. The process did not connect at all with what was real and motivating for them in their own classrooms. It is not that teachers in our study abandoned planning of any sort or that planning is a bad thing. But teachers were often able to subvert the approved planning process in ways that were more professionally energizing for them. Teachers planned not just abstractly and intellectually, but also practically and emotionally in relation to their images of and enthusiasms about real changes and improvements they could see happening in their own classrooms. Outcomes were not in the least bit neglected by the teachers in our project, but were introduced as a set of checks and balances once the creativity and emotionality of the initial planning phase had produced its first set of ideas. Perhaps a point can be reached when standards and outcomes naturally surface as the first things in teachers' minds when they plan, but the most effective way to reach that point might be using the checklist approach rather than forcing teachers to plan in a different, and initially more technical and linear, way that stifles their professional and emotional engagement.

Intellectually and emotionally engaged planning was enhanced when teachers planned with their colleagues. Student involvement in planning was also evident in the way some of our teachers approached common learning outcomes. Where it occurred, this process enriched the planning process for teachers and stimulated students to take more responsibility for their own learning. Planning a curriculum around common learning outcomes with students, and not just for them, is an extremely valuable part of the outcomes-based approach.

Some teachers also involved parents in understanding and engaging with common learning outcomes, and they developed clear, practical ways of doing so without using jargon. However, we also found that much of the communication and learning seemed to run in one direction, with parents being informed about outcomes and their significance, more than engaging in reciprocal dialogue with teachers about them. Considerable strides have yet to be made in developing partnerships with parents that are relationships of reciprocal collaboration rather than one-sided forms of support and communication.

In these respects, when a standards-based or outcomes-based approach pushes teachers to discuss and develop their teaching and learning plans with students and parents, it offers real possibilities for redistributing the power relationships of education within the classroom and the community. At its best, such an intellectually creative and educationally inclusive process is the antithesis of deskilling. Our evidence suggests that when teachers worked in shared communities of practice with others in this way, they were motivated to expand themselves professionally and empower their students concerning learning outcomes (Grundy & Bonser, 1997; Lieberman & McLaughlin, 2000).

Teachers' curriculum planning needs are often misunderstood and underestimated by the general public. What the public remembers are the kinds of teaching they witnessed when they were students—the teacher teaching a single lesson to the class as a whole (Hargreaves, 2000). The time needed to plan for such lessons, one might reasonably imagine, would not be great. However, we have shown that planning in relation to learning outcomes or standards, in classrooms characterized by cultural and linguistic diversity, with a wide range of abilities, and including many students with special needs, means that standards and how to achieve them have to be tailored to every student. These concerns for equity and diversity run against excessively standardized external prescriptions and point to the importance of teachers' being actively engaged in interpreting and developing more detailed standards.

The planning demands that teachers face are substantial. The time needed for planning is extensive, not perfunctory. And where standards or outcomes are complex and sophisticated, this planning time often needs to be spent with colleagues so that intellectual challenges can be met together. In short, our study shows that in a world of sophisticated learning standards, scheduled preparation or planning time is not an expendable luxury that teachers can make up for in their own time but a vital prerequisite of being able to work effectively with colleagues to create high-quality teaching and programming together.

The common learning standards and outcomes approach does not yet seem to have found a way to address credibly what will be done with students who do not reach the standards or Making political and administrative assertions that all child. and will learn them may provide the public with illusions of c dence and certainty, but teachers whose classrooms include ch. dren who have fetal alcohol syndrome, or were crack-cocaine babies, or were severely premature at birth (and there are more and more of these children in teachers' classes now), know just how vapid these illusions are.

Ron Edmonds's (1979) admirable school effectiveness dictum that "all children can learn," which served as a rallying cry to raise expectations and make a difference in disadvantaged children's lives, has been simplistically translated in some administrators' and policymakers' minds into the misleading belief or even demand that "all children can and will learn anything" or that "all children can and will learn as much as all other children do." Such beliefs hang like shadows over teachers who try in vain to get all of their students up to required standards—and who feel guilt and shame when they fall short of others' unrealistic expectations.

An alternate course is to modify the standards and outcomes so all children can attain them. But does that then not undermine what the outcomes mean and the standards they are supposed to uphold? Does it not reduce teachers to playing standards charades? Teachers are only too aware of the cleft stick in which policymakers have placed them. Before standards frameworks with their bellicose language of zero tolerance place teachers under intolerable burdens of guilt, it is a matter of great urgency that policymakers set demanding but achievable standards. They must acknowledge that not all children can learn anything and that although more and more children should certainly be pushed to reach higher and higher standards, it is unrealistic to insist or expect that everyone must achieve all of them.

| **Classroom Assessment**

Assessment-led reform has become one of the most widely favored strategies for promoting higher standards of teaching and learning, more powerful learning, and more credible forms of public accountability (Murphy & Broadfoot, 1995; Gipps, 1994; Black, 1998). Although large-scale, legislated assessments receive the most attention, classroom assessments matter most of all. They drive classroom pedagogy and student learning (Stiggins, 1991). Many educational reforms have heralded new classroom assessment approaches that go beyond traditional paper-and-pencil techniques to include strategies like performance- and portfolio-based assessment (Marzano, Pickering, & McTighe, 1993; Stiggins, 1995). Such alternative assessments are often intended to motivate students to take more responsibility for their own learning, make assessment an integral part of the learning experience, and embed it in authentic activities, which recognize and stimulate students' abilities to create and apply a wide range of knowledge rather than simply engage in acts of memorization and basic skill development (Earl & Cousins, 1995; Stiggins, 1996).

Changes in classroom assessment represent major paradigm shifts in thinking about learning, schools, and teaching. Alternative classroom assessment requires that teachers use their judgments about children's knowledge, understand how to include feedback in the teaching process, decide how to meet students' varying learning needs (Tunstall & Gipps, 1996), and learn how to share decision making about learning and teaching with colleagues, parents, and students (Stiggins, 1996; Gipps, 1994). It means rethinking what assessment and teaching are for, how they can best support learning, and what kinds of curriculum goals, coverage, and standards they can help fulfill (Wiggins & McTighe, 1998).

These changes in classroom assessment pose major challenges for teachers. They are the only ones who have the sustained contact with and intimate knowledge of their students and the curriculum that are required to paint vivid pictures of each student's learning over time (Earl & Cousins, 1995). At the same time, educators are becoming less comfortable with their ability to make good judgments using traditional testing methods. Universal, neutral tests are hard to devise and handle when classes are diverse. What is being tested is changing. Students are now expected to analyze and apply information, as well as simply recall it. The seeming certainties of what to assess and how to assess it are crumbling, and many teachers are now unclear or unsure about what to do as they struggle to serve all their students well.

The changes in classroom assessment present teachers with intriguing opportunities, confront them with great technical difficulties, and draw deeply on their intellectual and emotional energy. This chapter looks at how the teachers in our study coped with and often themselves initiated assessment reform in their classes, and it examines the conditions that supported or failed to support their efforts.

Perspectives on Educational Innovation

Classroom assessment is a multifaceted phenomenon, and many issues are at stake in reforming it. These can be seen by examining classroom assessment reform through different lenses. Drawing on House's (1981) classical treatment of educational innovation and on Habermas's (1972) discussion of different dimensions of human action, we draw attention to three such perspectives on educational innovation—technical, cultural, and political—and add a fourth of our own: the postmodern perspective.

The Technical Perspective

According to House (1981), the technical (or technological) perspective assumes that teaching and innovation are technologies with predictable solutions that can be transferred from one situation to another. The focus of this perspective is on the innovation itself—on its characteristics and component parts and on its production and introduction as a technology. The underlying assumption in a technical perspective is that everyone shares a common interest in advancing the innovation, that the goals of the innovation are settled or beyond question. All that remains is how best to implement it.

In the field of assessment reform, the technical perspective focuses on issues of organization, structure, strategy, and skill in developing new assessment techniques. Here, alternative assessment is a complex technology that requires sophisticated expertise in, for example, devising valid and reliable measures for performance-based assessments in classrooms, which will capture the complexities of student performance (Torrance, 1995). The challenge is to create defensible technologies that are meaningful and fair, and also help teachers develop the understanding and skills necessary to integrate new assessment techniques, such as performance-based assessment, portfolios, self-assessment, video journals, and exhibitions, into their practice. Stiggins (1995) writes about the assessment illiteracy that pervades schools and suggests that

> without a crystal clear view of the meaning of academic success and without the ability to translate that vision into high quality assessments, we will remain unable to assist students in attaining higher levels of academic achievement effectively and to be able to integrate them into their practice [p. 238].

Alternative assessments present a morass of technical issues:

- They take time (Stiggins, 1996).
- They raise concerns about reliability and validity (Linn, Baker, & Dunbar, 1991).
- Sometimes it is hard to untangle them from teaching and learning (Khattri, 1995).
- They are often not well described (Stiggins & Bridgeford, 1985).
- Frequently they presume that teachers already have the necessary skills to implement them (Earl & Cousins, 1995).

Alternative classroom assessment is a new world for teachers, most of whom have very little (if any) assessment training, often lack fundamental measurement knowledge, and generally feel uncomfortable about the quality of their assessments (Stiggins, 1991). Teachers are having to become more sophisticated in their implementation of new assessment strategies (Cunningham, 1998). In addition to teachers' struggles to master the skills of becoming proficient assessors, many institutional constraints create technical problems that make implementing these assessments difficult. Insufficient time, resources, professional development, and consultancy support for teachers to become virtuoso performers with the new strategies are but a few of the problems (Stiggins, 1996).

In summary, the technical perspective draws attention to the difficulties of devising and refining valid forms of measurement, the challenges teachers face when acquiring a wider range of assessment skills and strategies, the need to harmonize assessment expectations between home and school and across school levels, and the issue of time and resources that help or hinder the implementation of new assessment practices into the routines of the school.

The Cultural Perspective

The cultural perspective draws attention to how innovations are interpreted and integrated within the social and cultural context of schools. This perspective is basically concerned with questions of meaning, understanding, and human relationships. House (1981) suggests that the innovation process is actually an interaction of cultures, where change blends new ideas with the cultural history of a school. Within the cultural perspective, the challenge of assessment reform is one of reculturing (Fullan, 1993; Hargreaves, 1994) the human relationships that are involved in assessment processes—between and among students, teachers, and parents.

Alternative classroom assessment does not happen at the end of learning, in terms of a class, a unit, a semester, or a school year. It is an integral part of, or a window into, learning itself throughout the process (Earl & LeMahieu, 1997; Wiggins & McTighe, 1998; Broadfoot, 1996). It is concerned less with categorizing students or outputs of knowledge than with developing common understandings among people about when and how learning occurs. Such assessment must be sufficiently sensitive to detect the mental representations students hold of important ideas. It must be able to discern how well students bring their understanding to bear on solving problems (Sheppard, 1991). This kind of assessment has been described as authentic. Wiggins defines authentic assessment as

> student work that replicates/simulates the core tasks/criteria/ context done by performers in that field. Thus, finding a research problem, designing the experiment, de-bugging the design, publishing the results, defending them against counter-evidence and counter-argument is "doing" science authentically (as opposed to cookbook science labs that are really just hands-on lessons). Similarly, mathematicians don't fill out worksheets for a living—they apply math modelling to problems theoretical and practical, etc. Authentic assessment should not, in my judgment, be defined as relevant or meaningful to kids, as some writers do. This is a telling mistake to me, indicating that the definer is not thinking like an assessor worrying about validity and predictability (as opposed to thinking like a teacher making real work accessible and interesting in class) [Wiggins, 1999, personal communication].

"Authentic" assessment, in this sense, is multidirectional, direct, and deep and relies heavily on teachers' judgments. Students engage in real tasks under the watchful eye of a teacher (or teachers) who controls the agenda and makes positive use of the opportunities for feedback (Torrance & Pryor, 1998). The assessment criteria are not hidden or mysterious. Teachers are encouraged to teach to the test, because students' tasks comprise real situations that they need to master for success (Cunningham, 1998). This approach involves dialogue with and among students and includes constant reassessment, ongoing self-assessment, and mutual peer assessment. Students are active, engaged, and challenged contributors to their own learning.

In summary, the cultural perspective of classroom assessment emphasizes the interplay among viewpoints, values, and beliefs. The task of developing alternative assessment moves far beyond technical matters of measurement, skill, coordination, and existing relationships into the area of establishing communication and building understanding among all those involved in the assessment exercise.

The Political Perspective

All assessment entails acts of judgment, which involve the exercise and negotiation of power, authority, and competing interests among different groups. This brings us to the heart of the political perspective on alternative assessment. This perspective moves beyond issues of technical coordination and human communication to encompass the power struggles among ideologies and interest groups in schools and societies. It also treats alternative classroom assessment as a potentially problematic strategy that, instead of empowering people, can turn into a sophisticated new form of selection and surveillance. Three aspects of the political perspective are important to the assessment debate.

First, alternative or divergent classroom assessment (Torrance & Pryor, 1998) emphasizes the learner's understanding rather than the agenda of the assessor. It concentrates on discovering what the child knows, understands, or can do. Students have to accept some responsibility for learning, and teachers are charged with creating the conditions for this to occur. Assessment is part of the process; it is an essential part of learning that allows teachers, students, and parents to identify the extent to which learning has occurred and to set directions for the next stage (Earl & LeMahieu, 1997; Gipps, 1994; Stiggins, 1995). In this approach to assessment, it is important that assessment criteria are transparent, equally available to all, and publicly contestable in their application; that assessment criteria are known to students and often developed collaboratively with them so that better understanding can be developed and classroom power can be redistributed; that assessment judgments are acts of explicit negotiation among all those involved; and that assessment processes move in many directions, from student to student and student to teacher, and between parents and teachers, for example, as well as from teacher to student. This is a fundamental shift in the politics of assessment from decades of practice where teachers used their power to judge and classify students according to criteria and processes that were mysterious, secret, and often arbitrary.

Second, while alternative assessment promises to establish more positive micropolitical relationships among teachers, students, and parents, politics can also undermine the successful implementation of these new strategies. For example, high schools typically pressure their elementary colleagues to use more conventional forms of measurement and reporting. So do parents. Coordinating assessment expectations across communities and systems is a considerable political challenge for assessment reformers as well as a technical one.

Many of these contradictions that surface in our data are embedded in assessment policy itself. They represent different points of view about assessment held by teachers, on the one hand, and educational policymakers and the real and imagined public to whom they cater, on the other. These contradictory forces have made assessment reform a schizophrenic activity (Earl & LeMahieu, 1997; Firestone, Mayrowetz, & Fairman, 1998). It is hard to expect teachers to harmonize their assessment practices when policymakers and the wider public cannot.

These inconsistencies are deeply embedded in policy (Nuttall, 1994; Darling-Hammond, 1992). One group of reformers holds that educational change and improved student learning are the responsibility of some external individual or group in authority who has the power to judge quality, exercise control, and order compliance. Assessment is used as the mechanism to provide evidence for these decisions. Hard, numerical, standardized, and comparable assessment data culled from examinations or objective tests, applied consistently to large populations, are what these groups of reformers desire. This view is often based on the assumption that teachers have both the capacity and the ability to act in different, more productive ways but are unfocused, recalcitrant, lazy, or unmotivated. The obvious remedy for increasing student learning is to apply pressure and issue educational reform directives.

Other reformers believe that educational change and improved student learning are largely internal processes that the people who live and work in classrooms must undertake. The major purpose of assessment in this case is to help teachers and students improve classroom learning. Assessment is an opportunity for them to reflect, question, plan, teach, study, and learn. Assessment reform is not connected to compliance with mandates but is rooted in the constructivist view that learning depends on self-monitoring and reflection. Reformers committed to this stance assume that many teachers do not have current knowledge or skills about changing theories of learning or assessment (the technical perspective) and require support to acquire knowledge and training before they can change their practices. Assessment reform, in this view, provides an opportunity for teachers to share ideas and discuss their standards together, reach agreement about consistent and equitable expectations for quality, and create feedback loops directed toward changing the way they teach (the cultural perspective).

The political and practical conundrum for teachers is that pol-icy-makers often avoid choosing between these different value positions about educational change and the reform groups who support them. To maintain support and avoid criticism, they blur the issues and try to appeal to both camps (Hargreaves, Earl, & Ryan, 1996; Firestone, Mayrowetz, & Fairman, 1998) by embracing common standards and individual variation, numerical comparability, and descriptive sensitivity; improving individual student learning; and placating demands for systemwide accountability. Teachers are left to cope with the consequences—ones that, as we shall see, even our change-oriented teachers found exasperating. Resolving these contradictions should therefore be a political problem for policymakers to resolve, not merely a practical problem that is passed down to teachers.

The political perspective also highlights risks and excesses of alternative assessment practices themselves. This is especially true in the assessment of affect, where some teachers seem to exercise behavioral surveillance over everything their students do as an unending set of judgments from which there seems little escape (Foucault, 1977; Hargreaves, 1989). Continuous student assessment, self-assessment, peer assessment, and portfolio assessment can turn individual students into documented cases or dossiers that can be retrieved and referred to at any future point in order to classify, normalize, or exclude them in some way (Foucault, 1977). Such processes permit educational selection to be self-guided and allow failure to be disclosed gradually, in stages, as in the therapeutic, rather than the sudden and shocking, disclosures about terminal illness that medical staff are encouraged to make to hospital patients (Hopfl & Linstead, 1993). Alternative assessments can stage the gradual disclosure of failure the way modern medicine stages the disclosure of death.

In short, the political perspective draws attention to the acts and relationships of power embedded in assessment processes—whether these take the forms of empowering practices of shared, open, and negotiated assessment and reporting practices; the power plays of competing interest groups and their expectations on the terrain of assessment; or the more subtle and sinister forms of power that can infuse and infect alternative assessment practices themselves with processes of behavioral surveillance and covert, "therapeutic" selection practices that become the antithesis of what alternative assessment claims to be.

The Postmodern Perspective

A postmodern perspective on alternative assessment is based on the view that in today's complex, diverse, and uncertain world, human beings are not completely knowable. In culturally diverse classrooms, how children learn, think, feel, and believe is acknowledged as being complex (Ryan, 1995). What is important or real to children today in their world of "real virtuality"—of CDs, MTV, Walkmen, Discmen, computers, video games, and multi-channel TV—is also complex and constantly changing (Castells, 1997). Students, teachers say, have changed. They no longer seem knowable or predictable. Many teachers today feel that they have aliens in their classrooms (Green & Bigum, 1993).

In this complex and shifting scenario, no assessment process or system can be fully comprehensive, incontrovertibly accurate, or unshakably revelatory of the truth or essence of children's learning or achievement. Indeed, the meanings and assessment experiences that some describe as authentic are problematic in several senses. For one thing, little is unquestionably or indisputably true in a postmodern world. There are few right answers, or even best assessment processes. Alternative assessment may be diverse, wide ranging, negotiated, inclusive, and multifaceted, but this is precisely why it cannot be authentic in the sense of revealing some authoritative truth.

In the age of electronic education, when students have the power to cull instant information from multiple sources at the click of a mouse or to download pictures and pie charts rather than compiling and representing data themselves, it is more difficult to decide what is real and what is fake, to discern when students' work is their own, to determine whether the sources from which their work draws are reputable, and to decide if these things matter. In the postmodern paradigm, assessments clearly cannot be authentic in this second sense of indisputable origin either.

Third, while one meaning of *authentic* according to *Webster's Dictionary* is "close conformity to an original: accurately and satisfyingly reproducing essential features," as in a portrait, alternative assessments are actually less like realistic photographs or faithful portraits and more like cubist paintings—representing and interpreting rather than reproducing reality from multiple angles and perspectives.

Last, according to *Webster's, authentic* can also mean possessing "complete sincerity without feigning or hypocrisy." Yet the postmodern world of simulation is one where illusion is widespread and acceptable: new jeans are faded to look old, modern buildings are given traditional facades, digital music sounds better than a live performance, and fake rocks adorn the spectacular atriums of Las Vegas hotels because they look more real than real ones do (Ritzer, 1999). "Authentic" assessments simulate reality as much as they create it, producing beautiful fakes of grown-up book publications, theatrical performances, or artistic portfolios, for example. In all these ways, it is important to treat "authentic" assessment not as a cliché but as a point for critical inquiry (Meier, 1998).

The postmodern perspective points to both risks and opportunities in assessment reform. On the risk side, alternative assessments, especially portfolio assessments, can simulate rather than stimulate achievement. Students and teachers can be seduced into valuing form over substance, image over reality, with glossy covers, elegant fonts, and a sprinkling of multicolored graphs and flowcharts that mask mediocre content and analysis. Portfolios may become devices to drive and define students' achievement so that students perform community service or extracurricular activities not because of their moral value but because they want to have the right kind of curriculum vita or portfolio. In these ways, portfolio and performance assessments can trivialize and diminish the substance of learning, reducing it to surface appearances and "artificially contrived authenticity" (Mestrovic, 1997) in an unrigorous world of "feel good" improvement and what Ritzer (1999) calls a Disneyesque culture of niceness.

In more positive terms, postmodern assessment practices can offer multiple representations of students' learning in ways that give maximum voice and visibility to their diverse activities and accomplishments through written, numerical, oral, visual, technological, or dramatic media, which embody a mixture of styles, in a diverse portfolio of activity and achievement. Hierarchical distinctions of worth among these different forms of representation are diminished or eliminated so that the achievements of students from visually oriented cultures, for example, are not devalued compared to the achievements of students whose forte is more in the areas of writing or arithmetic. This approach allows students' work and achievements to be seen through multiple perspectives and allows the complexity of their abilities and identities to be acknowledged more readily.

Such a postmodern approach also involves the student's voice in the process of assessment and in determining how the products of assessment might be compiled and used. This student involvement is not just an act of empowerment; it is also a way for teachers to acknowledge that they cannot begin to know their students without having access to the self-understanding of students themselves.

Summary

In view of the contradictions and complexities surfaced by these different perspectives, it is scarcely surprising that teachers in our study told us that assessment was the hardest part of their work. Most of their conversations with us focused on trying to link their assessment and reporting practices to outcomes, trying to resolve contradictory expectations, communicating with parents, involving students, using a variety of alternative assessment procedures, and questioning their own and other people's assessment practices. The teachers also talked about their feelings of discomfort and uncertainty concerning assessment and evaluation and confessed that this anxiety had existed long before recent episodes of curriculum change. Let us look closely at how all these complexities and contradictions made themselves felt in the work of these teachers.

Assessing and Reporting Outcomes

An official educational priority at the time of our study was that outcomes or standards should drive the curriculum and that teachers should report student progress in relation to them. This requirement implied that teachers should assess students' performance on all of the outcomes and that reports to parents should reflect this kind of assessment. Teachers were blunt about their concerns. "How do we measure them?" they asked. They were unsure how to base their assessments on the outcomes and questioned their ability to speak confidently to parents about children's progress in terms of them.

A number of teachers identified assessment as their top professional development priority. They wanted to learn how to assess these outcomes. For these teachers, the technical complexity of the outcomes-based assessment system was formidable. One of them put it this way:

> How do we measure the indicators for the outcomes? We say this is the beginning and middle for this particular outcome, and you know at grade 9, you're talking about three-, four-, and five-dimensional matrices to really be able to understand it. There are too many twists and turns. If there's too much there to start with, how do you assess the "too much"?

The daunting profusion of assessment indicators was matched by the equally challenging problem of how to communicate with parents:

> There are specific outcomes for the end of grades 3, 6, and 9. But they're still meant to be general and you're going to have kids at the end of grade 3 who aren't there yet. How are we going to rationalize the evaluation to parents?

Reporting to parents was especially difficult because the reporting format was often discrepant with the new approaches to assessment that teachers were using:

> We had a lot of trouble this year because the marks don't mesh with the new outcomes-based report card. I can certainly see if a kid is exceeding or meeting the outcomes, but then when you have to match that with a mark, that's where we're having trouble.

Linking assessment and reporting practices to outcomes and indicators was difficult work, but teachers were not all at sea on this. With effort and experimentation, they generally became more aware of what they were trying to assess and devised a number of ways to approach this new task:

> I have all of the outcomes posted that we are addressing, and as we complete work, we write out the outcomes that the piece of work would address. Then every week, we have a reflection of the week's learning, and the kids identify what learning they had done, as well as what outcomes they specifically had addressed, and they set an academic goal and a social goal.

> We sat down, and we talked about the writing outcome—how to present material in different ways to different audiences. And then we looked at different ways in which this should be evaluated, and the kids and I made up the evaluation criteria together. Then they assessed what it should be out of a total score of 5 or 6 for each particular criterion that we came up with.

> The eighth graders did a skills-for-success continuum, and we targeted fourteen areas, many of the ones that the kids had already worked through, on a 0–3 continuum. The kids decided where they felt they were on the continuum, and then their core teacher and at least one other subject specialist teacher sat down and marked on the continuum where they saw the student. Then they sat down and did a gap analysis, and the kids had to set a goal out of it.

These quotations indicate how much importance teachers attached to the cultural, political, and even postmodern process of students' being involved in devising and applying the evaluation criteria. The following teacher's remarks echo the same themes:

> Ideally the students generate the criteria for the evaluation. They talk about it, and then we weight it. Last term, they wrote a creation myth as the major piece of writing. We talked about it as a class. What would you see in a creation myth? Well, these are the characteristics. And in a good piece of writing, these are the characteristics. And from that comes the evaluation. So they essentially generate the evaluation criteria, and that is what I use to evaluate their work.

Students were also encouraged to use specific criteria when they engaged in peer and self-evaluation:

I worked the unit so that they self-evaluate and peer-evaluate and have very specific criteria to go by. And they are really very good. They are pretty accurate. I thought they would all give themselves glowing marks, but they were pretty close to my own.

They had the mark sheet when they were given the assignment. They knew the criteria, knew what I was looking for, and that is the biggest change I think I've seen.

Using criteria and descriptors rather than letters and numbers to evaluate students' work does not mean that schoolwork can no longer be differentiated or that poorer and better quality cannot be discriminated. What matters is that the criteria are full and clear:

One of the things that I learned quickly was to move away from numbers. Don't ever put the numbers 1, 2, 3, down. Go to the descriptors, and yes there is a ranking of them, but they are far better. It's far better if we're developing the kids to say, "We have whatever ranking it is, but let's work through it." They know when we do it that it is much easier to explain it in words, if they have a word to work with, instead of a number.

Teachers genuinely tried to be clear about their outcomes and about linking the assessment to the outcomes. But they commented repeatedly on the difficulties this created for them, especially when they had to explain to parents what they were doing in the reporting process. At this stage of implementing changes in assessment, teachers felt ill at ease and had difficulty reconciling the contradictions they were experiencing.

Confronting Contradictions

Some of the contradictions seemed to exist in the curriculum policy itself. Teachers found it difficult to square the requirements of outcomes-based reporting with pressures for accountability and common standards that seemed to call for more traditional ways of recording and reporting their students' progress and achievements. This apparent inconsistency was not just a source of irritation and confusion for the teachers in our study. It is a massive and unresolved political issue in the assessment and accountability reform movement as a whole (Earl & LeMahieu, 1997; Firestone,

Mayrowetz, & Fairman, 1998). Is it even possible to use the same assessments for sorting and selecting students that are used as feedback for improving learning? How far were the change-oriented teachers in our study able to reconcile the emphasis on assessment as a way to improve learning in the classroom with the mounting pressure for testing and standardization? They certainly found this contradiction infuriating:

> It includes integrating all the subjects and looking for the outcomes of skills—not necessarily content driven, but they want them to do common testing. We're supposed to be teaching for those outcomes of learning skills and how to learn. What has that got to do with common testing?

> I worry, when they go to high school, will they be able to write a test in the amount of time that they need in order to produce what they know? In the end, we're not testing knowledge. Saying, "Okay—you have thirty seconds to answer this" is not testing knowledge.

As we saw in the previous chapter, these contradictions and confusions were seen as particularly problematic when the program had to be modified to meet the needs of students with learning or other special needs. How could teachers address and accommodate individual differences and have consistent standards at the same time? Our earlier discussion of the political aspects of classroom assessment reform makes it clear that there is no simple formula for finding a balance between conflicting reform orientations to assessment and accountability until we rethink accountability so that it supports rather than interferes with the classroom learning process (Earl & LeMahieu, 1997).

Another tension for teachers is between using assessment for educational selection and using it to support individual student learning and to promote students' motivation to be engaged in that learning (Hargreaves, 1989; Earl & Cousins, 1995). For example, if an assessment is to be diagnostic, the process should expose students' weaknesses and failures. However, it would be foolish to expect students (or their teachers) to take this risk of exposing weaknesses and failures in a selection exam or if the test were used to hold the school accountable for the performance of its students.

These different views about the purposes of educational assessment—for simple and standardized rank ordering and selection and for complex, individualized diagnosis and motivation—are still both present in political and public debate about assessment. Yet it is teachers who are left to deal with these contradictions, as well as their own ambivalence about the purposes of assessment.

Communicating with Parents

Another source of the contradictory orientations to assessment that teachers encounter is teachers' relationships with parents. One of the greatest areas of anxiety in teachers' work is the interaction that teachers must have with parents. Along with discipline, assessment and reporting are a prime focal point of this anxiety (Vincent, 1996). As one teacher said, "You're talking to a parent whose most precious possession is their child. You need to be accountable. And that's kind of scary sometimes." Wilson (1990) found that teachers generally engage in evaluation practices that are aimed primarily at producing defensible marks for reporting purposes. Many teachers need to feel they are able to account plausibly and persuasively for their students' progress.

Historically, teachers have translated all their detailed assessments into single numeric or letter summaries, by which students are either implicitly compared to their cohorts or measured against a standard. Parents understand these kinds of judgments because they themselves experienced them. Their representation in symbol or numeric form also gives them a semblance of certainty (which is hard to challenge if the criteria and evidence for reaching the letter or figure are kept secret or not made explicit). Against these historical, community-based, and to some extent political expectations for assessment and reporting, other policy emphases encourage teachers to differentiate and customize their programs according to individual student needs and to use sophisticated assessment strategies of diagnosis and self-monitoring that will enhance that process.

In our study, all four school districts had started to experiment with new procedures to make student reports more consistent with the outcomes, but there were still great mismatches between the goals of curriculum integration in the official policy document and the categories of subject specialization through which students' work had to be evaluated on existing report cards, as the following comments attest:

> There's a new report card, but when you get into the classroom, you still have a contradiction in the fact that you have subjects.

> Our report card has everything broken up in bits and pieces. If the teacher is doing an integrated unit, how does she suddenly separate geography from science from health?

Many teachers faced the problem of translating their changes in teaching and assessment into marks and then grades for the report card. Because of the internal contradictions, they were concerned about whether parents would understand the changes and interpret the report cards correctly. The greatest area of confusion was between ipsative (self-referenced) reporting that focused on student growth in relation to their own past performance and norm-referenced reporting that evaluated performance in relation to other students. It seemed impossible to do both with a single grade:

> The fault may lie with the modifications for students with learning disabilities. You still average in those modified students (that is, learning disabled), so it's not a true picture of where their child falls in the class. Even though you write on the report card "modified program," the parents don't see that; they see the mark. Parents would love to see how their child stacks up in relation to the position of others in the class.

Despite the immense difficulties of resolving contradictory assessment imperatives, finding better ways of reporting to parents was an area in which the teachers in our study showed exceptional imagination, creativity, and commitment, and they experienced considerable success. Teachers approached better communication not just as a technical task—as policies of clearly aligning learning standards and assessment practices are inclined to do. They treated this problem as one of creating better cultural understanding and changing the politics of teacher-parent relationships as well. Their efforts did not merely mollify parents by nipping potential criticism in the bud. For the most part, these teachers did not approach parents with an attitude of professional superiority or one of uncritical compliance. Rather, they approached the reporting process as one of open communication from which parents, teachers, and students would all learn in a quest for closer understanding. This reporting process was seen as being not only a way of communicating learning but as a form of learning in itself. Teachers brought this about in a variety of ways:

- Having students fill out a strengths, needs, and highlights of the term sheet to share with their parents:

  I feel that when we're interviewing and the students are also letting their parents know where they are at and where they should be going, the parents feel very comfortable.

- Sending outcomes and assessment criteria home with the students and including them in a newsletter so that they could be on the wall, on the refrigerator door, or in a notebook if parents wanted. The important thing was to create an atmosphere in which students were let in on the secret and assessment was no longer a mystery.

- Using portfolios to get students and their parents to talk together before the parent interview:

  I really liked the way the interviews went this time. I think it improved communication not only between the kids and the parents, but between the kids, the parents, and the teacher and the school. There just seemed to be a more comfortable air about the interviews. It wasn't as if people were worrying, "What am I going to hear about my child?" They basically knew ahead of time. It gave them time to sort through their thoughts so that they could come in and really discuss it, not just be talked at.

- Three-way interviews, involving parents, students, and teachers together:

  I like the idea of talking to both the students and the parents at the same time. The power of the portfolio conference is that the students have an opportunity to talk about what they have done, where they are going, and what their goals are. This is tremendous power, and you can see it in the parents' faces; they had really listened to what their son or daughter had been doing. They really understood it, and it related to the report card.

When we did reports this time, we had three staff interviews after the reports went home. Both the parents and the children came to the interviews. Before the children came in, they had a chance to go over what they thought their areas of strength and weaknesses were and ways they felt they could improve. So when they came to the interview, we had the report to go from. We had what the child felt were his or her areas of strength and weakness and the teacher's if they differed from the child's. The parents also had time ahead of time to write down things they wanted to talk about, so when we all came in—teacher, child, and parents—everybody was organized for the interview and knew the types of things that were going to be discussed. I think it really improved the communication not only between the kids and the parents but between the kids, the parents, and the teacher and the school. Not one parent came to the principal with concerns about the interview.

- Carefully disaggregating marks so that the criteria and evidence through which they have been created are open, accessible, and clear:

  I have all my marks broken down, so they can see exactly where they are in their marks. They like the fact that they know exactly how their mark was calculated. They might not like the mark, but they perceive it as being a lot more objective, so that when the parents come in for interviews, I have that ready for them. For the interviews, I have the whole list of their child's marks to date on paper for them, and I put it down in front of them.

- Using a daily agenda to maintain continuous contact with parents:

  The kids keep track in their agenda of the work that they have, and every night they need to get it signed by the parents. Parents or students can write me a note in their agenda if the student has had trouble with something, and I write back. I could be writing to the student; I could be writing to the parent. This is an area for continual contact with the parents daily.

- Informal contacts with parents beyond written reports and agendas or formal meetings:

> Last year I had time and actually called parents up from time to time when a kid had written a particularly good lab report and said, 'I just wanted to let you know that your child hadn't been doing so well, and all of a sudden she hands in this wonderful lab report and I'm impressed with it.' That earns me brownie points; the payoff is phenomenal. The parents are so happy.

While many of the contradictory assessment imperatives we have described are not open to easy resolution by classroom teachers, parents are potentially very accessible to teachers, and the long-standing assumptions they tend to hold about assessment and its purposes are by no means immutable if they are approached in a spirit of openness and with a view to bringing about learning.

Regressing to listing a child's position in relation to the existing class mean is an easy and popular way to respond to parents' reporting demands—ones that are based on their own nostalgic memories of schooling from three decades or so ago (Hargreaves, 2000). As these teachers have shown, the more difficult yet educationally valid and quite attainable task is to meet the challenge of reporting fully and openly to parents and help them understand how well their children are doing. The task of educational policy should not be to pander to popular prejudice, but to deepen everyone's understanding of learning and assessment issues in today's world (not the childhood world that parents remember) so that all children's learning can be elevated to a higher standard.

Later, we describe how teachers often feel like assessment impostors—so that secretly, they believe that beneath the categorical certainty of numbers and letters, most assessment judgments are suspect. One way to dispel the feeling of being an assessment impostor is to abandon any pretense that one's judgments or measurements of students' work are or can be scientifically certain and infallible. Instead, teachers can agree on reasonably clear and consistent criteria with their colleagues, then share openly with students and parents the uncertainty and the skilled sensitivity of how these criteria can be applied to those unique items of work with which students and their parents are immediately concerned. This is a cultural and political shift, not just a technical fix.

Openness takes the mystery out of marking and the magic out of judgment. Openness about assessment issues connects teachers to students and parents in a shared attempt to review progress together instead of placing teachers on pedestals of evaluative power and judgmental certainty above them. The teachers in our study were a long way on the road to achieving that more open state.

Involving Students

Classroom assessment reform involves a kind of cultural politics that changes relationships of power and communication, not merely technical procedures among all those involved in the assessment process. Nowhere is this more evident than in teachers' relationships with students. Many teachers in our study wanted evaluation to "be a comfortable interplay between student and teacher." By this, they meant:

- More emphasis on student self-assessment
- More joint reviews of progress between students and their teachers
- More sharing of assessment targets with students
- More active partnerships between teachers, students, and their parents in discussions about progress
- More attention to assessing and recognizing student achievement in the affective domain

In the area of self-assessment, teachers valued how students could assess their own individual progress or the progress of their group. They liked portfolios because they could help students develop greater independence by encouraging them to set up their own learning plan. Self-assessment could also help students identify what they still needed to know, enabling them to monitor their own learning more effectively over time. Teachers promoted student self-assessment in a number of ways:

When I do a rubric, I have "Teacher," "Peer," and "Self" at the top, and we use the same criteria. They use it and their peers use it, and we do a comparison. If you're going to demand excellence, you can set it so nobody can reach it, or you can build to it. We are building to it—really thinking about what we are assessing and how we are going to do it.

As we are completing work, we often stop and reflect, "All right, what outcome does this meet?" We begin to make connections. "What has been good is . . . " "If I had . . . it would have been much better."

They have a chart where they write the outcome and then they write the activities once they have done that related to that outcome. Then they self-assess how they have done on that specific outcome.

Some teachers' stories about the benefits of self-assessment were especially moving in their portrayals of how students achieved breakthroughs in self-awareness—for example:

I said to them something a little different today: "Instead of refiling your portfolio, I want you to keep it. I want you to look through it. I want you to make a statement in front of the whole class about how you feel about it at this stage in the game and the reason for your feeling, if you can say that." And they all go, "Oh, please Miss, don't make us say that!" Anyway they did it, and in fact it was sort of teary at one point. One kid said to me, said in front of the class, and this is an eighth-grade boy: "You know, my whole life, I thought I knew that I'm not very smart. I'm not very academic, and therefore I thought I wasn't very good at very many things." But then now he looks in the portfolio and even though he's still not very academic, there are so many things that he is good at.

A good thing happened to me last year about assessment. A girl came up to me who had started off completely lost at the beginning of the year. By May, she said the nicest thing I had heard in a long time. She said to me, "One day, after you assess something, is it okay if you feel good about yourself?" And I said to her, "What do you mean?" She said, "Well, I'm doing so much better, and I feel really good, but I don't want to feel conceited." And I said, "But you are not talking conceit; you are talking confidence, which means that you feel good." She may never be the brightest one in the classroom, but she feels good about herself and she is learning more than she thought she could.

In addition to promoting self-assessment, many teachers liked to share assessment targets and criteria with their classes. One teacher felt it very important that "the kids understand that whenever I evaluate on something, they generally know how they're going to be evaluated." Another took pride in "how everything I do, the kids get up front. Everything I want them to learn, they get up front. How they are going to be evaluated, they get up front. There is no mystery." Sharing outcomes with students was important: "Showing them first what exactly you are marking allows them to know exactly what the expectations are." One teacher reported letting students see on the computer how their marks had been calculated, which "they really like to see."

Specifying and sharing assessment criteria in this way could help increase students' own understanding:

> Students have a big problem with assessment because they are used to black and white. Either the question is right, or it is wrong; it is never gray or has shades. They say, "Well, I worked as hard as I could." And I say, "Effort is an important part of assessment; however, smart is important too." When I speak about smart, I speak about thinking skills, and I try to show them examples to help them understand this.

> Kids were student secretaries for the parent interview night. Instead of just saying to them, "Thanks for doing it; I really appreciate your help," I sent them all letters talking about their organizational skills and their punctuality and the things that made them do a good job. For us, it's really becoming important to get the kid to see it's not just a good job but why it's a good job, and to see they got a certain mark because they met this criterion or didn't meet this criterion.

Students were not only being expected to understand their learning but also to take responsibility for it as a personal and rigorous process, with rewards and consequences:

> It is interesting because they have to be accountable for what they are doing, and they are starting to see that this does matter, and we have a list of criteria to go through.

It really puts the onus on the children—makes them more responsible for their own learning.

Assessment is not only a vehicle for student learning; it is also a way of learning for teachers, helping them improve their teaching strategies. Teachers appreciated that their own practice could be opened to scrutiny, and they used assessment to help them reflect on and change how they taught. Teachers saw assessment as a reciprocal activity that allowed all the participants to pause, reflect, and learn from the assessment results in a continuous feedback loop. Sometimes teachers got feedback by asking students for their opinions—for example:

I ask the kids at the end, "Where could I have changed things? What was the most difficult thing in this unit? If you were the teacher, how would you change it?" to help me out so that next year when I teach, I look back and see where I can make those changes to help the kids. I'm getting feedback, and I'm trying to learn from their feedback so I can improve the course.

At other times, teachers summarized class results and used the patterns to identify how they needed to modify their teaching and plan the program:

I have all the skills at the top, and when we do our unit test, I'll have a look at that and see what reflection it has on what they've done on a day-to-day basis. We will see where we are, and I'll know who needs more help—both where and when.

I use evaluation to see the kids' development—how they are coming along the road to mastering things—as much as I can, where I'm starting with them.

Involving students in their own assessment was an unfamiliar and innovative activity for most of the teachers in our project, but it was also an insightful and productive one that furthered students' understanding, increased their responsibility for their own learning, and gave teachers useful feedback on their own teaching. In other words, the cultural politics of classroom assessment changes once teachers decide to get students actively involved in the assessment process.

Developing an Assessment Repertoire

The project teachers used a vast number of approaches to assess and evaluate student learning. Official curriculum policy emphasized the value of using a variety of assessment techniques, and teachers in our study responded positively to this direction. In their own words:

> Not so heavy on the testing, our guidelines stress conferences, essays, independent studies, interviews, inventions, journals, observations, peer evaluations, portfolios, presentations, projects, reports, self-evaluations, simulations, tests, and videos. Testing is just a very tiny spot for me as a teacher in assessing their knowledge.

> They have tests for that unit in the textbook, but I also have peer evaluations, group evaluations, and self-evaluations.

Narrowing the range of assessment strategies tends to restrict how and what teachers teach. A broader curriculum with more ambitious learning goals calls for a broader, more ambitious array of assessment strategies too. In this respect, when teachers (and policymakers) widen their repertoire of assessment strategies, they are better able to meet their students' learning needs and elevate standards of learning more effectively.

Assessing Affect

One growing tendency in widening the assessment domain is to embrace affective and attitudinal qualities more fully. Assessing the affective domain is notoriously difficult. It appears to be more prone to subjectivity and prejudicial judgment than any other area of assessment. It also runs serious risks of invading people's privacy and evaluating their emotions and behavior as a way of enforcing compliance and control (Hargreaves, 1989). Yet the most difficult and controversial areas of education—those that touch people's hearts as well as their minds—are often the most important. Developing and recognizing young people's emotional intelligence are significant achievements in their own rights, and ones that add value to intellectual achievement (Goleman, 1995).

In entering the affective domain of student assessment, beyond the customary preoccupation with "effort," teachers in our study were confronting serious and significant challenges. In general, most of our respondents tried to evaluate more than students' academic achievement. For them, student assessment should address the whole child. But often the way teachers described how they assessed affect seemed tantamount to exerting evaluative control: exercising behavioral surveillance over everything their students did as an unending set of judgments from which there seemed little escape (Foucault, 1977; Hargreaves, 1989).

Here, the politics of alternative assessment had the potential to work against students rather than in their favor. Assessing the affective domain for many teachers entailed using checklists to assess things like body language, the amount of work produced, making positive comments to one's group partners, paying attention in class, displaying positive attitudes toward the subject, completing homework, showing willingness to seek extra help from the teacher, "making a snarky comment," or categorizing "an exceptional student who really understands the concepts well but may have terrible cooperative team skills," which would therefore detract from his A grade. Some teachers kept things of this sort in mind or put check marks in their mark book to record them.

In one instance, peer evaluation, which can be extremely useful as an honest and valued form of feedback among students, had virtually degenerated into snitching and spying. This teacher reported how peer evaluation might involve

> having somebody else look at the number and say, "Why are you putting down 8 out of 10? I remember the times when you told so-and-so to f— off. You know, Mr. X, you didn't hear that, so maybe you should think about lowering that a bit."

In large part, many of the affective attributes that teachers assessed seemed to be synonyms for student compliance with the behavioral norms of schooling, not ones like questioning, risk taking, assertiveness, initiative, or creativity that might serve students better in the world beyond school (even if they might raise management problems for the teachers who taught them).

The assessment dangers for teachers in the affective domain lurk everywhere. Teachers may inadvertently use assessment for punishment and surveillance or as a way to control behavior. Students routinely received marks for compliant classroom behavior. In addition, concern for self-esteem and for maintaining feelings of success among some students might tempt teachers to hold back the real success of others in order to avoid invidious comparisons and feelings of inferiority. We came across only one instance of this sort, but it is a dramatic and cautionary one:

> I had a parent who came in. She and her daughter are from Eastern Europe. Her daughter is very strong, and she is doing very well. The mother said, "You are not challenging her enough." I said, "I agree." I'm not going to apologize for that. If I put my expectations up here, do you know how many kids in my class I am going to lose? Do you know how many are just going to fall by the wayside, fail, lose self-esteem and confidence, and just basically struggle through the whole year and not enjoy it? More than half. Way more than half. What do I do? I bring it down. Should I feel bad about that? I don't know. That is what I do, and what I have to do—both for my own sanity and to make them feel as if they are achieving something, that they are accomplishing things and feeling success.

In Chapter Six, we argue for more acknowledgment to be given to the emotional aspects of teaching, learning, and educational reform. In general, seventh- and eighth-grade classrooms probably need more emotion infused into them, not less. But more emotion is not always better. Affect can be used to control and manipulate, as well as to inspire. It can soften learning standards instead of engaging students in reaching for harder and higher ones. Mussolini's education minister, a great advocate of "progressive" education, once stated that from Italy's progressive schools would issue the fascist citizens of the future (Entwistle, 1979). Affect needs to be dealt with and assessed thoughtfully and reflectively in schools if it is to add to children's learning and not merely put them at their ease or make them easier to control.

In this sense, it is interesting that some teachers in our study pointed out that it was important not to assess everything or not to evaluate all of a child's portfolio. One teacher told a story that illustrated the sense of balance and perspective she felt it was important to maintain:

I have one little girl in my room who has a physical disability and has to deal with an awful lot in her life. If you question her in the class in front of the other kids, she is very self-conscious, and I think, "Oh, how can I mark a kid like that in communication skills?" I refuse to do that. It's a personality thing, and I'm not here to change a kid's personality. I will coax it along or I will try to develop it in certain ways—but that's all.

Assessment is inherently difficult work for teachers. If teachers fake the confidence and certainty with which their judgments are made, they are condemned to feel like impostors and to become defensive when others scrutinize those judgments. Really caring for students' intellectual and emotional development, and establishing caring relationships with students and parents to review that development, has led many teachers to develop new assessment practices and more open reporting systems that are demystifying the assessment and adding to, rather than undermining, teachers' professional judgments by bringing students and parents in on the secret of how these judgments are made.

Part of this new assessment technology is assessment of the affective domain itself. But while this offers the potential to recognize the development of students' emotional competence as an achievement in its own right, the affective qualities that teachers emphasize and assess often appear to be synonyms for classroom compliance. These assessments do not usually get much beyond the old idea of "effort." The emotional emphasis that pervades the work of many teachers is usually a good thing but not unilaterally so—and the confusion of care with control in assessment practices is an area about which we should remain especially vigilant.

Questioning Assessment

Assessment was clearly an area of heightened interest and concern for the teachers we interviewed. They expressed anxiety about an expanded notion of assessment and its many purposes and struggled hard with how to fit it all into their own conceptions of teaching and learning. These confusions and anxieties were far from resolved. Teachers felt like assessment impostors—people called on and expected to make judgments about which they remained unsure:

> I think for too long we've evaluated on a more subjective basis. I may think when I read a student's work, "It feels like an A to me when I'm reading this language, but what are the exact things?" And I don't think we've been very scientific about that.

> I have a hard time with subjective evaluation. It's very difficult for me, especially now, teaching language for the first time, I don't know what is an A paper or what is a B paper. I have to sort these things out, and so do my colleagues.

For some teachers, these questions and uncertainties were rooted in their own assumptions and long-standing beliefs about how assessment had been used in the past—for example:

> I struggle with assessment, against my background. I think part of keeping people subservient in the apartheid era [in South Africa, where she had taught] was to make them think they are not good enough.

In other cases, teachers talked about long-standing practices that needed to be reconsidered. One teacher expressed concern and frustration that the rich assessment data he had documented during grade 8 were virtually ignored at the high school in favor of a one-shot standardized test:

> The high school math department would like to issue to all of the feeder schools a standardized test so that they could get a sense of the kids who are coming in. It makes me think about all the evaluation that I've done on these kids through the year. I'm sending my kids over with three report cards that talk about decimals, or geometry, or integers, or whatever it is I've covered. What are they going to do with those results?

In other cases, assessment reform was leading teachers to question their own and not just other people's practices:

> I really stopped and thought, "Why am I evaluating everything?" and I started thinking about my kids—where we are going and

what I was really doing in assessment and whether I was really evaluating.

My approach to assessment has definitely changed from hard and fast to much more open. I make rubrics for the students from what an awareness would look like, or what a refined level would look like. I'm looking at more of a continuum for evaluation.

All of these uncertainties about assessment could expose teachers and make them feel vulnerable when they were questioned and confronted by parents. This drew some teachers toward preferring anecdotal assessments for their greater accuracy and completeness, along with portfolios, which could provide parents with more extensive information on which assessment judgments had been based. In a few cases, parents appeared to respond well to these more open and extensive assessment processes. But writing anecdotal comments, undertaking one-to-one conferencing, and generally managing the expanding armory of assessment technology raised additional problems by placing teachers under huge pressures of time. As one teacher put it, "I would really love to do anecdotal reports, but I resent the amount of time that it would take me to do. I would much rather parents come in and have an interview." Other teachers felt guilty about always being behind with their marking or about the fact that when they spent time with individuals in one-to-one conferencing, other students in the class might not be working.

Paradoxically, these constraints on teachers' classroom assessment practices could be increased by the time demands of imposed external testing. Teachers in one school district, for example, had to deal with a complex and demanding new literacy profile that had to be administered to all their students, as one teacher explained:

There is now this literacy report, which all students must have following them from kindergarten to grade 12. It is an amazing amount of work to be done by the teacher on each student. They have to have three samples of writing that has to have five pages of correlating check marks to go through, throughout each year, on each student they teach. And it involves assessment on an individual basis. I don't know how they are going to do this. We have just finished talking about all the other things on the plate. We earn a lot of money, but we bleed a lot and we sweat a lot, and this doesn't always come through.

The literacy assessment profile is a lot of work and a lot of testing. There's just so much going on that all you're doing is testing, all you're doing is assessment. There's very little so-called teaching-learning going on because we're spending so much time testing.

If more detailed and comprehensive forms of assessment took their toll on teachers' time, other kinds of assessment that demanded less effort from teachers were usually disliked because they were seen as superficial and inaccurate. One teacher resented report cards based on computer-generated comments:

You put in comment 234, and none of the comments even suit me, I want to change them all every time. When I was doing language arts and social studies, it drove me absolutely batty. And many teachers just have two comments for an A and two comments for a B, and everybody got the same stuff. It drove me nuts.

Another teacher disliked computer-based report cards because she did not feel that the reports really shared a good perception of the students. The comments were condensed and contrived and were often a poor match for the program goals that were based on integration or common learning outcomes.

Teachers in our study questioned assessment practices a lot. They questioned or were unsure about the validity of traditional patterns of grading and marking, they were critical about external testing that perpetuated such traditions and intruded on their own efforts to develop alternative forms of assessment, and they reflected on and reconstructed their own assessment practices. Sometimes this questioning did not extend far enough—for example, in differentiating purposes or addressing the problems of assessing the affective domain. But in general, teachers were highly reflective about their own and other people's assessment practices.

Implications

Assessment, evaluation, and reporting to parents will be central issues in educational reform for some time. Although teachers in our project were aware and sometimes critical of systemwide assessment initiatives, they were extremely interested in the assessments they carried out in their own classes and in how parents understood and used the resulting information. They had certainly made many changes to their assessment practices in an attempt to link assessment to outcomes, provide their students with different opportunities to show their learning, and use assessment as a vehicle for improving students' learning and their program. Although teachers worked diligently and sometimes expressed pride in their newfound understanding of assessment, they still conveyed a very strong sense that assessment was the Achilles' heel of educational reform.

Paradoxically, assessment was at one and the same time the most vulnerable aspect of teachers' work that had to be kept protected and the most public and visible part of the schooling process. Teachers were often almost schizoid in their views about assessment. They described complex and elaborate processes that they used to help students become accurate and wise self-assessors, and thereby more responsible for their own learning, in close conjunction with their need to prepare students for the exigencies of what they saw as impersonal and uncaring high school exams. They struggled and agonized over computer-generated report cards, which they felt were incompatible with their programs, while worrying that parents would discover the inconsistencies and not be able to interpret or understand the reports. They vacillated between their roles as judges of students' achievement and gatekeepers of their future and their roles as describers of student performance, as well as coaches and guides for students' own decision making. And they moved between using assessment as a kind of secret surveillance for regulating students' behavior and having open conversations with students and engaging them in defining assessment tasks and evaluative criteria.

Teachers were making great strides in expanding their assessment practices, but they found it hard to articulate or take a stand on assessment policy and practices as a whole. Assessment was clearly the area of work where they were most uncomfortable. They showed signs of suspecting that they were operating as assessment impostors, without the kind of confidence and certainty that they believed should accompany evaluative decisions.

It was not yet clear how teachers could resolve these uncertainties and dilemmas. One of them revealed her consternation and frustration by wishing out loud that teachers could just be plain honest with parents and have candid conversations about the students. A very small number of the teachers were tentatively beginning to abandon the pretense that their assessments of students were certain or infallible, and they tried to discuss all of the available information and possibilities openly with students and parents. This was rewarding but also unsettling for them.

There were and are no easy answers in the cultural politics of assessment reform. Encouragingly, these teachers had developed and expanded their assessment expertise considerably compared to teachers whom we had interviewed in related projects five years previously. This is exceptional technical progress. Yet assessment and accountability continued to define a complex and confusing terrain for teachers, and much in the way of formal training can still be done to improve teachers' knowledge and skill in this area. Stiggins (1991), for example, calls for more education of teachers in "the basics of assessment to know whether or not their achievement data are sound or unsound . . . [and] to be critical consumers of assessment data." At the same time, many of the confusions in assessment practice cannot be attributed to shortfalls in teacher competence or failure to master assessment technicalities. Assessment and accountability policy is shot through with unresolved political contradictions, and until these problems are addressed, teachers' difficulties with assessment reform are likely to persist.

| Curriculum Integration

The integrated or interdisciplinary curriculum is one of the most ambitious yet also contentious aspects of educational reform, as it seeks to connect classroom learning to the lives and understandings of all students. Integration is an attractive proposition for those who want the curriculum and the way students experience it to be less fragmented. Yet more than a quarter-century ago, Basil Bernstein (1971) prophetically argued that by reconceptualizing the subject-based and subject-segregated knowledge that has traditionally been at the basis of people's success and social mobility, curriculum integration threatens the fundamental structures of power and control in society—what he called its basic classifications and frames. Since then, Bernstein's predictions have often been realized in a series of onslaughts against integration and its excesses, and in related reassertions of a conventional, subject-based curriculum.

For example, the National Curriculum of England and Wales—prescriptive, subject based, and content loaded—was legislated in 1988 after widely publicized criticisms from conservative think tanks that increasingly popular initiatives in personal, social, and political education were not proper subjects, squeezed more important subjects out of the curriculum, exposed students to ideas that were too difficult for them, and contained ideological bias (Cox & Scruton, 1984; Scruton, Ellis-Jones, & O'Keefe, 1985; and see Hargreaves, Lieberman, Fullan, & Hopkins, 1998, for a critique). Meanwhile, in the United States, the battle over learning standards is being taken over by the school-subject associations. Their efforts to control the detail of what learning standards will be in each subject area perpetuate a historical and political role of defining and defending the curriculum through conventional subject categories in ways that serve the interests and careers of the members who belong to these subject-teaching associations (Goodson & Ball, 1985).

Initiatives in curriculum integration exist in uneasy tension and sometimes direct contradiction to these more subject-based and subject-centered curriculum reforms. Some national curriculum policies—in the predominantly Catholic countries of Ireland and Spain, for example—give stronger recognition to integrated knowledge and the idea of care in general as providing solid foundations for secondary school learning. Elsewhere, curriculum integration has emerged as a response to adolescent alienation and underachievement, especially in the early secondary school years—in some parts of Australia, for example (Eyers, 1992).

Within the United States, curriculum integration that takes place in more localized and voluntary ways coexists uneasily with federal and state prescriptions of subject-based standards. Integration continues to be important in middle school reform (Beane, 1991), curriculum areas such as language arts (Norton, 1988; Stanl & Miller, 1989), and many of the corporate- or foundation-supported reform movements that give priority to teachers' knowing their students well, such as the Coalition for Essential Schools (Wang, Haertel, & Walberg, 1998), the Annenberg Institute for Educational Reform (McAdoo, 1998), and the Comer Schools (Haynes, 1998).

Advocates of curriculum integration claim that it allows teachers to address important issues that cannot always be neatly packaged into subjects, develops wider views of subjects among students, reflects the seamless web of knowledge, and reduces redundancy of content (Case, 1991). They also argue that it encourages teachers to work as teams, sharing both content and children in common (Kain, 1996; Spies, 1996) and making it possible to bring teachers together by bringing content together. Integration, its advocates say, provides opportunities for information exchange among teachers about commonly held interests and talents, as well as about the teaching goals, themes, and organizing concepts in their subject areas (Gehrke, 1991). Most important of all, perhaps, curriculum integration is said to benefit all students by making learning more relevant to students' diverse lives.

Interdisciplinary curriculum has a long history, stretching back to the first half of the twentieth century (Wraga, 1997). For example, John Dewey (1938) emphasized the importance of connecting students' learning to their everyday experiences. In *Experience and Education,* he argued:

> A primary responsibility of educators is that they not only be aware of the general principle of the shaping of actual experience by environing conditions, but that they also recognize in the concrete what surroundings are conducive to having experiences that lead to growth. Above all, they should know how to utilize the surroundings, physical and social, that exist so as to extract from them all that they have to contribute to building up experiences that are worth while [p. 40].

More recently, psychologists of learning have stressed the necessity of connecting the curriculum, and how teachers teach it, to the prior knowledge that students possess through which they make sense of what they are asked to learn (Leinhardt, 1992). The burgeoning realities of ethnocultural diversity have also pressed educators to acknowledge the need to make the curriculum more responsive to the existing knowledge and learning styles of the diverse groups that make up a school (Cummins, 1998). Educators are struggling to define and bring to life principles of contextualization (Tharp, Dalton, & Yamauchi, 1994) or relevance (Hargreaves, Earl, & Ryan, 1996), which can connect learning to the experiences of all who undertake it and increase all students' engagement with and success in their learning (Smith, Donahue, & Vibert, 1998). The first part of our ensuing analysis examines what these principles of contextualization or relevance looked like in the practice of the teachers we studied.

Curriculum integration is intellectually and ideologically contested. In theory, this often confines integration and subject specialization to two ideological and political solitudes, each portrayed as a panacea by its proponents and an evil by its critics. Both advocates and adversaries of integration often adopt exaggerated justifications for their cause, locked in a battle between the essentialism of subject disciplines and the relativism of all knowledge.

As we have seen, however, where integration already exists in practice, this is almost always in conjunction with parallel systems of subject-based standards, curriculum content, and forms of assessment—in contexts where educators and policymakers want the benefits of both specialization and integration but do not want to alienate their opponents either (Sabar & Silberstein, 1998). This uneasy coexistence and the divisions that lurk beneath its surface create many tensions for educators who work within the field of curriculum integration and are keen to commit themselves to it. The second part of the analysis shows how these tensions are played out in the process of implementing curriculum integration and making it come to life in students' classrooms.

The Substance of Integration

The teachers we interviewed were eager to show us the integrated units of work they had prepared with colleagues and were using in teaching their students. They were proud of their curriculum writing efforts and freely leafed through newly produced binders and resource packs stocked with innovative ideas and materials. The themes and topics that were the focus of different integrated units were varied and included the following:

- Indigenous Communities
- Antiracism
- The International Year of the Family
- Conflict and Change
- Choices and Goal Setting
- Running a Political Campaign
- Life Cycles and Relationships
- Constructing Bridges
- Images
- Global Perspectives
- The Impact of Advertising

We examined what some of these themes, topics, and approaches had in common—how teachers chose them and justified them on grounds other than their thematic coherence.

The most powerful and consistent organizing principle underlying the integrated units that teachers had designed was relevance. Teachers emphasized learning activities that were connected with something or someone in the community or beyond and presented issues and ideas that had concrete, personal, and emotional relevance for students. Curriculum integration offered them a vehicle to link school with the self (Case, 1991), family life (Gedge, 1991), future work (Schlechty, 1990), and social and political citizenship. Beane (1995) goes so far as to argue that the only "authentic" curriculum integration is that which springs from students' interests and concerns (see also Hargreaves, Earl, & Ryan, 1996). Our analysis of the data revealed that relevance took three different forms: relevance to work, relevance to personal development and relationships, and relevance to social and political contexts.

Teachers organized units of study that made connections with real issues in students' lives and with people, ideas, and events beyond the boundaries of their classrooms. They took their students into the community through field trips or ventured into the community imaginatively through role playing and simulations. They brought the world into their classrooms and took their classrooms into the world.

Relevance to Work

Teachers have been bombarded by policymakers and organizations about the sweeping changes occurring in national and global economies and about the need to alter and strengthen the way schools prepare young people for these changes. Governments and others have emphasized that the curriculum should provide students with broad generic skills for the high-technology, service-oriented economy. These generic skills, they argue, include academic skills (communicating, thinking, and learning), skills in applying knowledge to real problems, personal management skills (responsibility, adaptability, and willingness to take initiative), and teamwork skills (the ability to work with others). Such pressures and pronouncements challenge teachers to develop curricula that promote and integrate generic skills of creative thinking and communication alongside more specific vocational competencies.

But not everyone accepts this corporate script of economic and employment transformation. Critics argue that high-skilled jobs in the restructured economy are available to only a relatively small elite (Hargreaves, 1994), that there will not be a significant number of new jobs to employ the "knowledge workers" who leave our schools (Barlow & Robertson, 1994), and that educational change for adolescents is being driven by exaggerated preoccupations with corporate agendas (Wyn, 1994). Nevertheless, the rapidity of economic change and the uncertainties surrounding it are indisputable realities of which adolescents are all too aware and that educators would be foolish to ignore (Hargreaves & Fullan, 1998).

The teachers we studied appreciated and worried about this. Would their students be ready for the changing workplace? What skills would they need to survive or prosper in the future world of work? The criticisms that employers have directed at schools and teachers for failing to prepare students for the workplace had hit home with many educators, and they had started to respond:

> The big thing that I've always said to the kids is that when you're an adult and you're out doing your job, you don't do forty minutes of this and forty minutes of that. If you have to use your language skills to solve a problem or your mathematics skills or your science skills or whatever else, you've got the skills and you just use them. That's what we're trying to focus on with integration. We've got a problem that you may need math, you may need some science, and you may have to use the computers to help you solve the problem—all at the same time.

Many of the teachers were particularly concerned that their integrated units should incorporate knowledge, skills, and values relevant to the workplace. A conversation with her business-employed husband about the "real" world made one teacher think about the implications of the changing workplace for her classroom, her teaching, and her students:

> My husband had challenged me, "What do you know about the real world, the business world?" But then one day I was looking in the newspaper just when the Conference Board of Canada was doing the first material on employability skills, and I thought, "This I can handle." Since then we've built a whole program around employability skills, called Skills for Success. I deliver the informational material in the guidance class. I do a lot of self-awareness activities on individual styles of learning and multiple intelligences. Also, one of our eighth-grade teachers is doing a huge project called Envirohouse that's bringing together career information, measurement, science, and math.

Changes in the workplace are pointing to more contract-based and short-term employment roles and more career changes than in the past (Castells, 1996). A few teachers mentioned that teaching a specific set of skills and practical knowledge to prepare students for one career choice would be inadequate in the long run. They instead emphasized general attitudes, values, and lifelong learning skills that would equip their students to manage change in the workplace and in their work roles more effectively, as this teacher noted:

> In grade 8 we really focus from a career angle: How are you going to handle change? What changes are coming? The kids have a cross-curricular, extracurricular portfolio that's equal between academic skills, personal management skills, and teamwork skills. Once a week, the kids administer their portfolios. They put in a piece, or they write about an event or an activity. They have to reflect on the skills. In every classroom we have the employability skills posted. The teachers are getting kids to make choices about their groupings and [with] whom they choose to be partners based on learning styles and dealing with other people.

Some teachers designed units that focused specifically on strategies for researching career opportunities, career planning, and acquiring skills for preparing résumés and applying for work:

> My students are analyzing the newspaper and categorizing all the jobs according to seven different topics, and then they're going to bar-graph, line-graph, and pie-graph them. These students need résumé writing and job applications skills. They soon have to be out there looking for jobs, applying themselves. They're going to research seven different careers, bringing in the idea: What is the relationship between school and career?

Some writers argue that the future workplace will require more interpersonal and social skills for working effectively in teams (Shmerling, 1996; Woloszyk, 1996; Donofrio & Davis, 1997). Many teachers organized their integrated units using cooperative learning approaches that emphasized and promoted such teamwork skills:

> I also try to incorporate cooperative learning. I try to incorporate math and language arts with process writing, which was new to them. The Japan manufacturing unit was a great opportunity to

change it into the "jigsaw" [a method of cooperative learning] for expert groups and base groups.

One teacher taught a unit of study called "The Real Game" with her seventh-grade students over several weeks. This was structured according to different work roles that had been assigned to students, each with a number of characteristics, such as income and amount of leisure time, associated with these roles. Students made financial, leisure, and career plans, and new contingencies were factored into their lives at various points through a process of engaging simulations. Students we interviewed commented on how intellectually and emotionally engaging this process had been. It had made them take their career decisions and even approaches to their current school work more seriously, and it had stimulated considerable dialogue with their families about life outside school.

Teachers also made integrated curriculum relevant to the world of work by involving business partners in the life of the school and simulating workplace processes. One teacher taught a unit on images about self and society, the impact of advertising, and how advertisers get consumers to buy certain things. She brought in "a speaker who does advertising for GM and Ford to talk to the kids."

A few teachers brought the world into the school by drawing on local expertise to help formulate and design integrated units and materials. They combined the talents on their staff with those of other professionals outside the school to make the programs more relevant for their students. One teacher's hands-on unit exemplified this approach:

> I had used this commercial unit on bridges before with my own kids, so we presented the idea to the staff. One teacher got in touch with a community member, who then got in touch with some engineers and with a pasta-making company, so the unit changed from a project using Popsicle sticks and toothpicks to using pasta so the company would agree to sponsor it. We presented it to the staff, then rewrote it, and built it all up as a long unit.

> The kids were divided into groups of four with different roles. They had to buy pasta and land, and they had to build a bridge with the idea that the bridge supporting the greatest weight would win. We incorporated a lot of integration into it across the curriculum: visual arts, literacy, geography, history, science. For six days we basi-

cally shut down the school and re-timetabled. The kids worked every day from 9:00 A.M. to 11:15 A.M. Then on one day they worked a double lunch and the whole afternoon. They worked in companies making these bridges. Then we had a pasta dinner sponsored by the company, and we had an awards presentation for them. It worked really well.

This project connected several subject disciplines, involved the use of higher-order conceptual skills (such as theorizing, modeling, inquiring, testing, and reasoning), and also entailed social group skills. In some ways, the corporate connections were superficial (using pasta for the building materials) and ethically problematic (using the learning process of public education to develop consumer attachments to particular corporate products). But there were also opportunities to inform and educate the corporate world about the quality of teaching and learning that took place under the banner of curriculum integration.

Another instance of involving corporate partners and educating them about the learning process and the value of curriculum integration was a school's inventors' festival:

We have a Creativity Festival where students become entrepreneurs. They develop their own invention, and an outside support team comes in to work with them. Those outside people are mainly from the bank and securities firms. They're the real-world experts.

Relevance to the world of work is and should be an important component of teaching and learning and curriculum integration for young people who are beginning to think seriously about future jobs and careers for the first time. But excursions into corporate partnerships and engaging with corporate agendas can also be an ethical quagmire, in which educational independence and integrity can soon be lost. Are teachers sometimes selling their educational souls for a pile of pasta or similar corporate products? How can teachers succeed in building constructive partnerships while also keeping their educational integrity (Hargreaves & Fullan, 1998)?

Occasionally teachers went deeper and were critical of aspects of the corporate context. In addressing career choices and strategies, some engaged their classes in discussions of gender issues and ethnocultural inequities. The students who simulated "The Real

Game" became highly critical of many aspects of the working world they would enter. Relevance to the world of work does not mean uncritical acceptance and endorsement of it. In general, however, critical approaches to the corporate world were minimized or muted in the classrooms of the teachers we interviewed, and deserved considerably more emphasis.

Relevance to Personal Development and Relationships

Young people are not only concerned about their future work prospects and career choices. As they grow and mature, adolescents are also intensely interested in finding love, developing their independence, and having successful relationships (Wyn, 1994).

Early adolescence is an exciting and also emotionally turbulent time for students as they struggle to find a personal sense of identity and direction and grow toward more independence and confidence in making crucial life decisions (Hargreaves, Earl, & Ryan, 1996). Teachers can provide moral, emotional, and intellectual support as well as be positive role models for their students at this time. As we will show later, the teachers in our study ranked caring for their students, establishing emotional connections with them, and helping them develop and work through their relationships with others as high priorities. This acknowledgment of and engagement with the emotional dimensions of young adolescents' lives underpinned many of the decisions that teachers made about teaching and learning, including their commitment to and the way they designed curriculum integration.

Teachers were highly sensitive to the life dilemmas facing their students and tried to design curricula that could tap into their students' personal experiences and interpersonal relationships. In some cases, programs of study helped students to develop life skills in which they could identify and clarify their goals and guiding values as a context for making choices. Two teachers, working as a team, used the ideas of choice and survival as a basis for designing their integrated program:

> We did a lot of work about choices and goal setting right from the beginning in our mentor classes. I started out with a novel study on this in literacy. It's a story about a boy who goes into northern

Canada. The plane crashes and the pilot is killed, and the boy has to survive on his own. We brought in a lot of ideas about life skills that are necessary. Then we related these life skills to everyday life in the classroom. We related the choices to our history unit on conflict. We talked about choices in the schools, changes in the schools, changes in the community. That's how we got into our geography and history. I did math on predicting and decision making.

Some teachers drew on the concept of family to address not only the choices that students faced but also the very broad processes of growing up and of passage through distinct stages of life that make up the adolescent experience. The emotional issues and distractions that once got in the way of teaching teenagers, and that many high school teachers regard as being intrusions in the classroom (Hargreaves, 1999), were now made the focal point of learning itself:

> We started looking at creation myths—the ways in which different religions and different cultures look at the creation of the world. From there we moved to self-exploration of the different cultures. We looked at music, religion, foods. I called my unit "The Passages of Rite." We looked at the way families in different cultures celebrated birth, coming of age, becoming a teenager, marriage, and death and the different ways people address these issues. Students had to interview someone in their family. We generated questions about those different times of life that they would be interested in or that would be relevant. They wrote an essay based on the interviews with either an elder or parent, explaining one of those passages of rite.

This unit integrated music, social studies, and history, and it promoted language skills, especially in conversation, reporting, and writing, as well as skills of inquiry and research. It tied these outcomes to students' personal family experience and to their interest in the passage from adolescence to adulthood. A wide range of subject material was closely integrated with the emotionally charged and engaging experiences of growing up in our complex and changing world. The unit stimulated thoughtful discussion about young people's present and future life passages by looking at their own personal and family experiences and linking them to broader religious and cultural values and life patterns.

Another way teachers approached these issues was through the concept of relationships. They drew on ideas and activities from several program areas to help students acquire and apply a range of knowledge and skills outcomes, and to engage in group problem solving and inquiry:

> In the novel *Tuck Everlasting* we started with our theme of relationships. We used a concept attainment lesson, where we had the kids sorting pictures. They had to develop their own rules. The pictures involved people in some kind of a relationship or by themselves. From that sorting the children developed a definition for *relationship*. Then we started the novel because there are a lot of relationships in *Tuck*. We taught them the plot line. At the beginning of *Tuck*, they talk about the forest floor where the eternal spring is. From that, we went to the forest in the community. Using the same process, we developed a definition for the forest floor and developed a hypothesis.

Teachers frequently used the concept of family to make links between content areas and to integrate the knowledge, skills, and values they were trying to teach. Family experiences shape our personalities, attitudes, and values; family biography provides our most direct links with social history; and families provide frameworks of values about learning and education that affect our later life choices and self-images as persons and as learners. Given this fundamental role of the family in students' lives, teachers often turned to it as an organizing concept for integration.

Teachers were not sentimental in their references to the family, nor were they single-minded or presumptuous about the kinds of families from which students came or the ways that families should be. Teachers put students' own families in the context of other kinds of family life in history and around the world:

> I'll do the family because of the International Year of the Family. I tried to design a family unit that crossed over English, history, and geography mainly. I really tried to involve the graphic organizers [math] and thinking skills as part of the proposal, along with the language, basic reading, and writing and listening as well. We started off with the kids using brainstorming techniques of what they think a family is in this day and age. Then I used media saying

what the traditional family was like and how it has changed to bring across the idea of the changes in society. We went into personal family surveys of their origin, mapping skills, and the history of their family. They were collecting articles and artifacts to go into their memory box of their family, as well as their personal achievements and treasures.

The culmination was the sharing of these boxes. It was a lot of writing. We showed *A Raisin in the Sun* [Hansberry, 1959] and analyzed the family dynamics there. Students compared that to their own family dynamics. We talked about values, and what a value is, and how personal values and family values and society values sometimes can be integrated, sometimes conflicting, and the problems of parenting with children at different stages of development.

I do what we call a cycle report, where students reflect on what they're learning. The culmination of the unit led into the next unit, "Conflict and Change," because of the family conflicts that can come with change, such as divorce and stages of development. Students got together in a group and made a very large graphic organizer, contrasting family situations under five conditions.

This unit emphasized connections among significant learning experiences, students' own family backgrounds, and both immediate and global contexts of cultural diversity. The teacher interwove a number of curricular elements by means of conceptual cohesion (family), cross-curricular learning outcomes (math, English, history, and geography), and cooperative group work. The theme of family was linked with the concept of conflict resolution, which had immediate implications for students in their everyday interpersonal relationships. Integration of the unit within the wider International Year of the Family connected students with a global celebration beyond their own immediate experience. Studying traditional family structures and values in relation to students' own families and families across the world deepened the sociological as well as personal understanding of what family means. Discussions about parenting helped prepare many students for their future roles and responsibilities. The cycle report embedded general concepts in students' personal learning and in what they found most relevant.

Another teacher drew on literature, history, and geography in order to explore the concept of family and the personal and social

relevance it had for her students. The process was mutually en-
riching. The subject of family makes history, geography, and literature more meaningful and helps articulate the connections
among them, and the different areas both deepen and provide a
broader context for the study of family:

> An example is the unit we are starting now in language arts, "War
> and Peace." The kids have been working on war journalism. In lan-
> guage arts we've been doing writing about the history and a play on
> the Holocaust. In geography we're doing world patterns, labeling
> maps. Then we are going to be talking about where the kids' ances-
> tors have come from and where the wars have been in the world
> and labeling them on the map to make the two coincide. Then, fur-
> ther on in the unit, we are having an element where on their world
> maps, they are going to put down where their ancestors—their par-
> ents and grandparents—came from. Then they are going to find
> someone from that country and interview him or her over the
> Christmas holidays and develop questions so they can find out why
> that person emigrated to Canada. What made him or her come
> here? What is different, and what is the same?

Like many other important issues in education, those that are
most relevant to and engaging for students are also often the most
controversial and difficult. Teachers in culturally diverse classrooms
in our study appreciated that no one model of the family was appropriate for all their students. They also recognized that family
structures were changing over time and that even passing references in the classroom to students' parents and families could not
be made easily and casually.

Many of today's students come from postmodern families that
are single parent, divorced, and blended (Elkind, 1997). Their
parents may be unemployed or part of the working poor. Some immigrant students may be living with relatives or even alone. Other
students come from cultural backgrounds where family structures,
values, and attitudes toward gender relations, discipline, and education differ sharply from conventional North American standards.
Yet it is possible to broach these issues sensitively, thoughtfully, and
with realism—for example:

> There isn't a greater relationship for kids than their own family. We
> generated a dozen questions about relationships, for example,

"How would my life change if I were an only child?" "How would my life change if my father stayed at home and didn't go to work?" They developed their own questions too. At the same time we're teaching them how to do a hypercard stack [a computer program for creating presentations of graphics, text, and sound]. They do their interview at home with their parents or at school with a person who is an only child.

Families are changing. Students' cultural differences can create value conflicts, but they can also create powerful opportunities for learning. This is also true for students from single-parent and nonconventional families. Teachers who used an integrated curriculum to address students' personal experiences through projects that focused on the family posed the question, "What is a family?" rather than asserting, "This is a family!"

In a postmodern world of diverse shifting and sometimes conflicting cultural values, making the curriculum relevant to students' personal development and social relationships is an intellectually demanding and emotionally sensitive undertaking. Yet by addressing rather than avoiding or downplaying these differences, teachers are able to use the family as a meaningful touchstone for many other aspects of learning and to increase knowledge and understanding of the family and students' relationships to their past, present, and future families at the same time.

Relevance to Social and Political Contexts

Some of the curriculum outcomes in the provincial policy document (Ontario Ministry of Education, 1995, pp. 85–97) were explicitly designed to raise students' awareness of themselves and their society and to develop their sense of social responsibility. One way teachers promoted these outcomes was to link their integrated learning programs with outside humanitarian agencies:

> We hooked up with an agency called Share, an international organization that focuses on global education. We did a webbing on how we could touch on different disciplines and different ideas through shared cultures, global vision. The kids worked with inquiry-type questions. We wanted them to see people as resources. This is human geography. Students were comparing and contrasting always with how others see us and how we as Canadians see ourselves.

Many teachers developed integrated units that drew on current events in order to underscore to students the severity of health and economic conditions in other parts of the world:

> One of the units is "Countries in the News." To make it valid for the kids in terms of the grade 8 concepts that they have learned in human geography, I keep newspaper clippings on Third World countries. We compare Canada to various Third World countries and with almanac data. They get an idea that in Canada there are seven infant deaths per thousand population; in Ethiopia it's fifty deaths or higher. They do a written project and an oral report. The material we use is in the newspaper today. It's in the here-and-now.

Such studies of international agencies and global comparisons take students beyond parochial visions of themselves to address outcomes that promote their understanding of cultural diversity and international inequities. This wider appreciation of cultural diversity was sometimes also approached historically:

> We were asked by our principal last year to put together a unit, and I did one on antiracism, so we integrated history as part of Black History Month. I took a workshop on African infusion in our Canadian history curriculum. I took what I learned from there and infused it into my history of the rebellions of 1837. We did some work on antiracism. We entered the "Let's Stop Racism" contest by the Canadian Immigration Organization. The students' project was to come up with a way of advertising antiracism. Then we presented our different projects to the sixth-grade classes.

In another case, music was the entry point for this socially broad approach to integration:

> We had a series of five speakers from Africa. They made a very personal connection. One of them was a young man, a refugee from Somalia. He was a musician. They explored the field of music and shared cultures through music. Students were so taken with him. He was going through the process of seeing if he could gain refugee status. The next day, he was to present himself for this hearing. He was very tense and nervous. When we came to understand this, the kids were so empathetic, realizing that his whole future lay in the balance. We asked that they keep us informed.

Students asked me every day after that, "Have you heard?" They became so involved on a personal level. They raised some money, which they donated to one of the speakers who was going back to Somalia to start up a school, in order to make sure that the school was able to function for those who were able to get education.

Integrated curricula that bring together music, history, geography, literature, and other areas of content to address issues of cultural diversity can serve as powerful tools for enhancing interpersonal empathy and international understanding, developing wider and comparative senses of social justice and social consciousness, and helping young people address the realities and the possibilities of the culturally diverse society that surrounds them, and in ways that deepen students' knowledge and cognitive skills as well.

In classrooms of increasing cultural and linguistic diversity, a curriculum that makes these kinds of connections is not only socially desirable for the sort of society that many people want schools to help shape, but also educationally essential because of the backgrounds and prior understanding that students with different family cultures and life histories bring into the school.

As well as addressing cross-cultural comparisons and culturally diverse histories, teachers were able to identify and cultivate other points of social and political relevance. In one ingenious experiment, students designed a balcony ramp for their school to accommodate people with wheelchairs. This unit blended science and mathematics outcomes with meaningful participation in a program of immediate social relevance and possible benefit, demonstrating that social consciousness in the integrated curriculum need not be achieved only by drawing on the humanities:

> We were doing a unit on inventions. We were trying to have the children develop an innovation that would be beneficial to a disabled person. Upstairs in our science lab, we do a lot of experiments off the balcony. There's a big step up, and it's uneven. The challenge we gave to the children, who had been studying forces in science, was: How could we develop an innovation or come up with an invention that would allow someone who's in a wheelchair to have access to the balcony? Then, in the Design and Technology course, they came up with their plans. We talked about the forces

involved in science. They used some of the simple machines. In Design and Technology, students actually built a model of the structure. We pulled in the math. I had them calculate the force involved, and we tested all that.

Thinking globally means acting locally. Changing the world begins by making changes in your own backyard (Postman, 1995). Caring about the global environment starts by caring about one's local neighborhood. These kinds of social and political questions, about which many young people care and worry deeply, also provide prime opportunities for showing how scientific knowledge and investigation can contribute to students' understanding of important issues in their local community. In turn, this kind of integration can make science more personally and immediately relevant in students' lives.

One teacher in a rural school had taught there for many years and knew the community well. He believed in extending learning into the community and using local knowledge and resources to enhance his program. That he knew his students' families and their backgrounds and cultures very well and was an active member of his local community, widely involved in clubs and social events, helped him to make strong and persuasive linkages between the school and the community in relation to environmental issues—for example:

> I developed a unit with the librarian around science about pond study and creek study, because we had the creek right here. We made up this mapping and looked at all the ways of integrating different types into this map study. I brought history into it in terms of fur trading, highways, and water highways. Then we did geography with the land profile maps. It was all done with the librarian in putting it together. There's a river here that is heavily polluted with chemicals. The unit gave the librarian a chance to get into the science and math when students did graphing. Students found data on the number of farmers who used to live along the river and ballpark figures on how many cattle they had. They did a projection to see how many cattle should be using that river now. That was worked into a graph. Then students read various stories that she found about ponds and rivers and an art unit. It really showed us that we could make almost any unit work as a totally integrated whole.

Local community politics could provide another point of social relevance and focus for curriculum integration. Drawing on current events in the community that paralleled the program of study in real time was particularly effective, especially if students were able to simulate outside events in their classroom activities. Many teachers found that using standard text resources alone was less effective than when they introduced real-life examples of the concepts and ideas being studied. Making learning like real life, using the principle of what Woods (1993) calls "verisimilitude," was a creative and compelling stimulus for student learning in relation to wider social issues as well as the skills and understanding through which these issues were investigated—for example:

> The community was having municipal elections. It was a natural thing to do elections because we were doing community studies and learning about the cities and municipalities. This gets us out of the textbook. Each student was given the task of running his or her own campaign. They had to select a number of things that bridged all of the subjects being taught. They learned how to write a ré-sumé. We brought in campaign literature and compared it and talked about opinions versus facts and the way people are presented. What is important? What isn't important? That was the English component. Also, students did surveys and graphs in math, along with an actual presentation. They are learning to display by making bulletin board displays, signs, and buttons. Students had to speak to other people and learn how to speak effectively. They ran their own campaigns. Then we made predictions and assumptions about who would win the municipal campaign. For me, moving back and forth from the actual municipal election to students' own candidacy and what was important to them was the best part.

Simulations could also be used to make past as well as present connections with political processes and events—to bring political and social history to life by having students act out events, assume roles, and recreate the social and political context of the time—filtering curriculum content through students' own awareness, experiences, and interests.

In general, the teachers in our study embraced the principle of relevance to wider social and political issues and contexts by designing units that activated students' feelings of empathy and compassion in relation to people whose experiences and life circumstances were different from theirs. Teachers designed integrated units that heightened students' social consciousness and helped break down cultural and social stereotypes.

To achieve these goals, teachers used school, community, and international issues to link subject material with students' developing sense of social awareness. At the same time, social and political issues acted as a catalyst for using skills in inquiry, investigation, and representation of knowledge and results. In these ways, social and political relevance seemed to be not the enemy of rigorous study but its invigorating partner.

Teachers' use of social and political relevance in the integrated curriculum was not unproblematic. Although problems of inequity, prejudice, and social injustice were confronted in several of the integrated units that teachers had developed, these problems were usually distant in time and space from the society in which students lived. They were other people's inequities and injustices, in faraway cultures or distant times. It was as if the integrated curriculum presented a great national myth—of Canada as a safe haven or refuge from injustices and inequities that people had suffered in other countries or earlier times. The nation and the local community were not presented as places that generated their own kinds of injustice and inequity—of increasing poverty, marginalization of indigenous peoples, racial and gender inequities in the workplace, and so on. The nation was not presented as a source of social and political problems but as a sanctuary from them. In this respect, although the integrated curriculum was bold and critical in making connections with society, it seemed to be silent on many of the most controversial social and political issues of the day that were relevant to students' present and future lives. If teachers of young adolescents can apply critical social thinking to societies outside their own, it is important that they use the integrated curriculum to critique the social realities of their own country, and not just of other societies before and beyond it. As renowned cultural theorist Edward Said argues, "It is part of morality not to be at home in one's home" (1994, p. 57)

The Process of Integration

Curriculum integration is not easy to implement. It is hard to conceptualize, time-consuming to plan, and not at all easy to square with subject-based traditions and secondary school requirements. Commitment to integration also increases the extent to which teachers need to collaborate with their colleagues. Our analysis of the implementation process probed beyond the usual problems of time, leadership, resources, and collegiality (Kain, 1996; also Chapter Five). It also addressed the deeper structural and political tensions and contradictions of integrated curriculum reform in general. In this second part of our analysis of curriculum integration, we explore three tension-filled implementation problems: curriculum traditions, curriculum exceptions, and curriculum discontinuities.

Curriculum Traditions

Many teachers in this project seemed highly preoccupied with how curriculum changes affected them personally (even more than their students). This is a common feature of any change process: people first ask how it will affect them (Hall & Loucks, 1977). Some teachers spoke animatedly about the freedom and flow afforded by curriculum reform or about the excitement of teaching in thematic or integrated ways. Others told of their struggles to relinquish subject attachments, and their fear and shame of feeling incompetent when new subjects and areas of content were unfamiliar to them. A few specialist teachers who were committed to other parts of the curriculum reform agenda but not to integrated curriculum as such poured scorn on the idea of integration or on those who interpreted and implemented it in trivial ways.

These teachers' feelings about curriculum categories and attempts to change them reflect how secondary or middle-level teachers' identities are often closely tied to the content of what they teach, to their comfort and familiarity with that content, and to how that content is labeled and organized (Eisner, 1992). Subjects clearly matter for many teachers (Siskin & Little 1995; Stodolsky, 1988; McLaughlin & Talbert, 1993; Goodson & Ball, 1985). Especially at the secondary level, teachers have traditionally guarded their subject specializations with great vigor. Many middle-level and secondary teachers and their identities have been shaped by subject traditions. Their interests and careers have become embedded in departmentally based secondary school structures that have grown up around the subject system. For these reasons, the history, politics, and psychology of subjects and subject allegiances present significant obstacles to efforts to bring about curriculum integration (see Hargreaves, Earl, & Ryan, 1996 for a more extended analysis; see also Siskin, 1995, and Fink, 2000).

A number of teachers in our study seemed able to conquer their own anxieties and elevate students' curricular needs above them (Muncey & McQuillan, 1996), or their own needs were less aligned with subject commitments in the first place. Advocates of curriculum integration considered it valuable in part because almost anything was worthwhile to teach "as long as it connects for kids." A teacher of guidance and family studies described how "I feel like my role is to really point out connections to kids, and that's where I think teachers have failed." When the integrated curriculum was initiated in one school, another teacher reached back into her own experience and described how

> I could feel the other side—what it felt like for someone to do things in very little pieces. And I could feel what it was like for the child to do things in little pieces, because that's what my high school was like. So for me, when I said, "Let's divide the curriculum up into four main groups, put all these subjects into four main groups, and see how they blend," it just made perfect sense. I saw the connections for the kids. The connections are there for them to grab and for us to start building with.

Not all teachers were unqualified advocates of curriculum integration. A few were extremely reluctant to give up their own subject specializations. Teachers' justifications for this position included fear of not knowing the content, concerns about treading on the toes of colleagues in other subject areas, and dislike of having to do additional preparation to familiarize themselves with new subject matter. Some of their worries were also genuinely grounded in concerns for their students' learning needs. Curriculum competence and professional confidence were integrally related to each other (Helsby, 1999). One teacher worried about teaching "areas that I find I am not comfortable with and knowledgeable enough to bring to the students." A music specialist who was now also teaching history as part of her core program responsibilities described her fellow grade colleague as a "history buff":

He can tell things about history that I wouldn't have a clue about. So what do my kids lose?—the little tidbit that he can throw in, that he has in the back of his head. I haven't got that, so when I work with them alone they've got only the bare bones. Am I doing the best job? I don't know.

Similarly, an art specialist said:

I wouldn't want to move out of my specialization because I couldn't do it. And I wouldn't want to try because this is what I'm really good at. Why would I want to do something that I'm really poor at doing? The kids would lose, and I would lose, and I would hate it.

Although the particular systems of subject categories and the particular firmness of the subject boundaries that currently exist are very much products of history, politics, and organizational traditions in education, this does not mean that subjects and disciplines in general are entirely the result of historical contrivance, that they are tired anachronisms and educationally irrelevant (Lawton, 1975). Nor does it mean that all teachers who cannot know or teach in every subject area are lacking in commitment, unconcerned about their students, or professionally inferior. Yet this is how subject specialization and curriculum integration are sometimes contrasted. It is as if integration increases professional virtue, while being unable or unwilling to let go of specialization keeps teachers in sin (Drake, 1991).

What really matters is deciding on clear grounds and in a rigorous way what should and should not be integrated and for what purposes. Ill-considered integration can lead to the watered-down themes and badly organized topic work of which critics complain, because they contain no real challenge for students and confuse rather than enlighten them. One teacher eloquently illustrated these concerns about curriculum integration:

A lot of integration doesn't worry enough about the content, the knowledge base. It's, "I connected math; see, I connected." Sometimes the connections you make have hidden things in them that are very confusing. So then if you throw in the integration part, can the various levels of my class handle it? I find with these kids that to make the integration really work, they have to see the integration. I'm very careful in doing art integration because I want to keep the integrity of the visual arts or the performing arts, as well as what I am doing. And so the battle really comes in. Once they start to lose the integrity of one discipline or the other, then I'd better stop. I think if I tried to integrate my whole day, I could do it. But there is going to come a time when I find it just too odious and ineffective. If I'm going to be accountable to those kids, and their parents in particular, then I'd better be sure that I am meeting the criteria that are in the official curriculum outcomes. I can't do it all through integration. There are certain disciplines that go well together, and there are times when it is best not to do it.

Effective integration seems to require that teachers and administrators engage with and find the right point of balance between two poles of a difficult dilemma. On the one hand, it requires teachers to take risks by extending their own comfort zone and stepping beyond the boundaries of their own familiar, traditional subject territories—putting the needs of their students' learning before their own insecurities about curriculum content. On the other hand, integration may best be approached as a judicious, not a promiscuous, practice, based on clear criteria that both teachers and students understand. There is a wealth of resources outlining clear, philosophical principles and strategic options on which rigorous programs of integrated study can be based (Drake, 1998; Fogerty, 1991; Case, 1991, 1994). Not everything needs to be integrated, and it may be best if teachers are not drawn so far beyond their knowledge base of familiar subject content that they feel incompetent and exposed in front of their classes and their colleagues as a result. If this tension cannot be resolved judiciously, on a case-by-case basis, then damaging consequences may well ensue:

> I knew that the intermediate division could become civil war–like very easily if some teachers wanted to stay with their specialty subjects and were not happy with what they had to teach. We thought we had the timetable all set. Then it just fell apart, and no one could cooperate. People were practically shouting at each other. I just sat back and watched the whole thing. It was very frightening.

Curriculum Exceptions

The most frequently integrated subjects in our study were English, history, geography, and science. Subjects like languages other than

English, music, and mathematics were seen as much more difficult to integrate. These difficulties were sometimes attributed to the nature of the subject itself. At other times, teachers felt that their own knowledge and expertise were especially wanting in these subject areas.

Mathematics was viewed as being particularly problematic, for it is a subject that occupies a larger part of the curriculum than other "difficult" subjects like music. Many teachers do not feel highly proficient in it, and it is often seen to stand apart from most other curriculum areas. The following responses give a strong sense of the interlocking nature of these various sources of difficulty:

> It is not impossible, but it is difficult to integrate math in studies of history. You know, something like: "If 3 rebels were killed and 2 escaped . . ."

> We integrate language and social science. We're supposed to integrate math, but we found that math does not integrate very well.

> We still have not integrated the subjects together. I really struggle with some of those concepts. I don't see how you are going to move math and science together. I see the requirements for children at the age I have been teaching as vastly different in those two subject areas, and I don't see a correlation.

> The math I never worry about trying to integrate. I don't push to integrate that. But obviously the language you integrate into the research. Math I've let stay separate. But other subjects integrate naturally.

Alongside these doubts, other teachers had successfully integrated mathematical components into the wider curriculum, as did the teacher who used mathematics in an integrated unit on inventions as part of a project to design imaginary wheelchair-accessible facilities. Sociologists of curriculum are sometimes critical of the claims that subject teachers in mathematics or languages make that it has a more linear structure—claims that are used to excuse teachers from student-centered innovations like integration and mixed ability grouping (Ball, 1990). But whatever the historical and ideological arguments, when even committed and leading-edge teachers question whether these subjects can be integrated as well as any other, then their criticisms should be taken seriously.

Perhaps not all integrated curriculum units are amenable to including mathematical (or certain other subject) components. And perhaps not all mathematical skills and concepts may be able to be handled efficiently in an integrated way. Mathematics and other "difficult" subjects may be ones where some of the material can be integrated some of the time, but the rest of it might best be taught in more specialized ways. Even in this more modest scenario for integration, though, teachers whose training and previous teaching experience have largely excluded mathematics (or other "difficult" subjects) might best overcome some of their shortcomings in subject confidence and competence by collaborating closely with other teachers to bring together different specializations. Just as competence leads to greater confidence, so too does the professional confidence built in collaborative teams of shared knowledge lead to greater competence (Helsby, 1999), as the following quote indicates:

> Over the past couple of years, we've had a lot of the specialist subject areas more involved in teaching classes. Last year, I was on the team with the family studies teacher and the design and technology teacher. We did a lot of work together where we looked at units that combined computers, math and science, and design and technology. We're trying to integrate those, and I think we've come a long way.

Curriculum Discontinuities

Teachers of young adolescents often sacrifice their students' needs for a relevant curriculum to the immediate pressures of preparing them for high school (Hargreaves, Earl, & Ryan, 1996; Tye, 1985). Even with their commitments to curriculum integration, a few teachers in our project still made preparation for high school their paramount priority. As one teacher explained:

> Even though we're doing a very integrated program and it's very creative and we're not very knowledge based, we still cover a lot of the skills that kids are going to do in high school. We've done a lot on essay writing and learning how to support answers. Our philosophy is that basically our role is to get the kids ready for high school.

Teachers were acutely aware that relevance to the "real world" also included relevance to high school. For seventh- and eighth-grade teachers and their students, the imminent world of high school is a pressing one:

> The high schools, of course, work on grades, so we've been trying to let the kids know their actual percentage as part of a transition to high school, when all of a sudden they're faced with a real number.

Teachers appreciated the fundamental differences between elementary and secondary schools in their structures, cultures, and the way they organized their curriculum. They saw their role as helping to smooth the transition between the elementary and secondary years for their students:

> To me elementary school should be elementary school. I still feel kids in elementary maybe should be here until they're fourteen or fifteen. If they don't really grasp the concepts, if their maturity isn't such to make responsible decisions, maybe they're not ready for the more independent high school environment.

Yet many became frustrated by their high school colleagues who seemed oblivious to or dismissive of their efforts. Teachers in one school, for example, found that the sophisticated portfolio assessments they had developed with grade 8 students were derided by their high school colleagues as childish. These colleagues made no use of them in their communication with incoming students.

The strong subject focus in secondary school runs contrary to many seventh- and eighth-grade teachers' efforts to integrate the curriculum and develop cross-curricular skills through it. If teachers emphasized curriculum integration, how could they adequately prepare their students for the subject-oriented secondary school world that their students would soon enter? Some teachers settled for a trade-off. They prepared their students in the skills of research, writing, and critical thinking that would help them perform well academically in the long term, while acknowledging that these students would be less prepared for recalling specific facts and subject area knowledge:

A lot of our kids don't have the knowledge base, but they are very good at the skills. That's helped them out when they go to high school. They may not know all there is to know about the opening of the West and the railroad, but when it comes to essay writing, they're really good at it. When it comes to supporting their answers or reading for context or detail, they are good at that. If they are told that they have to develop a research project, they're great at coming up with an inquiry question. They're really good at using key words in context and finding the information that they need. But they don't know all the facts. So you're kind of damned if you do and damned if you don't.

This difficult dilemma of trying to integrate effectively in the shadow of a specialized secondary school system cannot be one that seventh- and eighth-grade teachers can solve entirely by themselves. Aligning learning standards and assessments across the entire span of schooling is one way to address this dilemma, with the provisos that these standards are not so subject driven that they destroy opportunities for integration and that they are not so detailed that they undermine teachers' professional discretion and opportunities to connect with the relevant interests and concerns of their diverse classes. Secondary school teachers, too, must take shared responsibility in relationships of equal and open dialogue with their upper-elementary and junior high school colleagues, recognizing that these dilemmas also affect and challenge their own teaching. Instead of elementary teachers' being expected to make all the curriculum adjustments, elementary and secondary teachers must build a shared community of practice that can address the issues of curriculum continuity together (Cochran-Smith & Lytle, 1992). Continuity is an achievement of human trust and communication, not just paper coordination.

Implications

A common misconception about curriculum integration is that it is not rigorous for students or their teachers. In reality, the teachers in our study who had committed to curriculum integration found it rewarding but also difficult and demanding. Successful curriculum integration is intellectually demanding for teachers to master; it needs careful thought, sensitive adaptation to students of all abilities, time for teachers to plan, and opportunities for them to share their complementary expertise (Rasinski & Padak, 1995).

In part, integration was challenging for teachers not because it was based on abstract conceptualizations of topics and themes but because these themes, and teachers' approaches to them, were rooted in deep understandings of how content and ideas must be made relevant to students' lives—to their personal relationships, career prospects and choices, and growing sense of social awareness. Successful and stimulating integration was most likely when teachers put students and what was relevant to and meaningful for students first, and when they had the knowledge and imagination to draw widely on their own and others' subject expertise to make that relevance into an experience that was also rigorous. Developing effective integrated units demanded high levels of subject knowledge on the part of teachers, not the cursory understanding of a generalist (Bernstein, 1971).

Among the committed integration enthusiasts we studied, the choices between integration and specialization were not absolute. Exemptions to integration may be warranted in some subjects or when teachers feel they lack confidence or competence in those subjects. These exemptions are best decided not according to a universal principle or ideology but on a discretionary case-by-case basis.

Implementing curriculum integration in this respect is likely to be most effective in meeting the needs of all students when it does not try to aspire to faithful compliance with "true" or "pure" integration, but when it adapts to local circumstances, and to the competence and confidence that teachers have to implement it in those circumstances.

This more pragmatic approach to implementing curriculum integration entails teachers' being allowed to adjust their implementation to local conditions and their own collective capacities, and being encouraged to unleash their energies and enthusiasms in curriculum development by being accorded a high degree of professional discretion. This discretion enables teachers to create a curriculum that is rigorous and relevant for culturally and intellectually diverse groups of students who bring different forms of prior knowledge, understanding, interests, and concerns to their classrooms. Incompatible with any such approach is excessively centralized curriculum control that overloads teachers with detailed curriculum content, nails them down to a complex apparatus of subject-based standards, or assesses the fruits of their labors by the exclusive (in both senses) use of subject-based tests and examinations.

Much of what the study's teachers were able to create in integrated units of study developed forms of knowledge and learning that are increasingly valued in today's rapidly changing and complex postmodern society:

- Higher-order thinking skills
- Problem-solving capacities
- Applications of knowledge to real problems
- Creativity and invention
- Embedding of learning in real time and real life
- Learning collaboratively as well as individually

Teachers also fostered the skills of critical thinking:

- Questioning and not just adjusting to the working world that teenagers would enter
- Inquiring into the diverse forms of family life rather than advocating a simple and singular version of it
- Critiquing forms of injustice, intolerance, and inequity in other times and other parts of the world

At the same time, these more critical aspects of relevance could and perhaps should have been pushed further, especially in the areas of corporate influence on the curriculum and in relation to students' own society as a source of inequality and injustice and not simply a sanctuary from it.

At their best, notwithstanding these reservations, the practices of these teachers suggest that integration advances the rigor and relevance of classroom learning. It makes learning more applied, more critical, more inventive, and more meaningful for students. All this requires significant intellectual and emotional work on the teacher's part, the subject of the chapters in Part Three.

Part Two

The Process of Change

Chapter Five

The Intellectual Work of Change

The changes described in the previous chapters have presented and continue to present teachers with enormous challenges—not just in our own study, but in thousands of schools and school systems across the world. Integrating the curriculum when the dominant practice for decades has been to divide it into subjects and specialisms is difficult work conceptually and practically. Designing teaching in terms of standards to be met rather than content to be covered requires fundamental shifts in teachers' classroom strategies and, for many teachers, considerable leaps forward in their levels of skill. New forms of classroom assessment also have their own unique paraphernalia of techniques and special languages to be mastered.

New standards, new curriculum, and new assessments all involve change for teachers. Change of any sort is rarely straightforward, and certain kinds of change can be inordinately difficult to achieve. Policymakers and senior administrators often underestimate, overlook, or are oblivious to the difficulties of implementing change. The history of educational reform has, in this sense, largely been one of "predictable failure" (Sarason, 1990; Goodlad, 1984; Tyack & Tobin, 1994). Power holders have issued edicts, legislated mandates, and reconfigured whole systems, but few of their changes have made a difference at the classroom level or had a significant impact on student learning (McLaughlin, 1990; Fullan, 2000). Adopting an innovation or reform is straightforward enough. Developing, supporting, and sustaining it is a far more difficult matter.

Four Perspectives Revisited

One way to understand why educational change can be so challenging for teachers is to return to the four perspectives we reviewed in Chapter Three. These perspectives apply not just to assessment reform but also, as in House's (1981) original article, to processes of change and innovation in general.

The Technical Perspective

"If a teacher isn't able to do it, it can't be done!"

The technical perspective draws attention to the technical difficulties of changing knowledge, skill, and behavior, whether in teaching or in other occupations. Successful change in this respect means learning how to master a new and technically complex curriculum or a demanding new set of teaching strategies. This might mean teaching mixed-ability classes, learning how to integrate ideas and materials from different disciplines, knowing how to create a rubric or identify indicators so that one would know when particular standards had been met, being able to undertake different kinds of performance assessment, and so on. Much of the new educational orthodoxy of standards, aligned assessments, and forms of teaching and learning that are often more creative, applied, and open-ended in character calls for very high levels of technical skill among today's teachers. Indeed, in a systematic comparison of the skills and tasks involved in different occupations and professions, Cohen (1995) ranks teaching among the most complex.

If performing these skills and strategies is technically difficult, so too is the process of learning to become competent and expert in them. Like learning to change your golf swing, write with the left hand when your right arm has been broken, or drive a standard shift car after years of driving automatics, the task of learning to assess children cooperatively instead of individually or of integrating computers effortlessly into the rest of classroom learning is technically hard work.

Understanding how technically complex it can be to master some of the contemporary educational changes in teaching and learning is important. Teachers do not and cannot alter their practices simply because a directive arrives and they feel compelled to comply. They cannot conjure new practices from thin air or transpose them straight from the textbook to the classroom. Teachers require opportunities to experience observation, modeling, training, one-to-one coaching, practice, and feedback so they can develop new skills and make them an integral part of their classroom routines.

Reformers typically acknowledge the existence of these technical challenges and provide at least some degree of in-service training to support the implementation process, but the levels of support that are provided are usually limited to a small number of off-site workshops or to short and superficial approaches to training trainers, who are then supposed to train teachers in their own schools. The chance to observe other teachers' practice or to get one-to-one feedback on one's own is a rarity. As a result, too many teachers repeatedly make only the most limited progress in implementing classroom changes. By contrast, as we will see in this chapter and the next two, a striking feature of how teachers in this study experienced change was the exceptional degree of support they often received from systems, leaders, or colleagues to develop the technical skills of the new curriculum. These teachers were not only given the chance to practice their skills; they were given opportunities to understand the changes they were supposed to be practicing as well.

The Cultural Perspective

"If a teacher doesn't know how to do it or doesn't ultimately feel confident doing it, it can't be done."

Successful innovation entails more than improving technical skills. It also demands and draws on teachers' capacity to understand the changes they are confronting. The cultural perspective is concerned with the meanings and interpretations teachers assign to change, how changes affect and even confront teachers' beliefs as well as their practices, how teachers (alone or together) understand the changes that face them, and the impact of change on teachers' ideas, beliefs, emotions, experiences, and lives.

Placing curriculum documents in teachers' mailboxes and expecting their contents to make their way unsullied and untransformed into teachers' brains and belief systems is a naive strategy. Indeed, it is scarcely a strategy at all. Just like their students, teachers are not vessels to be filled, and learning is not osmotic. Changing beliefs and practices is extremely hard work.

Elmore (1995) argues that the problem of educational reform is one of "changing the core of educational practice—how teachers understand the nature of knowledge and the student's role in learning, and how these ideas about knowledge and learning are manifested in teaching and class work." Change, in this respect, has its indispensable human side, as well as its technical one (Evans, 1997). This human dimension of understanding educational change is both intellectual and emotional in nature.

Intellectually, teachers need to be able to figure out or make sense of what any particular change means. The change needs to have sufficient clarity for them to do this and not be so complex, vague, or incoherent that it defies reasonable understanding. Teachers need to be able to see the reasons for change, grasp the point of it, and be convinced it is feasible and will benefit their students (Fullan, 1991). These reasons must be explicit and compelling in policy, and they also must be ones that teachers have time and opportunity to figure out for themselves, alone and together.

Teachers also need to know what a change looks like in practice as well as in theory so that they can gauge exactly what it means for their own work. They particularly need opportunities to see exemplars of the change in their own school or elsewhere so that they can develop images of it and apply it to their own practice and experience.

This hard thinking or deep intellectual work does not stop once a change is adopted. The change may falter or take unexpected turns. At these points, teachers need time, encouragement, and support to reflect on how the change is proceeding, monitor its progress, ensure that its purposes are being met while not also pushing other purposes in the curriculum to one side, and make adjustments as they learn from their attempts to innovate. To say, as Fullan (1991) does, that change is a process, not an event, is to recognize that positive change involves continuous learning and therefore always has an intellectual element. Time to plan and reflect, and opportunities to do so in collaboration with colleagues and others, are essential supports for a successful change process. Later in this chapter, we will see how well these intellectual dimensions of educational change were addressed by the teachers and schools in our study.

In a five-year study of school improvement in which one of us was involved (Earl & Lee, 1998), there was a distinctive spiral pattern of urgency, energy, agency, then more energy in schools where teachers made significant changes in their practices. The process typically began when something prompted teachers to feel a sense of urgency about changing the way they did their work. Successful schools experienced a call to action or a critical incident that precipitated this sense of urgency. Something occurred in these schools that jarred teachers and led them to believe that change must be made, and quickly. The staff (and sometimes also the students and community) experienced something compelling enough for them to recognize that the existing state of affairs was no longer acceptable or tolerable. The change in question might be a rapid shift in the cultural makeup of the school population, a feeling that some students were not being well served by the school, an escalation of complaints from parents and the community, the imposition of a new curriculum or assessment system, the arrival of a new principal, the threat of school closure, the injection of new technologies, or some combination of these things.

Whatever the change was, it presented teachers with a problem, need, or sense of dissonance that they felt to be compelling and were motivated to resolve. According to Bandura (1986) and Ford (1992), motivation is future oriented and helps individuals evaluate the need for change or action. It also generates the energy they need to engage with the innovation and undertake the intellectual work of making sense of it and translating it into practice by engaging in tough reflections about their own practice, in decisions about what ought to be changed, and in efforts to acquire the skills and capacities that would turn their ideas into reality. From urgency and energy, in other words, teachers sought agency, showing confidence in their ability to acquire the training they needed. It is not only students who need to be engaged with their learning. Teachers need to do so as well. When the conditions were right and the necessary supports were provided, these bursts of energy led in an upward spiral to an increased sense of agency and productivity, which in time released even more energy as the spiral continued. When proper supports were not present, however, the energy could drive teachers in the opposite direction, toward frustration and despair.

Chapter Six describes the emotional work of change among teachers in our study when it was often at its best—when teachers were intensely engaged and involved in creative processes of curriculum planning, for example. Chapter Seven then describes the supports needed to sustain teachers through the emotionally and intellectually challenging work of changing their practice, to enable them to persevere through difficulty, and to help them move beyond the "implementation dip" (Fullan, 1991), when teachers typically stumble through their early efforts at change and often find that things get worse before they improve.

Teachers' motivation to change their practices, we will see, is influenced by the extent to which they think that their personal goals are consistent with the details of the reform, feel that they have or can acquire the knowledge and skills necessary to implement the changes, and believe that the reform will be supported over time.

Being motivated to explore a new way of teaching is not enough. Without the proper supports, the fragile resource of human energy can drain teachers instead of sustaining them. It can rob them of their chance to rest, reflect, and celebrate success, or strip them of their time to find emotional succor from and support among their colleagues. Where work and reform conditions are unsupportive, intellectual and emotional labor easily degenerate into a process of draining perspiration rather than energizing inspiration for teachers (Blackmore, 1996).

Meaning, motivation, and relationships are all at the heart of the change process, therefore, by either design or default. They emerge as important recurring themes in the following two chapters on the change process that teachers in our study encountered.

The Political Perspective

"If a teacher won't do it, it can't be done."

The political perspective is concerned with how power is exercised over others or developed with them, the ways that groups and their interests influence the innovation and reform process, and how the ends of education address, comply with, or challenge the existing distributions of power in society.

Politically, it is important that when teachers engage in the intellectual work of change, they not only reflect on their practice and their change efforts but do so critically—with a view to considering the social ends that their practice serves, as well as which students (mainstream or special education, dominant culture or cultural minority, affluent or poor) will benefit or suffer most from their initiatives.

All people, Antonio Gramsci (1971) says, are intellectuals, but only some have the function of intellectuals. Teachers are one such group (Aronowitz & Giroux, 1991). Teachers help to create the generations of the future. Their work cannot and must not be reduced to skill and technique alone. Teaching should also be imbued with moral purpose and a social mission that ultimately develops the citizens of tomorrow. This means that teachers must sift all their curriculum and teaching decisions through a social and political sieve. Oakes and Lipton (1998), for example, advise rejecting behaviorist systems of "positive discipline" because they do not address the content, structures, and relationships that disengage many poor and minority students from schooling in the first place. They also advocate putting the benefits of detracking for students before the inconveniences it poses for teachers and before the challenges it poses to high-status parents who wish to retain exclusionary gifted and honors programs for their own children. As we saw in the previous chapter, taking a critical perspective also means teachers' thinking deeply about how they address issues of cultural difference in their classes, even in virtually all-white schools.

The political perspective also raises questions about who is in charge of change and about whose agenda the change itself serves. Not all change is good. Educational reform is sometimes superficial, driven by political popularity and economic stringency rather than educational values. It can be harmful to less successful students. It can also destroy working conditions that enable teachers to do their jobs well. In a study one of us has undertaken on the emotions of teaching and educational change, when the fifty-three teachers we interviewed were asked to describe characteristics of positive and negative change in their experience, they described positive change as change that benefited students. It was usually also change that teachers developed themselves. One teacher reflected, "I find the only change that has ever happened has come from within, never from without. It's never come from someone telling me." Negative change was seen to serve a political rather than educational agenda and was "imposed on," "dictated to," "forced," or "thrust on" teachers by governments (Hargreaves et al., forthcoming). Interestingly, in this vocabulary of imposed change, teachers represented themselves as being intruded on, violated, and even abused. Resistance to change is therefore not always a problem or an obstacle. When the change is educationally or morally suspect, resistance can be a great professional virtue (Maurer, 1996).

Conversely, when educational changes promise to benefit all students and boost their learning, then providing teachers with the time, discretion, collaborative opportunities, and other resources to implement them properly is a political act as well as a technical one. Teachers also need to recognize that their own needs for empowerment and inclusion in the change process are replicated among students and parents and that the involvement of students and parents as well as teachers in change is an important part of its political dimension. We address these issues in Chapter Seven.

The Postmodern Perspective

"If the teacher has too much to do, it won't be done well."

Postmodern society is synonymous with chaos, uncertainty, paradox, complexity, and ongoing change. In postmodern societies, communities, schools, and classes are more diverse, so change is more complex. Electronic and other communications are faster, so change occurs at an ever increasing speed. Knowledge overturns quickly and solutions are contested by growing numbers of interest groups, so change is more and more uncertain. Multiple innovation, changing communities, and rapid communications mean that schools and their problems change quickly. Old-style, locked-in approaches to linear, planned change no longer suffice.

Some teachers, including many of those in our study, thrive on working in conditions of uncertainty, complexity, and continuous change. Changes are opportunities; problems are their friends

(Fullan, 1993). New experiences provide chances for learning, development, and improvements in their work and themselves. Flexibility, adaptability, optimism, and teamwork define their approaches to change—ones that are ultimately anchored in their concern to do the very best they can for their students. This, in postmodern terms, is educational change at its best—and we will see much of it in the ensuing chapters.

At the same time, change in postmodern society can become an obsession rather than an opportunity. The worthy pursuit of continuous improvement can turn into an exhausting process of ceaseless change. People may repeatedly take flights into the future because they disparage the present and dismiss the past. Indeed, from a psychoanalytic perspective, Shave (1979) argues that people who are attracted and even addicted to change are often fundamentally dissatisfied with some basic aspect of themselves. If people are forever in a state of becoming, they never have the chance simply to be. Tradition, consolidation, and contemplative reflection have no place in this postmodern excess. As Pirsig (1991) writes in his novel *Lila*, quality requires both dynamic and static activity. And as schoolteacher Gutierrez (2000) argues, moments of measured pace, consolidated achievement, and simply time to rest are as essential to educational success as is the quest for continuous improvement and ever higher standards. As a teacher inundated by reform pressures said to one of us in another study of school improvement, "You don't take swimming lessons when you're drowning."

Thinking Through Change

Teaching is hard intellectual work that involves tough thinking about educational changes, and their desirability and consequences, as well as thinking through what these changes mean or look like in classrooms. The teachers in our study worked hard as they set about developing and implementing curriculum integration and learning outcomes and broad-based classroom assessment. They had to make sense of broadly defined principles and policy guidelines and transform them into workable classroom activities. They deliberated about whether and what to implement, invested time and energy in acquiring new knowledge and skills, and struggled to plan lessons that fit their purposes, teaching styles, and existing classroom practices. Moreover, all of this occurred at the same time. Teachers, in typically nonlinear fashion, worked on the fly to incorporate and integrate their understanding and efforts into a coherent pattern of curriculum response and development.

Understanding Change: Meaning and Mastery

Teachers, like their students, are learners. Making changes in teaching practices always requires new learning. In the case of the complex practices being addressed by these teachers, this learning is a sophisticated process of high-level thinking and conceptual understanding. This kind of thinking enables teachers to

- Solve complex curriculum and classroom problems
- Engage in multistep reasoning through developing curriculum rubrics and new assessment formats
- Extract defensible and workable ideas from complex and sometimes jargon-ridden material
- Make judgments about the veracity and utility of arguments
- Anticipate the implications of their implementation decisions and evaluate those implications in a critical way that is consistent with their educational and social mission

First, the intellectual work of educational change involves establishing moral and philosophical clarity and agreement about what the change means (Tom, 1983; Sockett, 1989; Sergiovanni, 1990). Although some teachers understood from a social and political perspective, from the standpoint of their social mission in teaching, that the philosophy of reform in the transition years was rooted in caring for students effectively and keeping them switched on to learning at a highly vulnerable point in their development, many teachers found policy documents too "nebulous" and "far too involved," without "a clear focus." As one teacher expressed it:

I'm not sure that the framework is in place yet. Well, here are your ten learning outcomes and how are you going to address them, and what part do they play in curriculum design or evaluation? I'm not really clear. I think one of the shortcomings is there are too many twists and turns and too many blocks upon blocks and within blocks that need to be dealt with. There's too much there. Help me meet an outcome. Give me something I can grab onto because the outcomes are too nebulous.

Teachers had to decode the language of the policy documents and determine if the policy's intentions were in line with their own social and educational mission. In Chapter Four, for example, we saw how teachers drew on the intentions and opportunities within the policy to develop integrated curriculum units that addressed their own curriculum concerns to educate students about the environment, global awareness, cultural tolerance and diversity, and the nature of the world of work. Teachers also had to decode the policy in practical terms in order to discern what precisely it might mean for their own classroom practice. This process of decoding was no intellectual cakewalk. One teacher commented:

I find it overwhelming when I get sheets of paper coming down to me, and until I can digest some of it and look at it, it's mind-boggling. I get bogged down with the lingo and the verbiage and everything else. I have to look at it and analyze it and translate it and decide, "This is what it really means in the day-to-day classroom work."

Another teacher complained that "we use too much jargon, and we are afraid to decide what it means. Were the people who put together that document being deliberately vague?" Before teachers could actually do anything, they spent time reading, thinking, and talking about what the documents meant and what should change. Individually and together, they had to consider the documents in relation to their own beliefs and practices. They judiciously selected which areas of the change to work on first and tried to establish a clear focus (Werner, 1988). This involved significant intellectual work in deciding what to keep and what not to keep, what to do now and what to do later, which things to attend to quickly and which ones to slow down. Because the sheer scope and volume of many educational changes can seem overwhelming, educators often bite off chunks instead of consuming everything at once. One teacher remarked, "There's no way I can do this job. I've got to break it down into manageable pieces, just one piece so I can see some results right away. At least then I'll feel that I'm accomplishing something."

After wading through confusing documents, some teachers would persuade themselves that much of what was being recommended was what they were doing already:

> At first I started reading the curriculum outcomes document and I thought, This makes no sense to me. I don't understand this strand learning, outcomes, indicators—all this new stuff. Then when I got thinking about it, I thought, despite its intimidation, that I'm really doing a lot of this already.

This approach of "doing it already" could offer teachers personal and professional reassurance, but it could sometimes also lead to smugness and complacency, preventing teachers from forging ahead. Other teachers, however, explored the differences between their own practice and the policy recommendations more actively by pinpointing where the gaps were (sometimes this is called gap analysis)—for example:

> We're looking at learning outcomes and identifying where in our programs they are being addressed and to what degree, so that we can really begin to see where it's happening and where we could make more connections.

In cultural terms, this process of deciphering and sense making was best undertaken collaboratively, with other colleagues:

> People took turns reading the books or viewing the videos concerned with the province's curriculum reform, and they would do a brief presentation at staff meetings. We would decide how beneficial the reform was, what was in it for a class.

Such collegial work is a vital and frequently necessary prerequisite for and accompaniment to the intellectual work of educational change. It helps to make the change process seem sensible, real, and practical. This is especially true when the task of understanding change extends beyond discussion to practical observation:

> I found the change very difficult at first. I was comfortable going in one direction, but I was intrigued that this school is heavy on coop-

erative learning. I was invited to go into other classrooms and watch and talk to the teachers. When I saw that my interpretation was not totally correct, I agreed to go to a cooperative learning session to see what it was all about.

In addition to deciphering what the curriculum intended, the teachers in our study were sometimes pulled between different principles or values. The curriculum itself raised a number of value conflicts regarding how education is perceived, organized, and delivered. Outcomes-based learning of a broad kind is based on beliefs and values about education that are not necessarily widely shared or understood by many educators, and still less by members of the public. The student-centered emphasis and focus on equality of both opportunity and outcomes for all students represents a dramatic shift from many practices of the past. The focus on preparing students for broad-based experientially relevant learning is often incompatible with subject-specific "academic" courses. Even within the curriculum policy document, the concept of integration emphasizing broad connections and relationships among ideas, people, and things was potentially inconsistent with the specific outcomes and clear expectations for learning at key stages in schooling and with assessment and reporting formats that were organized in terms of subject specialist categories. One teacher reflected:

> I find there's a big contradiction in the curriculum when I read it. It talks about integrating all of the subjects and looking for outcomes of skills, not content, but they want to have common testing. Isn't that a contradiction?

Although policy documents often fudge these competing purposes and perceptions in an effort to appeal to the wishes of all, teachers must somehow choose between, balance, or reconcile them within their practice. As a result, teachers found themselves balancing different purposes, choosing between better and worse courses of action rather than self-evidently right and wrong ones, and settling for optimum solutions instead of perfect ones. All of this is intellectual work of the most serious and sustained kind—work that makes a difference to whether the changes are meaningful, practical, and sustainable among teachers who understand and are committed to them.

Deciding to Change: Urgency and Energy

In addition to understanding change, teachers' commitment to any particular change, and not just change in general, is at the core of successful implementation. A common administrative and legislative delusion and conceit is that reform can be imposed, even forced, on teachers, without any regard for their values or inclusion of their voice. Historically, this pattern of forced implementation has enjoyed little or no success. Reviewing the impact of numerous innovations in education over many decades, McLaughlin (1990) concludes that "you cannot mandate what matters to effective practice."

Ten years of large-scale, legislated reform in education in England and Wales provide some salutary lessons for others who may be considering the option of forced implementation. In that context, Nias (1991) reported that many primary (elementary) teachers expressed senses of loss, bereavement, and demoralization or loss of purpose when they were required to implement a detailed, subject-based National Curriculum with stringent and repeated procedures of student testing. Although teachers did not all respond to English educational reform in the same way (Pollard, Broadfoot, Croll, Osborn, & Abbott, 1994; Webb & Vulliamy, 1993), as the reforms persisted and were backed up by the relentless enforcement of a high-stakes school inspection system (known as OFSTED), more and more teachers adapted to reform in ways that were negative, cynical, and professionally limiting.

In intensive interviews with fifty-five primary teachers, Woods and his colleagues (1997) found that only five regarded themselves as experiencing "unequivocal enhancement" as a result of the reforms. Ten others felt some enhancement but were also suffering from overload, intensification, burn-out, and loss of control. Interestingly (though this is not acknowledged in the study itself), all of the "enhanced" teachers cited by the authors were in positions of administrative responsibility, where they would experience some degree of influence and control over others and derive some career benefits from reform implementation. Of the remaining forty teachers, most of whom were not in administrative positions, twenty-nine were categorized as compliant—but in their compliance, they often narrowed their conception of their role, distanced themselves from what they were required to do, devised cynical and expedient strategies to secure implementation with the minimum fuss or effort, and patrolled their time commitments to their work, compared to other areas of their life, with great vigilance. While these teachers might, in technical terms, have implemented educational reform accurately, they became lesser teachers because of their compliance. The remaining eleven teachers (20 percent of the sample) actively defied the reform requirements, left the profession altogether for other careers and early retirement, or sank into debilitating illness or mental turmoil. The most disturbing part of Woods and his colleagues' study is that over time, as the reforms persisted, more and more teachers moved from the "enhanced" category into categories that were professionally diminishing in nature. Force might win reformers the battle for short-term implementation, but it will mainly lose them the war of long-term improvement. In these respects, how teachers relate to the purposes embedded in educational reform as well as to its patterns of implementation is a key factor in securing or failing to secure long-term improvement.

Most teachers in our study, like the "enhanced" ones in the research of Woods et al. (1997), were comfortable with and positive about the changes in the new curriculum, at least in principle. In part, this was because the purposes seemed educationally desirable. Teachers also enjoyed the discretion the changes gave them to design and develop their own curriculum and assessment initiatives within very broad parameters. These teachers' "enhanced" responses were not surprising, as they were selected for the study precisely because of their perceived commitments to the new curriculum.

It is important to remember that the responses of our teachers were not always matched by their colleagues elsewhere in the system. In grade 9 especially (the beginning of secondary schooling in Ontario), there was widespread teacher resistance to legislated detracking (destreaming)—both to the idea of forced implementation and, in common with many teachers elsewhere (Oakes, Wells, Yonezawa, & Ray, 1997), to the very idea of detracking itself, which, despite research evidence to the contrary, contradicted secondary teachers' own beliefs about student ability and the initiative's achievability (Hargreaves et al., 1993). Although the teachers in our study may not be representative of all teachers encountering change of this sort, they nevertheless provide important insights into the intellectual work that successful change requires, even among those already committed to it.

The seventh- and eighth-grade teachers in our sample had been thinking about their approaches to curriculum, teaching, and learning for a long time. What was it that prompted them to commit to this new curriculum? Were they characteristically early adopters of change, always keen to join a new team or pilot a new program? Or was there something in particular about this curriculum that drew them toward it? What drove them or drew them to change their practices?

We found that most teachers agreed to develop and implement curriculum changes because they saw them as being largely consistent with their own educational and sociopolitical beliefs. The curriculum reform was congruent with the social and educational missions that these teachers invested in and pursued through their work. Their own philosophies and beliefs were reflected in many parts of the change. They repeatedly articulated their conviction that education in the middle years was not serving students as well as it might and that an outcomes-based, integrated curriculum held great promise for their students. Some could see the direct benefits for students:

> When people ask me what I teach, my answer is "children." I have adopted a lot of the curriculum because it helps reach children better. I'm adopting the substance because it fits, and I believe a lot of it. I think you have to believe the philosophy before you can truly implement something.

> I'm all for changes. I see a number of really positive things. First of all, the kids are becoming more responsible for their own learning. There can be more partnerships with the community. Over the past few years, I have done far less direct teaching. I let the kids do a lot more investigating. The new curriculum allows this kind of teaching.

This latter comment suggests that teachers saw benefits for making positive connections with students' learning beyond the walls of the school, as well as within them (Hargreaves & Fullan, 1998). The power of social relevance was most obvious in teachers' willingness to integrate curricula and establish relationships across traditional boundaries—to be, in a sense, transformative intellectuals with their students, helping them to think critically about the world around them:

> We did simulation games to get them to understand concepts like world hunger and distribution of wealth. We used global education and did an assembly called "Under the Same Sun." In one class, they had done a study of immigration—tracing our connections and our heritage. Another class had done a unit called "The World in a Chocolate Bar," which showed the concept of interdependence and connectedness with other places through the world economy.

> I get really excited when the students make connections back to their world. We wanted to teach them about plot line. *Tuck Everlasting* was a great novel to use for plot. Well, the unit mushroomed. The novel talks about the cycle of life and how the characters cannot get back on the cycle because of their immortality. From that, we went to cycles in science and connected to water cycles and air cycles. Then we went to life cycle stories and through them asked kids to connect something from the story with their own lives. It just flowed.

These teachers prepared integrated units that were almost always connected to real issues in students' lives, the world around them, or social questions. As we indicated in Chapter Four, teachers believed that relevance was essential for students to engage fully in their learning, and they often involved students in planning and developing ideas. These teachers, in other words, approached the intellectual work of educational change not just as a technical process of mastery, or even as a cultural one of meaning and understanding, but also as a critical and political process of inclusion, empowerment, and fulfillment of education's social mission.

Developing Capacity to Change: Agency and Opportunity

Teachers as learners are at the center of educational change. The teachers in our study had to learn a whole new set of skills, knowledge, and practices. This kind of change does not happen by osmosis, administrative mandate, or even sheer will and determination.

Successful implementation requires opportunities to clarify policy initiatives and understand reforms (declarative knowledge), opportunities to develop procedural knowledge associated with the innovation, and opportunities to explore new routines and modify practices (Leithwood, Jantzi, & Steinbach, 1999). All of this demanding work requires deliberate, sustained learning by teachers.

The teachers in the study were keenly aware of how much they had to learn, and most believed they were capable of making the necessary changes. They found many ways to create the conditions for their own learning. To begin with, they used their own practical knowledge and experience to think through the changes so that they made sense in the classroom. As we discussed in Chapter Two, teachers grounded learning outcomes in the practical world of their students and in their own accumulated knowledge and experiences about what does and does not work with such students. They built integrated units on this foundation of practical knowledge before considering how these units connected to the outcomes. Outside-in knowledge made sense only when it was filtered through inside-out experience. Although drawing on this practical knowledge could breathe life into curriculum units, it sometimes created inconsistencies in how outcomes were interpreted and implemented, and it imposed limits on what was possible. Teachers often found that they needed more, and they searched for outside-in knowledge to complement and extend their own inside-out experience (see Hargreaves, 1996).

They found more by engaging in explicit professional learning about new practices and strategies in an embedded way, both within their own workplace and through specific workshops and other events. The consortium of which their districts were part offered many professional development sessions ranging from five-day institutes on cooperative learning to professional sharing sessions where teachers could think through how to implement the curriculum.

Teachers found professional learning by coming together to share ideas, engage in problem solving, undertake joint planning, pool expertise and resources, and explore ways of integrating their work more effectively. Many seemed to value ongoing forms of "interactive professionalism" (Fullan & Hargreaves, 1996) with their colleagues more than traditional attendance at one-shot workshops. The importance of professional dialogue among colleagues was reiterated time and time again. Two teachers described the value of dividing attendance at workshops in order to cut down on their workload. Another indicated that

> the biggest change for me hasn't been in the reforms; it has been working with my partner. Whenever I go to a workshop, I just say all this stuff is totally secondary to actually sitting down with one person and collaborating.

The sheer size and complexity of the curriculum pushed teachers to search for help beyond the confines of their own classrooms. Some teachers went outside their school to find colleagues who could discuss with them the changes that were occurring. One teacher, among many with similar sentiments, stated, "I think teachers need to be given a chance to workshop together and talk about what we really need and what meeting these outcomes really means to us in our classrooms."

For many teachers, there was a conviction that their best units came from thoughtful and extensive collaboration with other teachers in their school and in other schools within their district. Not only were they proud of units that emerged, they also found that the planning process itself was a highly valuable form of job-embedded professional development. At the same time, developing original units was exhausting and time-consuming work. Consultants attached to the schools provided invaluable technical and moral support in this sense as they helped teachers through complex processes of planning and design.

Many of these teachers were accustomed to seeking out new learning for themselves. They regularly read papers in professional magazines and journals, went to workshops, worked together, and shared their professional lives with spouses and colleagues. A number of the teachers we interviewed had accumulated a variety of teaching experiences across the elementary age range or throughout a range of subject areas. Some had taught at both elementary and secondary levels through teacher exchange programs or over the course of their careers. Yet although they had been and were still engaged in many professional growth experiences, they also recognized that they still had a great deal to learn and that it would take time before they would feel comfortable with the new practices. At the same time, amid the feelings of frustration and overload, many had little doubt that the changes were achievable and that they already had or could readily acquire the capacity or agency to fulfill them. Developing this vital capacity for change, though, is not only a matter of individual or even collective commitment and determination. It is also a political matter of providing the conditions, the leadership, and the broad support that make the school a learning organization for its teachers, as well as for students. We explore the nature and effects of these supports and the political challenges of providing them in Chapter Seven.

Implications

Making sense out of complex educational change agendas is intellectually demanding. Engaging with the philosophy, seeing the underlying coherence, aligning the change with one's own social mission in teaching, learning new practices, integrating them into one's routines, and checking that they are valid and practical—all these things and more make up the intellectual work of educational change. Without time to engage in serious thinking, without the staff development (especially of a job-embedded nature) to know what to think about, and without colleagues who are willing to discuss and clarify ideas, the sheer conceptual and intellectual challenge of deciphering the clutter of policy demands can be overwhelming.

Some of the difficulties teachers faced were open to relatively straightforward (although not always politically popular) solutions of more time, more human resources, and better professional support of the kind we discuss in Chapter Seven. At the same time, changes in how policymakers present reform would give teachers invaluable help in undertaking the demanding intellectual work of reform. For instance, outcomes (or standards) and report cards that are written clearly by policymakers without sacrificing the ambitious goals that such standards push teachers to reach are more helpful to teachers than outcomes that are written so vaguely and obscurely that they cannot be understood, or so narrowly and simplistically that they restrict the scope of what teachers strive to achieve.

Equally, educational reform must become considerably less schizophrenic. Integrated curriculum that clashed with subject-based report cards and open-ended classroom assessments alongside systemwide tests were just two contradictory reform imperatives that placed teachers in the seemingly impossible dilemma of having to move in opposite directions at the same time. These dilemmas are largely insoluble at the individual school level. Assessment directions can and must be made more consistent, tensions between specialization and integration must be resolved more clearly, and accountability needs to be fundamentally rethought and redefined. Although everyone wants to change the teacher, it is also time for change agents and change addicts in the command centers of educational reform to begin to change themselves.

Chapter Six

The Emotional Work of Change

Educational change requires more than technical and intellectual effort and mastery and relies on more than exercising knowledge, skill, and problem-solving capacity. Educational change is also emotional work that draws on and affects a vast web of important, meaningful human relationships that make up the work of schools. Educational change efforts affect teachers' relationships with their students, the parents of those students, and one another. Teachers make heavy emotional investments in these relationships. Their sense of success and satisfaction depends on them.

Key Concepts

This chapter focuses on the nature and importance of teachers' socioemotional goals for and relationships with their students and the implications of these relationships for how teachers respond to various kinds of educational change. (A more detailed literature review on emotions and teaching and our theoretical framework for understanding the emotions of teaching and educational change are outlined in Hargreaves, 1998b, 1998c; and Hargreaves et al., forthcoming). In this opening section, we concentrate more specifically on some key concepts that cast light on what teachers told us about the emotional aspects of their work. We will see that virtually all aspects of teachers' work—the ways they teach, the timetable structures they prefer, and even how they plan—are affected by the importance they attach to the emotional goals and relationships of their jobs.

Emotional Practice

For all teachers, good and bad, child centered or subject centered, by design or default, teaching, like other work in caring professions or service occupations, is always an emotional practice. An emotional practice is one that activates, colors, and expresses people's feelings and the feelings of those with whom they interact (Denzin, 1984). This is especially true in teaching. What teachers do enthuses their students or bores them, makes them approachable to parents or keeps parents at arm's length, inspires their colleagues to collaborate closely with them or restricts staff relationships to patterns of politeness and noninterference. How teachers conduct and express themselves emotionally always matters. Emotions, in this sense, are central, not peripheral, to the learning, standards, and improvement agenda.

What is at stake here is partly a matter of what is variously called emotional competence, emotional literacy, or emotional intelligence. Being able to master the five basic emotional competencies that Goleman (1995, 1998) described—knowing how to express one's emotions, manage one's moods, empathize with the emotional states of others, motivate oneself and others, and exercise a wide range of social skills—is essential for being highly effective as a teacher. Yet, this is not only a matter of personal choice or individual skill development. Emotions should not be reduced to technical competencies. Indeed, Boler (1999) criticizes Goleman's view of emotional intelligence and argues that presenting emotion management as just another set of skills to be mastered, in which people can be trained, limits how we approach, understand, and try to shape the emotional work that people do.

Emotional Understanding

How people are emotionally is shaped by the emotional experiences they have developed within their culture, through their upbringing, and in their relationships. Organizations and workplaces are prime sites in which adults experience and learn to express their emotions in particular ways. Central to this cultural dimension of emotions is the idea of emotional understanding—and of how people develop or fail to develop it with their clients and associates.

For sociologist Norman Denzin (1984), emotional understanding does not take place like cognitive understanding in a linear, step-by-step way. Instead, emotional understanding occurs
instantaneously, at a glance, as people reach down into their past
emotional experiences and read the emotional responses of those
around them. Teachers scan their students all the time, for example, checking their appearance of engagement or responsiveness.

When teachers' emotional scanning goes awry, what they actually experience is emotional misunderstanding; they think they
know what their students are feeling, but they are completely
wrong (Hargreaves, 1998b, 1998c). Students who seem studious
are actually bored; ones who appear hostile are really embarrassed
or ashamed that they cannot succeed. Because emotional misunderstanding leads teachers to misread their students' learning, it
seriously threatens learning standards. In this sense, emotion, as
well as cognition, is foundational to the standards agenda.

Importantly, emotional engagement and understanding in
schools (as elsewhere) require strong, continuous relationships between teachers and students so that they learn to read each other
over time. Yet this is just what treating standards like hurdles can
easily threaten. They can create a frenetic pace of teaching that allows no time for relationships and understanding to develop and
that reinforces a subject-centered organization of schooling that
makes integration difficult and fragments the interactions between
teachers and the excessive number of students they are required
to teach. In this sense, emotional understanding in schools is either fostered or frustrated by curriculum structures and priorities
and by the way standards are designed and imposed.

Emotional Labor

Many jobs that involve interactions with others call on workers to
manufacture or mask their emotions on many occasions. The po-
lite waitress, enthusiastic salesman, solicitous undertaker, and irri-
tated debt collector are all expressions of this phenomenon.
Teachers manufacture and mask their emotions too—when they
enthuse about a new initiative, are overjoyed with a student's break-
through, show patience with a frustrating colleague, or are calm
in the face of parental criticism. This does not mean that teachers'

emotions are somehow artificial or inauthentic—that teachers are just acting and are not in tune with themselves. The point, rather, is that emotions do not always arise spontaneously or naturally. Creating and sustaining a dynamic, engaging lesson, for example, requires hard emotional work, investment, or labor. So, too, does remaining calm and unruffled when confronted by threatening student behavior.

At its best, emotional labor in teaching (and other occupations) is pleasurable and rewarding when people are able to pursue their own purposes through it and work in conditions that allow them to do their jobs well (Oatley, 1991; Ashforth & Humphrey, 1993). At times like these, emotional labor is at the heart of the passion to teach (Fried, 1995). But as Hochschild (1983) shows in her classic text on the subject, emotional labor can be negative and draining when people feel they are masking or manufacturing their emotions to suit the purposes of others or when poor working conditions make it impossible for them to perform their work well.

Blackmore (1996) has shown how women principals who work in repressive policy environments can become what she calls emotional middle managers of educational reform—leaders who motivate their staffs to implement or make the best of the impractical and unpalatable policies of government, and lose something of themselves—their health and their personal relationships—in the process. In these sorts of circumstances, the emotions of teaching and leading are not just emotional matters but also highly politically charged ones.

Emotional Goals and Bonds

Many teachers' relations with their students are significantly and deliberately emotional in nature. Like many elementary teachers, a number of the teachers we interviewed spoke of these relationships in terms of love (Nias, 1989). One teacher described her basic teaching technique as "I love you to death and work you to death, and we can still have fun doing it." Another proclaimed:

> I love children. I love all ages. I have a great deal of trouble with teachers who say, "Oh, I only like first graders. I won't teach anybody else. All other kids are awful." That just gets my back up. I

think to myself, "If you don't like kids, you shouldn't be teaching." You have to like kids. You have to like what you are doing a lot, and I do.

Many of the rewards of teaching among the teachers in our sample were what Lortie (1975) calls psychic in nature. They came from relationships with students, from seeing adolescents change as a result of teachers' own commitments and efforts. "Working with young people and watching them grow" was "a real turn on," said one teacher. That was where her real strength was—"with individual kids." Indeed, as in Lortie's study, many teachers' psychic rewards were found in successes with individuals. "The kids," said one teacher. "What keeps me going is helping just one in a year." Individual students who came back later and had succeeded, who remembered and were grateful, were particularly valued. One teacher said, "I'd love to meet them in five years and say, 'I really remember when we did . . . ' To me that's valuable." Another commented:

> I feel very proud when students come back and say, "We're doing very well. We've got good marks. We feel good about that, so give us some strokes for it." At the end of it all they come back and thank you. That makes you feel good that you are doing a lot of the right things.

Teachers liked to celebrate stories of their efforts with individuals and of what they had learned from them. One spoke of a "wonderful boy" just arrived at her school from the United States, for whom she had had to make a wide range of curriculum adjustments.

The psychic and emotional rewards of teaching fundamentally affected what teachers did as they adjusted their teaching to what they learned about individual students through conferencing, peer evaluation, and other kinds of personal interaction. Teacher after teacher commented on why their emotional relationships with students mattered for the social outcomes they were trying to achieve and for establishing an appropriate emotional climate in which other kinds of learning could take place.

The emotional relationships that teachers cultivated with students and the emotional qualities they tried to develop in their students were part of the wider social mission of their teaching.

One teacher's "underlying truths" in the classroom included students' having respect for themselves and each other. Another also felt that mutual respect was essential and was proud that none of her children was mean-spirited. Many teachers talked about the value of developing and displaying tolerance, especially in contexts of increasing cultural diversity so that "there's not a lot of this 'Oh, you're so stupid! You mean you can't do that?' Instead, they say, 'No, it's not right, but look what you've done here. It's just a small mistake.'" Cooperative groupwork was seen as especially valuable for fostering this kind of tolerance. Running through all of these qualities of tolerance and respect, and through the ways teachers tried to develop them, was an underlying ethic of care (Gilligan, 1982; Noddings, 1992). One younger teacher felt that the whole reform philosophy was very much centered on providing better care for intermediate-level students:

> I got a copy of the transition years reform document and looked through it. What I think it means is working with students, mentoring them, showing them the connections between school and the real world, showing them the connections between subjects that they are learning in the real world, helping them to develop at a very difficult time in their lives, and just being caring and at the same time giving them an academic base for the future.

This teacher wanted students to know that teachers cared about their lives. She was proud she had built a reputation for being fair and caring and felt it important to know the students well if she was going to teach them well. This caring, as a way of pursuing emotional understanding, involved great emotional labor, which could potentially exact costs on herself. This teacher was keenly aware she could be criticized for caring too much; she reported:

> People would say to me in my first few years of teaching, "You've got to toughen up. You're too soft, you're too sensitive, and you take everything so seriously." And I'd say to them, even in my first year, "When I get tough and when I stop caring about what I'm doing, then I won't be a teacher anymore. I will stay teaching, so I refuse to change now. My philosophy of teaching—to be a caring and effective teacher—has not changed.

Teachers in our study wanted to provide a safe, secure, caring environment; they wanted it to be a place of comfort that was "not like high school." Indeed, some teachers worried about their students' "getting lost" in high school. Other research that one of us has conducted suggests these fears are not unfounded (Hargreaves, forthcoming; Hargreaves et al., forthcoming). Secondary school teachers stated that although they attempted to be aware of and responsive to emotions that students brought with them into the classroom from their troubles with family or friends, they mainly did so when these emotions were regarded as disturbances interfering with students' learning. They did not see emotions as part of students' learning, as something that they were themselves responsible for creating and not merely controlling. Furthermore, when elementary and secondary teachers were asked to describe memorable incidents of positive emotions with their students, all elementary teachers referred to incidents involving students they taught in their own classes; only secondary teachers referred to incidents outside their classes, in extracurricular activities or elsewhere, where they saw students "in a new light." Here, it seemed, secondary teachers sometimes had to meet and interact with their students outside the classroom to know them emotionally. The secondary school classroom was not itself a place to develop shared emotional goals with students or establish close emotional bonds with them.

In this study, the emotional goals and bonds of working with students were especially important in relation to student differences, such as those involving cultural diversity or special educational needs. In many countries, educational policies over the previous decade have brought a wider range of special education students into ordinary classes. Teachers' caring orientations were especially visible where this group was concerned. This care did not take the form of pity for or protectiveness toward children who were seen as fundamentally deficient. Rather, teachers were particularly pleased when special needs children were successfully integrated with all the others. "I love the fact that they are sitting in groups right now working with everybody else," said one. In another teacher's class, if one special needs child needed a mathematics resource pack as a learning support, every child got the resource pack. Teachers generally took pride when colleagues came into their classes and could not distinguish children who had learning disabilities from the rest.

In the area of cultural diversity, one teacher whose school was in a mainly all-white community felt that it was these sorts of students in particular who needed to have their cultural horizons broadened to gain a better sense of being part of a wider global community. But it was teachers in the three other and more culturally diverse districts in our study whose teaching was most directly confronted by the changing multicultural context of their communities and society. Whereas teachers in the first district could increase students' awareness of cultural diversity through introducing "global education" into their integrated curriculum or by bringing visiting speakers of color into the school, cultural diversity in the other districts was a feature of the student body itself.

In the main, teachers welcomed the opportunities that working in culturally diverse settings provided. One teacher said of her school that she "would be so bored if it wasn't multicultural." Other teachers pointed to dramatic and moving instances of multicultural engagement, such as linking the Holocaust to the lives of children whose relatives had died in wars in Somalia, Vietnam, or Japan. One recalled how "the little Japanese boy had tears coming down his face as he told how his grandfather had been killed." Another described one way in which he had connected the curriculum cognitively and emotionally to his students' diverse lives:

> I really enjoy the multicultural dimension of my work. For example, we have a student who has just arrived from Turkey. He speaks very little English. He stays with us for math and then he has English as a Second Language. They (people from Turkey) divide differently. He didn't recognize the symbol when I was doing division. They do it some other way. It is nice to share that. Turkish children don't do order of operation at all, and the concept just floored him. Some other kids backed that up and said, "Yeah, my parents don't do that; they don't understand order of operation. They've never seen it before." So it is kind of neat for us to go, "Yeah, just because we are doing this doesn't mean that it is the be-all and end-all, or it doesn't mean that everybody else is doing it." It allows me to do things like that and to celebrate differences.

By focusing on teachers' emotional responses, we were able to rethink what is important about educational change and what its purpose should be. Our data clearly show that teachers' classroom commitments extend beyond issues of cognitive learning to encompass their emotional relationships with and connections to students, to care for students, to pursue a strong social mission of teaching their students in ways that develop them as tolerant and respectful citizens and not merely high-performing learners and future workers, to develop their social skills as well as their academic knowledge, and to create an inclusive atmosphere where students with special needs or from diverse backgrounds or nonconventional home circumstances can feel equally comfortable and accepted.

In Japanese culture, teachers make relentless efforts to establish an emotional bond or ligature with every student in their care as a basis for learning (Shimahara & Sakai, 1995). In every cultural context, high standards of student learning depend on teachers' developing successful emotional understanding with students and creating conditions in teaching that make such understanding possible. This is even more important when students and classrooms are demonstrably diverse.

In our study, teachers' emotional connections to students and the social and emotional goals they wanted to achieve as they taught those students shaped and influenced almost everything they did, along with how they responded to changes that affected what they did. Teachers wanted to become better so that they could help their students. The emotional understanding they sought to develop with their students was central to how they taught them, how they evaluated them, what kinds of curricula they planned and selected for them, and what kinds of structures they adopted as a context for teaching them.

Emotions and School Structure

The emotional relationships that teachers have with their students and with the work of teaching students are shaped in many ways by how the work of teaching is structured. Structures are often imagined or conceptualized in almost physical ways, like frameworks or architectural designs. Among people, however, structures mean more than this. Organizational structures are mechanisms for arranging and regulating the ways people interact with each other in time and space. Structures bring people together or keep them apart. They can make human interactions brief, episodic, and superficial, or allow them to develop into deeper, sustained relationships. Structures can shape our actions and relationships, opening up opportunities for and imposing constraints on them. Structures need not be cast in stone. They can also be changed by our actions so that they better suit our purposes.

School structures, particularly those that affect teachers, consist of timetables, length of lessons, curriculum choices, the organization of school subjects, subject departments, the assignment of teachers to grade levels, patterns of decision making, and so on. Some very familiar school structures have been part of the accepted "grammar of schooling" for decades or more (Tyack & Tobin, 1994), but they are also open to change.

How teachers felt about something as seemingly abstract as the structures in which they worked was influenced by whether they felt these structures would benefit their students. The majority of teachers' remarks about structures and structural change came from a district where the most systematic attempts had been made to build curriculum integration, establish a core block of time for integrated studies within the timetable, and in some cases encourage teachers to follow their classes from one grade to the next (a structure known in some places as "looping"). Teachers were consistently positive about the benefits of the new core structures for students and for their relationships with students. They did not like the way conventional timetables with separate teachers, separate subjects, and short lesson periods fragmented their relationships with students. "The kids really need that one person they can relate to in school," said one teacher. A core-blocked timetable, where teachers were with the same class of students for at least half the day, made such relationships and emotional understandings possible. It was now easier for "children through their adolescence to bond with one teacher." In one school, this had been very important for being able to care for one particularly difficult group of students, the so-called "hell kids," who created immense problems for teachers with whom they did not have this kind of bond. Following students through from one year to the next meant that "because you know them so well, you know their moods, and you can start right in with them. "You can see the change in growth." By following the same students year to year, one teacher said, "I know my kids, and I call them my kids, and I know what they're about. I know what they're doing inside and outside of school. I know their families, especially if I have them for more than a year." And as teachers see students grow and mature, "it's wonderful to see that process."

A number of teachers commented on the advantages of the more open time structures that core blocking allowed. They "felt comfortable" with the open time lines and did not "feel constricted" by them and would "love having those students the whole day" if they could. Open time lines enabled teachers to keep "rolling" with the projects—to "go with the flow," as they often put it:

> Where you have the children for a morning and there are no time lines, if you find you are rolling with a project or they start asking, "Can we go into the library to look up this?" or "We want to find out more about this," there are a lot of teachers who feel comfortable saying, "Go for it! and maybe we don't get to math this morning, but we'll do more math later on during the week."

> I can help any kid learn anything as long as he is motivated. I feel that I can motivate a kid through reality and natural situations, but in order to do that, I have to be able to have block periods of time to set up situations where I can show them the reality of what we are doing, and to me that's a great thing. I get rolling on something, and if the kids get rolling on something, I don't want to be stopped by a bell telling me to move on

> We had some kids involved in smoking in my class, and I was really upset with them. They were all upset too. How could they have done that! One kid had smoked so much that she literally was drunk on it; she could not walk a straight line. They were so concerned. Whereas if it's a specialist class in a conventional timetable, pack up, away you go! The other kids were really concerned; they could see her suffering. It was a good learning experience for the other kids. She sat there, and we talked about it. It was a wonderful learning experience that you won't get out of a textbook and that I'm not dictated to by a clock. These things don't come up every day, but when they do, you really appreciate the time that you can bond with the kids.

The alternative structures made these change-oriented teachers feel they could care for their students and teach them more effectively, but the persistence of more conventional structural arrangements could make it harder for them to do so, fracturing their relationships, undermining their planning, and overloading them with other obligations. For example, a guidance teacher who taught many classes wanted time to do team building to connect more with the students. And another teacher mentioned how, before the core blocking arrangements, the previous timetable was "horrible, "just brutal" in the way it fragmented contacts with students into forty-minute slots. Such conventional structural arrangements account for the findings in our other research that secondary teachers often seem unable to develop the depth of emotional understanding with their students that their elementary colleagues are better able to achieve (Hargreaves, forthcoming; Hargreaves et al., forthcoming).

When teachers in this study supported structures that supported their students, they did not do so in a self-sacrificial way. The teachers we interviewed who worked in more open time structures felt extremely comfortable with them. Many of their colleagues did not, however. When one school printed out its new timetable with a large allocation to core blocking, some teachers were "more comfortable getting out their rulers and blocking the periods off and putting specific subjects back in." But teachers who worked in a larger core liked to adjust the time to the learning rather than squeezing the learning into the time, and they welcomed the flexibility to do that. In this respect, their desires for structures that would support students and their own sense of what kinds of structures were comfortable for themselves as teachers were closely aligned with each other. Their students' emotional needs and their own emotional rewards were attuned to each other.

Emotions and Pedagogy

Pedagogy, or instruction as it is sometimes called, is one of the great rhetorical battlegrounds of educational reform. Many studies portray classroom teachers as being predominantly wedded to traditional patterns of teaching, such as lecturing, seatwork, and question-and-answer methods (Goodlad, 1984; Tye, 1985). Conversely, in many countries there has been an assault on the supposed pervasiveness of and excessive adherence to group work and project work in elementary and intermediate teachers' classes at the expense of whole-class teaching (Nikiforuk, 1993; Woodhead, 1995). Meanwhile, new pedagogical approaches like reading recovery, cooperative learning, and manipulative mathematics surface regularly, each with its own bold claims about achieving significant gains in student learning.

Interestingly, very few of our interviewees seemed to believe in one best approach to teaching. Most of them valued and said they used a wide variety of teaching strategies. Among them, teachers listed a formidable array of methods that they used in their teaching:

- Concept attainment
- Mind mapping
- Individual conferencing
- Traditional teaching
- Cooperative learning
- Individualization
- "Real-time" assignments
- Visiting speakers
- Twinning with high school classes
- Special events such as inventors' festivals, video, television, visual things in general
- Humor
- Enthusing students by doing "crazy things"
- Creating hands-on experiences
- Setting puzzles or problems
- Organizing student oral presentations
- Using natural situations
- Having a "talking bucket" that children can use to speak about items of concern to them
- Computer data analysis
- Portfolios
- Out-of-school visits
- Kinesthetic learning, such as walking around the circumference of circles
- Peer coaching and peer teaching
- Reading and writing workshops
- Roundtable discussions

- Working in pairs
- Role-play
- Brainstorming
- Dramatic presentation

Not all teachers claimed to use all these methods, but the overall range is extensive, and having and using a broad repertoire of teaching strategies mattered greatly to almost every teacher in this group. Teachers used "a lot of variety," "a combination of methods," and multiple strategies. They "liked to mix things." "I can't say that I have one strategy that I use," said one. Another teacher said that ideally, he would "love to see every teacher using a variety of strategies." Even a teacher who referred to being "indoctrinated with cooperative learning" said:

> I don't do one thing all the time. I do direct teaching at the front of the room. I do pair work with the kids. I do cooperative learning. I do social skills teaching. I like an eclectic mix so that I can make things as interesting and effective as possible.

In opting for variety, what mattered most was making things interesting and effective for students. Having a wide repertoire could enable the teacher to "help any kid learn anything as long as he is motivated." One teacher put it this way: "All I know is that I like to use as many different things as I can in my classroom to reach as many kids as I can in different ways and make things interesting." "Just anything that will work" would be a good pedagogical motto for most of the teachers in our sample.

Most of the teachers also included traditional teaching in what they felt would work with students. Few, if any, were happy to be quiet facilitators, mere "guides by the side." Although they favored cooperative learning, hands-on learning, and learning that was like real life, these teachers also saw a strong place for traditional teaching, or "old teaching" as one called it, within their wider repertoire. One interviewee said about her teaching:

> You'd see a lot of variety, and you'd see some pretty aggressive teaching. I like to be seen. I like to be heard. I like to move. I like to make sure that people are still with me. I like to be excited about what I'm teaching, even if it's bland material.

Many teachers portrayed themselves as vivid and vital presences in their own classrooms. One teacher was "not ashamed" that she "loved to present." She took pride in the fact. A teacher of French immersion (where French is the language of all or most instruction) said, "I think in second-language teaching, you have to be prepared to dance and stand on your head and do just about anything to get kids to understand and respond and participate." As an example, she said that in one class, she had jumped from one table to the next as she role-played a historic naval battle.

The teachers drew on a broad repertoire of strategies to try to reach their students, get them motivated, and help them understand. The methods they used were determined, in many ways, by what they sensed their students needed most. Teachers talked about

- Changing their teaching so that it meshed with what their students wanted
- Using support strategies that raised the comfort level of students with learning difficulties
- Trying "to involve the kids as much as possible by finding out their interests"
- Taking pride when their special education students shone
- Using portfolios to discover what children found fun so that this could be incorporated into teaching them
- Not "acting as if I am the boss and as if I know everything" so that the classroom could "be a safe place where people can be free to express their ideas"
- Creating an atmosphere in which students could feel comfortable interrupting or asking questions
- Playing with students
- Encouraging students to share their feelings
- Finding ways to get students to support each other
- Playing soft background music if it helped children perform better on tests

Through all this, some teachers felt that one of the most important strategies was humor. "I love to use humor as an effective tool," said one, "because it's a great equalizer. It breaks the tension and the stress." More than this, they agreed that it was important to be themselves as teachers, and to let their own emotions and feelings show through from time to time. As Farson (1996) says, it is indeed in moments when we *lose* control rather than exert it that our humanity as leaders shines through. One teacher recalled that "the more I imposed superstructures that were not me—and the kids knew it—it didn't function as well." Another described how he and his teaching partner would sometimes "do silly things together, in front of the kids," like throwing pies at each other. Humor made them human to each other and to their students. It was important that their emotional selves shone through, that they could let go occasionally, even to the point where students could sometimes scarcely believe what their teachers did. For these teachers, the emotional labor of teaching was a labor of love, a passionate investment, a giving and fulfillment of the self.

The teaching strategies that the teachers used were shaped in part by their own emotional needs as well as those of their students. Excitement and enjoyment figured strongly among those needs. Teachers would talk about how they would really enjoy getting their students involved or about the excitement of special events or performances, like an innovation festival, where students could present their work authentically to real audiences outside school. One teacher described her concept attainment lesson on relationships in ways that connected her own excitement to that of the students:

> I was so excited about it, and really when I started, I didn't know how it was going to work, and it took a long time. But oh, it was ever so powerful. I'm sure if I went out in the schoolyard now, they'd tell me what *relationship* means because they developed it.

Another teacher recalled how he had caused laughter in an inservice workshop by saying that cooperative learning had now surpassed sex on his list of priorities. A third teacher talked more generally about her ongoing emotional needs as a teacher:

> As a person, I have to change every year. I have to get excited about what I'm doing, and if I see myself going forward, I'm fine. Probably the most exciting things are the fact that we are bringing in more "real time" people with the junior program and we're doing some more twinning with the high school. I think that if you're looking at global customs or man-made hazards globally,

for example, those are "real-time" things and the kids get excited about those too.

As with many of her colleagues, this teacher's remarks pointed to the positive aspects of her work as emotional labor (Hochschild, 1983), one that was often a labor of love, a passionate investment of the self in the work of teaching that was an act of self-fulfillment. She cared for her clients and worked hard to get herself excited so that she could meet their needs while staving off the ever-present threat of boredom, routine, and stagnation. Going forward, and developing and changing as a teacher in pedagogical terms, was important for many teachers in our sample (who by definition had been identified for the project as having a serious and sustained commitment to certain kinds of educational change):

> I'm a much better teacher than I ever was. I am much more aware of the kids' needs. I don't think I would say I was afraid of dealing with special education kids or gifted kids, but I don't think I was really confident in what I was doing and what was best for them. But now I know what works for them.

For some, this sense of growing confidence and competence was especially accented in their early years of becoming a teacher. This time is typically one of early classroom survival: establishing authority as a teacher and moving beyond preoccupations with self and one's own insecurities, to addressing the needs of students through a bank of knowledge and strategies that begin to accumulate over time (Sikes, 1985; Huberman, 1993):

> My first year, I never even looked at the kids. Looking back, I kind of think, "That's okay. It was my first year, and they all warned me that I would do that." You are so concerned with yourself and where you are at and whether your attendance is done and all of that stuff, that you have forgotten to look out to the kids and see where they are at and what their needs are. I am doing that a lot more now because I am feeling more comfortable about what I am doing. And I am realizing that the more interesting I make things and the more that what I do here is different from other classrooms, the more interested they are going to be. I feel freer to try new things and not worry if it goes overtime. If I don't finish one unit, I don't mind it.

Part of the challenge of change and development for teachers was struggling with letting go of old conceptions, familiar practices, and comforting routines:

> I taught math the first two years I was on staff, and I was in a portable classroom. The desks were in rows. Getting the groupwork going in the core area was a big change. I thought during the first couple of weeks that I was going to go nuts with the noise. But then I realized this is very productive.

Integrating new ideas and techniques recently acquired from professional development courses was equally challenging in both technical and emotional terms:

> What I've been doing over my last two years of teaching is to learn as much as I can and do things over and over again until I feel comfortable with them. So things that I learned in the cooperative learning institute the first time, I may have used only once or twice. But I have them in my teaching repertoire now, and when I know that it's going to be effective, I will use it again.

Most teachers were committed to having or developing a broad repertoire of teaching strategies. How they drew on this repertoire at any time was shaped by their relationships with students, their feelings about what would excite and engage students emotionally, and their feelings about what would excite and engage themselves as teachers. Building and maintaining such excitement and enjoyment was at the heart of the positive emotional labor of teaching, of what made teachers want to change and develop pedagogically, and of what made them take pride in that development over time.

Emotions and Planning

Few other areas of teachers' work seem as ostensibly unemotional as planning. As we described in Chapter Two, curriculum planning for these teachers was not constrained by stilted formats, excessively packed with overly detailed targets, or mapped backward from abstract ends. Rather, teachers started with knowledge and feelings about their students, with intuitive understanding about what would be likely to excite and engage those students, and with their own passions and enthusiasms about ideas, topics, materials, and methods that they could picture working within their classes. Teachers described how they loved writing curricula, making things "richer for kids" in ways that were "practical" and "exciting."

Emotions are about psychological movement. The Latin origin of emotion is *emovere*, meaning "to move out, stir up." When we are emotional, we are overcome by joy, fall in love, or sink into despair. In this sense, it is interesting that teachers described their excitement of developing ideas with colleagues in vivid, kinesthetic metaphors that portrayed planning as being full of creativity, movement, and emotional intensity. Planning for outcomes began with teachers' own passions and feelings about their students. Ideas for new integrated units were brainstormed by teachers together and sometimes with students, who were made part of the planning process too. They were "piggy-backed" on one another, "bounced off" people, or generally "bashed around." Teachers would work together in teams to "capture those learners," be "springboards" for each other, "spin off" one another's ideas, "take risks," "go nuts," and engage in a "free-for-all" so that the planning process became "like a pinball machine" for them.

The feeling of freedom in planning was exceptionally important for our teachers. It offered the opportunity to let the ideas and the brainstorming with colleagues flow. Indeed, two of the teachers specifically talked about their experiences of planning in terms of recognizing the flow and making the meetings really flow. Csikzentmihalyi (1990) describes *flow* as a state of concentration so focused that it amounts to absolute absorption in an activity. Flow, he says, is the necessary ingredient for optimal experience and quality of life. For Goleman (1995, p. 90), "flow represents the ultimate in harnessing the emotions in the service of performance and learning. In flow, the emotions are not just contained and channeled, but positive, energized, and aligned with the task in hand." "To be caught in the ennui of depression or the agitation of anxiety," Goleman continues, "is to be barred from flow." This is exactly what happened when planning processes and formats were imposed, when planning partners were not chosen, when planning purposes were unclear or not owned by those engaged in the planning, and when the "connections for the kids" were not evident. Teachers used very different metaphors to describe these kinds of planning: "stifled," coming across "stumbling blocks," or being "bogged down in cement." Rational planning has come in for criticism in recent years because of its failure to deal with the highly complex, nonlinear, and rapidly changing environments of today (Mintzberg, 1994). Our data suggest that rational planning models are also flawed because they do not account for the emotions.

Freer, flowing approaches to planning among our leading-edge teachers did not exclude attention to goals or outcomes. But it was only later, as the course of study started to take shape, that many teachers would return to the list of prescribed outcomes, as a checklist, to see if they missed anything and to ensure that their curriculum was balanced. Overall, while outcomes were still included in these more open-ended and flexible forms of planning, the emotionally charged way that our sample teachers appeared to plan in practice seemed sharply at odds with the more purely rational process of backward mapping implied by outcomes-based (and also standards-driven) education. For them, curriculum planning engaged their emotions. It flowed. It was attentive to general goals and ends but not dominated by them. Such planning began with the teachers' emotional connections to students and was sustained by their emotional engagement and excitement about the creative, interactive aspects of the process itself. Students' emotional needs and teachers' emotional engagements in a creative, flexible process of teaching were reciprocally attuned to each other.

Implications

Teaching and improving teaching cannot be reduced to technical competence or clinical standards. There is more at stake even than teachers' becoming thoughtful, reflective practitioners. Teaching and its improvement also involve significant emotional labor. Establishing emotional understanding with students was central to reaching high standards in teachers' work. Connecting teaching and learning to their social mission of educating also gave their work critical depth. The teachers in our study valued the emotional bonds they established with students and valued educating their students as emotional and social beings, as well as intellectual ones. Teachers' emotional commitments and connections to students energized and articulated everything these teachers did: how they taught, what they taught, how they planned, and the structures in which they preferred to teach. One important way in which teachers interpreted the educational changes that were imposed on them, as well as the ones they developed themselves, was in terms of their impact on their own emotional goals and relationships. It is time for educational change strategies, reform efforts, and definitions of teaching and learning standards to come to terms with and embrace these emotional dimensions of teaching and learning. Without attention to the emotions, educational reform efforts may ignore and even damage some of the most fundamental aspects of what teachers do.

What does our analysis mean for policy and practice? In our view, it suggests the following:

- Standards and outcomes should include social and emotional goals for student learning as well as strictly cognitive ones.
- Standards and outcomes should not be so numerous and detailed that they squeeze out time and discretion for teachers to develop emotional understanding with their students.
- Schools' structures need to be redesigned so that teachers can develop the sustained relationships with their students that are at the basis of effective emotional understanding. Core blocks of curriculum time, longer lesson periods, less highly specialized roles for teachers, and opportunities for "looping" or following students from one grade to the next are key components of a structural design that supports emotional understanding.

It is also important that the work of teaching be constructed and supported in such a way that it makes the intellectual and emotional labor of the job feel exhilarating rather than draining and exhausting. Ensuring that curriculum planning formats are flexible and engaged; encouraging pedagogical breadth and growth rather than compliance with singular, dogmatic approaches; and having opportunity and encouragement to work in many different ways with colleagues provide key supports for this necessary intellectual and emotional labor. These supports are the focus of our next chapter.

Chapter Seven

Supporting and Sustaining Change

Encountering and internalizing new educational ideas and practices do not occur in a vacuum. Teachers are creators of their work, but they are also creatures of their workplaces. How the workplace of teaching is organized significantly affects how well the intellectual and emotional work of teaching and of change is done. This places a heavy responsibility on the shoulders of policymakers, system administrators, and school leaders to create and maintain the supportive conditions in which teachers can do their best work. People in these leadership and support roles have three fundamental tasks:

- To *support* teachers and, where necessary, push them to be able to implement appropriate changes that matter
- To ensure that the changes that teachers make can be *sustained* over time
- To ensure that the changes can be *generalized* beyond a few enthusiastic teachers or specially supported pilot schools (like the ones in this study) to affect whole systems

Although the issue of generalizability is an exceptionally important one in educational change (Hargreaves & Fink, 2000; Fullan, 2000), for the most part it cannot be addressed by the database of our study. This chapter therefore concentrates more on the issues of support and sustainability in educational change.

Institutionalizing change, sustaining it, and generalizing it are some of the fundamental tasks of large-scale educational reform and of leadership within and beyond the school. These tasks involve attending to a whole infrastructure for change, including curriculum resources, coalitions and alignments of agencies and policies, professional development and capacity-building processes, and procedures for monitoring and feedback.

What kinds of supports seemed important for helping teachers in our study with the intellectually and emotionally demanding work of educational change, and what obstacles seemed to impede them? And what can we learn from the effects of these obstacles and supports on leading-edge teachers, working in pilot projects, in a snapshot of time, for the long-term sustainability of positive educational change?

Support

The first task is that of supporting teachers in the change process—helping them to develop and implement important changes in their work. This is not merely a matter of ensuring that teachers faithfully implement particular innovations or reforms but of teachers' being able to respond to multiple innovations, deal with constant change, and always be open to and interested in exploring ways to improve their teaching on a continuous basis. In getting teachers to implement particular reforms, governments are often drawn to strategies of compliance and control such as legislation, inspection, and linking funding to performance. Although control strategies sometimes work with short-term imposition of change, their longer-term effectiveness in places like Kentucky and the imposition of the Kentucky Education Reform Act has been questioned (Whitford, 2000). Moreover, as imposition is heaped cumulatively upon imposition, as in the more than a decade of national educational reform in England and Wales, teachers appear to withdraw their interest and investments from change in general, and even from their fundamental commitments to their work, as their scope for professional judgment is significantly reduced (Woods, Jeffrey, Troman, & Boyle, 1997).

Openness to and ability to work effectively with continuous change rather than specific reforms depend not on control strategies but on what change theorists call strategies of capacity building. If the capacity of the system is insufficient, it can be increased by developing teachers' knowledge, skills, dispositions, and views of self (O'Day, Goertz, & Floden, 1995). Capacity can also be influenced by creating professional communities within the organization (Fullan, 2000; Stoll, 1999). Although educational change can be initiated and imposed by heavy-handed edicts, only the deeper human capacity of individuals and schools can sustain reform efforts over time.

Sustainability

Much of the history of educational reform is one of promising educational experiments that fade and fizzle after the first few years of innovation (Tyack & Tobin, 1994; Smith, Dwyer, Prunty, & Kleine, 1987). Successful educational strategies are therefore ones that do more than promote and implement change in particular sites; they also need to anticipate and overcome obstacles to sustaining change over time. This is the problem of sustainability of change.

Longitudinal studies of innovative schools, model schools, lighthouse schools, special pilot projects, and whole-school change initiatives repeatedly reveal that over time, their success is eroded or sabotaged by a predictable set of factors (Smith, Dwyer, Prunty, & Kline, 1987; Fink, 2000; Huberman & Miles, 1984; Siskin, 1995; Hargreaves & Fink, 2000). These include:

- Lack of continuity in or inconsistency of exceptional school leadership. When initial charismatic leaders are administratively rotated between schools, they become hard acts to follow.
- Problems of staff recruitment and retention. Initial (sometimes hand-picked) enthusiasts lose their energy, or get promoted, and are hard to replace with teachers of similar vision or levels of commitment.
- Governments and administrators change, and so do their policy emphases, often running counter to the changes to which teachers originally committed themselves.

Loss of initial promise, fading of enthusiasm, and eclipsing of local initiative and change capacity by the pressures and changing demands of district and government policies loom like shadows over all promising educational change efforts, including the ones described in this book. The kinds of support that can help sustain educational change over time include developing widespread leadership capacity rather than making change reliant on small numbers of exceptional leaders in a system; developing widespread (and job-embedded) staff development rather than investing all hope in special groups of change enthusiasts; and maintaining policy consistency or at least a policy framework that leaves schools and teachers with sufficient scope and discretion to establish their own consistency over time. All of these threats to sustainability, we will see, were already present even in the earliest, most optimistic stages of innovation that we observed in this study.

The teachers in our study identified five major areas that significantly influenced their attempts to incorporate major policy changes into their daily routines and that were important for supporting and sustaining these changes in their work:

- School structures
- Teacher culture
- Professional learning
- Professional discretion
- School leadership

School Structures

Deep changes like the ones addressed by the teachers in this study often run against the grain of existing school and classroom structures. Structures of schooling have often become so institutionalized or entrenched over years and even decades that they define the essence of schooling itself for the teachers and students who work there. They become an accepted part of the school's culture, of the way people routinely do their work (Deal & Kennedy, 1982). Among teachers, parents, policymakers, and the wider public, structures such as lesson periods of a particular length, a subject-based curriculum, or numerical or letter-based systems of assessing students' work are often regarded as not just one version of schooling but as synonymous with school itself (Metz, 1991). Parents typically reinforce this view and indeed may press to reinstate it if their children's school begins to diverge too sharply from what is familiar to them (Fink, 2000; Hargreaves, 2000).

When educational structures become firmly inscribed in the public and professional imagination, they can seriously impede efforts to define and achieve new purposes or solve new problems. Educators find themselves trying to squeeze new projects and initiatives into old, unsympathetic structures rather than transforming the structures so that they accommodate and support the new purposes and practices. The teachers in our study were no different in this respect as their innovative practices challenged existing structures of time and space.

Traditionally, the years of early secondary or even junior high schools have been organized around forty-minute time blocks of subject teaching. This time structure sets a familiar rhythm to the school day, to how teachers organize the content and regulate the pace of their teaching. Not surprisingly, for many teachers, especially colleagues who are not involved in the first phases of innovation, this timetable is not to be tampered with.

A number of teachers tried hard to engage in common planning, team teaching, and the development and delivery of integrated units together. Yet these initiatives cannot be implemented effectively without addressing and altering the traditional forty-minute time blocks designated for core and elective subject teaching. "The timetable certainly runs things around here," one teacher complained. Another wanted to be involved in team teaching, but arranging it was "hard." "I'm out on my own," she said, "and that is the fault of the timetable." A third teacher felt that "we are certainly making progress, as much as possible," but only "given the structure of the timetable, where we're still very much locked into forty-minute periods."

Traditional timetables, with each teacher teaching his or her own specialty, stymied the flexibility that schools needed to foster collaborative work cultures among students and teachers—cultures that teachers felt were vital to effective development and delivery of the curriculum:

> The school structure, the system of each teacher teaching their specialty, has got to be much more flexible. If you're doing a unit together, you've got to have a block of time, and the way our

programs are set up at the moment, once that seventy-five minutes is over, you've got to move because everybody is moving.

Learning standards that are exclusively and excessively subject based will, regrettably, reinforce timetable structures and priorities that impede teachers' efforts to achieve the kinds of integration and innovation that will benefit their students.

Some writers have argued that important as structure is, changing it need not always be a school's first priority when pursuing improvement or reform. Indeed, classroom practice may need to change to a degree where teachers feel a need for structural changes that will support the emerging practices that they are starting to value. Similarly, staff relationships may need to develop to a point where teachers feel able to pursue structural change together, without treading on their colleagues' toes or threatening the sense of security the existing timetable has given them. Structural change, in other words, often needs to be preceded by cultural change—where teachers do not have restructuring imposed on them but pursue it together as staff relationships become more collaborative (Newman & Wehlage, 1996; Fullan, 1993).

In some schools, teachers had been encouraged to get involved in restructuring the timetable. Other schools had experimented with block timetables or flexible timetables where teachers did not have to shut their textbooks and begin another subject every forty minutes. As we saw in the previous chapter, these more open time periods gave teachers more curriculum flexibility to follow the classroom momentum in learning. One school altered the timetable so that teachers could work in pairs to plan and share ideas and experiences about cooperative learning. One teacher noted that "scheduling changes have given us a lot of flexibility. We can move kids around to best suit their needs." Another "started to dabble with" the timetable and thought, "Well, who cares what the timetable says? Let's try a little bit more of this."

The other important structural factor for teachers who are trying to change is space. Winston Churchill once said, "We shape our buildings and afterwards our buildings shape us." Various studies (Davis, 1992; Manning, Freeman, & Earl, 1991) have identified how school architecture influences a school's culture in terms of its norms, beliefs, and patterns of relationship. Designed (and inherited) space brings people together or keeps them apart. Space establishes what is central and what is peripheral. It comprises a social geography of schooling (Hargreaves, 1995) that reflects and reinforces the school's principles of organization, educational priorities, and distinctions of power. It delineates the contours of schooling that can support or impede educators in their efforts to pursue new purposes and priorities.

Among the schools in our study, some of their buildings were two stories high. In one school, two teachers who were trying to work together were separated by two floors. The physical distance between them, coupled with incompatible timetables, left them isolated from each other and unable to talk or plan together. Although the teachers had been able to collaborate with colleagues outside their school, their physical and professional isolation from each other due to time and space factors remained a source of difficulty in their own building.

Although adjacent classrooms did not guarantee the existence of collaborative work cultures among the teachers concerned, suitable spatial arrangements create opportunities for joint planning and implementation. In one school, two teachers took full advantage of the close quarters they shared on the same floor across the hall from each other. They combined their seventh- and eighth-grade classes to deliver six major integrated units and engage in joint evaluations. They planned together and shared ideas on a regular basis. They also shared a computer lab, with one of the partners mentoring the other, who was less comfortable with computers.

Paradoxically, however, as these two teachers established close relationships with each other, they felt isolated from the rest of their colleagues. The closer they became to each other, the further away they grew from their colleagues. One of them remarked, "People are starting to talk. We are just together too much." In part, the location of the staff room on the floor below them reinforced this isolation. However, the social geographies of schooling are not unalterable; when they realized their growing isolation, these teachers "made a real point of going down to the staff room a lot more again."

Because structural changes affect whole schools, they require collective action and support. If people are committed to the same purposes, structural change is less difficult. But such change is exceptionally hard when staff have more diverse commitments and beliefs. Teachers in our study often had to try to implement changes on their own, because many of their colleagues did not necessarily support the philosophy of curriculum reform. The "grammar of schooling" that was laid down in the late nineteenth and early twentieth centuries defines the very essence of contemporary schooling. Its structures include classes graded by age, taught by individual teachers, segmented into separate classrooms, organized into subjects, and compartmentalized into different lessons of relatively short time periods, where assessment is undertaken individually by paper-and-pencil means (Tyack & Tobin, 1994; Hamilton, 1989; Goodson, 1988). Some of these structures have become so bound up with teachers' professional identities and senses of security that they have come to be regarded as sacred and beyond possibilities for change (Sarason, 1971).

Students and teachers in many schools have become captives of space and prisoners of time (National Commission on Time and Learning, 1994; Adelman & Walking-Eagle, 1997; Hargreaves, 1997a), locked into existing structures of classroom-based organization and timetabling that are ill suited to the kinds of reforms to which teachers like those in our study were committed. These same structures are also sources of security for many teachers, are recognizable to students, and give schools (and their teachers) credibility among parents. Changing them is no easy matter. This was one of the key problems teachers faced: having, indeed wanting, to implement a set of mandated changes within school structures that did not easily accommodate those changes.

When embarking on challenging cross-curricular reforms that affect teaching and learning, it is important to understand how existing structures of space, time, curriculum organization, and decision making will support or impede the new purposes that teachers are trying to pursue. It may also be necessary to change these structures at some point. They need not be treated as sacrosanct, but sudden and widespread structural change may destabilize the routines and identities of teachers who have grown accustomed to them to such a degree that curriculum innovation and classroom learning will suffer rather than prosper. We have seen that when some teachers were moved away from subject specialist teaching too suddenly or extensively, they felt weaker in their mastery of content and their ability to meet their students' needs. Structural change therefore often needs to be preceded or paralleled by changes in teachers' practices and relationships within their schools.

Teacher Culture

Strong collaborative cultures (Hargreaves, 1994; Nias, Southworth, & Yeomans, 1989; Fullan & Hargreaves, 1996) or professional communities (McLaughlin & Talbert, 1993) in teaching are powerfully linked to effective classroom learning (Newman & Wehlage, 1995; Rosenholtz, 1989), stronger professional confidence, and feelings of self-efficacy among teachers (Helsby, 1999; Ashton & Webb, 1986) and teachers' capacity to initiate and respond to change (Fullan, 1999).

Against the demonstrable strengths of professional cultures of collaboration stands a well-documented and deep-seated tradition of teacher isolation (Lortie, 1975; Fullan, 1991; Rudduck, 1991; Little, 1990). This isolation might afford teachers some protection to exercise their discretionary judgment in the interests of the children they know best, but it also cuts them off from clear, meaningful feedback about how effective they are.

Elsewhere, we have described the causes and consequences of teacher isolation in some detail (Fullan & Hargreaves, 1996; Hargreaves, 1994). Such isolation is in part a structural legacy of the historical grammar of schooling, with its one-teacher, one-class system that kept teachers inside their own classrooms and apart from one another. The contemporary time constraints of teaching and the seemingly endless intensification of teachers' work further serve to keep teachers confined to their classroom boxes (McTaggart, 1989). The habits that come from history and that are often perpetuated by policy have inscribed isolation and individualism into the imaginations of many teachers. Isolation protects teachers from scrutiny, insulates them from invidious comparisons with their colleagues, seems to elevate them beyond help and the implications of weakness or incompetence that come with it, and underlines teachers' rights to professional independence—to follow their own consciences and teach as they wish.

As the teachers in our study worked with curriculum and assessment change, they realized that the reforms were intended to be implemented within communities of teachers working and planning together. Yet many schools do not possess the kind of learning community that makes this possible. When we asked teachers about the obstacles they encountered in their attempts to change, the major one they mentioned was having to implement the changes alone. They often felt unsure about how well they were interpreting the new material. The intellectual work of thinking one's way through new programs and practices is never more difficult than when it is undertaken alone, as this teacher noted:

> I'm basically on my own with the philosophy, and you really have to have the support system of the team around you. What I've done all these years is try to make changes on my own. I don't see much collaboration because teachers are all so busy, and I think they are scared of something new. It just blows me away that there are a lot of teachers who in effect say, "Just don't enter my door; don't infringe on my space." I feel like it is just me having problems with curriculum reform, and this is because I am looking at this document alone at home or here at school.

Collaborative work cultures or professional communities have many components. When teachers did experience them, they valued the opportunities and encouragement such cultures provided to implement a number of initiatives. Collaborative work cultures helped teachers make sense together of the reform initiatives they were expected to implement. They also helped to stimulate teacher creativity (Woods, 1993), provided the teachers with the confidence to experiment with new ideas (Helsby, 1999), and offered a support network in which teachers were more prepared to persevere when they experienced setbacks (Nias, 1989). Working together can provide teachers with "emotional support, so you don't feel like you're alone, and then you feel a lot more confident. You can laugh when you screwed up and blame it on the other person."

Such support also encourages teachers to take risks when they know that failures will be treated as opportunities for learning, not occasions for blame (Rosenholtz, 1989):

> I was always uptight and very concerned about what other people thought. I was very reluctant to try new things. I'm a risk taker now, and if something doesn't work, it doesn't work. I can accept that, but I couldn't have ten years ago. The security comes from the fact

of having someone to talk to, to give me the feedback and say, "It's okay; it doesn't always work."

When teachers within and beyond our immediate sample had taken the risk of developing collaborative relationships together, the exuberance and excitement were evident. Energy led to agency in which collective optimism inspired and energized teachers to keep forging ahead (Goleman, 1998):

> I like a support system around me of teachers who have experience and expertise to brainstorm and come up with different strategies. I think it's a confidence builder, plus it gives you ideas to try. You can think of only so many as an individual person, and I think it's great to be finally out there and listen to other people talk. If I had stayed in my own classroom alone, without such a partner, I don't know that I'd have said everything I said today or been as interested as I've been today. It's so much fun to work with someone else toward the same goal and to bounce ideas off someone else and always to be encouraged by someone else.

In some schools, cultures of collaboration pervaded the entire institution; in others, they were confined, more problematically, to smaller pockets of innovation. In the latter case, teachers were conscious that many of their colleagues did not share their interest in the new curriculum. Here, both teachers and administrators worried about becoming an exclusive group and alienating the rest of the staff by making too many changes too fast or forcing their colleagues to accept them. As one teacher said, "I think that we were so far ahead of the rest of the school, we were being isolated. We were cutting ourselves off." She then described how she and her innovative colleagues "made a real attempt to sort of pull back a little bit." Other teachers avoided professional conflict and competition by using more informal methods to discuss ideas and provide helpful suggestions to colleagues. This often opened a door of trust, which led to more robust forms of joint planning and teaching.

Among researchers on teacher collaboration, there is considerable debate about how intense or formal collaborative arrangements should be. Little (1990), for example, argues that shared planning and joint work comprise more robust forms of collaboration than, say, exchanging materials or mutual storytelling. Fielding (1999) argues for the value of a more formal, talk-centered collegium over informal collaborative relations as a way of establishing working norms that embrace rather than avoid disagreement as a professional value. And Lima (2000) contends that close friendship may be less valuable than more distanced friendliness among colleagues if teachers are to be able to discuss and resolve difficult questions together about which they might differ professionally.

Conversely, others argue that productive disagreement and debate that lead to beneficial change (rather than argumentation for its own sake) are more likely to develop on a foundation of informal trust and emotional as well as intellectual understanding (Hargreaves, 1994; Nias, Southworth, & Yeomans, 1989). Indeed, some feminist writers argue, these informal aspects of collaboration may be especially important in professional cultures comprising many women (Acker, 1999). Although we would not want to generalize too much on the basis of what we observed, our own data point to collaboration mainly preceding collegiality among the teachers we studied.

Professional collaboration and isolation are important issues not only for teachers within schools but for colleagues across schools as well. Many teachers in our study were isolated from their colleagues at the secondary level who would be responsible for their students in years to come. In *Schooling for Change* (Hargreaves, Earl, & Ryan, 1996), we argued that stronger connections, closer collaboration, and better continuity needed to be established between teachers in elementary and secondary schools to provide better support and a more coherent educational program for young adolescents. The importance of these connections was reinforced by the teachers in our project:

> I think we need more interaction with the high school, and when I say *we*, I mean teachers, students, and parents. Get those kids over there; get them into the classroom to observe sooner, not at the end of the year.

Some teachers attempted to form alliances with their secondary partners to engage in shared projects within similar subject divisions or simply to enable their students to visit their secondary schools. Although teachers were eager to share information and engage in cross-site visits with their secondary colleagues, and even pass on students' portfolios to them, these good intentions were often thwarted because secondary school teachers seemed less ready to make such shifts in practice. In Chapter Three we saw that secondary teachers could too easily disregard the portfolios of work that their entering students had carefully compiled in eighth grade. More generally, another teacher reflected:

> I think that what I was really angry about was that I went to all the staff development sessions—the history, curriculum, the geography. The high school, for whatever reason, hadn't come on board at all.

Strong collaborative cultures and collegial relations within and among schools provide essential supports for implementing effective and sustained changes of the sort that have been addressed in this book. They support the emotional and intellectual work of educational change, and by ensuring that changes do not leave with the one or two individuals who have pioneered them, they enable those changes to be sustained over time. Collaborative school cultures provide a context for and sometimes themselves comprise especially effective forms of professional development for teachers—and their creation and perpetuation depend a great deal on high-quality school leadership. We turn to these other supports next.

Professional Learning

Complex changes cannot be achieved without considerable learning. For this reason, educational innovation and reform often include some provision for professional development and training to support the process of implementation. Unfortunately, the most common and typical forms of professional development are chosen mainly because they are administratively familiar, simple to organize, and politically easy to account for and defend, rather than because they are the most pedagogically effective (Little, 1993). Individual or short series of workshops provided off-site, away from the school, by external experts are the staple diet of professional development in the context of change (Guskey, 1986). Yet such patterns of professional development give teachers little opportunity or encouragement to try out the new strategies that are being advocated in their own classrooms, puzzle them through with colleagues, seek out feedback on how effective they are in implementing them, or find moral support when the experience of implementation threatens to discourage or defeat them (Wideen, Mayer-Smith, & Moon, 1996). Moving toward more school-based patterns of professional development does not guarantee reversing these trends. Indeed, even when schools determine staff development priorities locally, they still seem to place a premium on purchasing services from external experts and delivering packaged forms of training (Little, 1993).

Some of the most effective forms of professional development and learning appear to be ones that are embedded in the job and ingrained in the culture of teaching so that learning how to teach better is not separated in time and space from the work of teaching itself (Day, 1998). Job-embedded professional learning gives teachers routine access to the ideas and emotional support of colleagues (Fullan & Hargreaves, 1996); it provides teachers as a matter of course with opportunities to observe other teachers' teaching and receive feedback on their own (Joyce & Showers, 1988); and it makes learning integral to the work of teaching—in how teachers plan curricula or lead and mentor their colleagues, for example—rather than something separate from teaching, added on at the end of the teaching day or the school year (Day, 1998). Job-embedded professional learning is more complex to administer organizationally and more difficult to justify politically, as it seems to take up teachers' time from their classes. Yet our own evidence points to its immense value for making complex change processes successful.

Time is one of the scarcest yet most important resources for educational innovation: time to plan, think through new themes, find resources, understand outcomes, write new units, experiment with new assessments, and do all this with colleagues (Goodlad, 1984). It was often hard for teachers to meet with colleagues for sustained collaborative work other than outside of the school day. One teacher expressed her frustration with time constraints this way:

> We don't have enough time to do team-building techniques where you have the trust built in and can really work with one another. That's all I really want: time to work through some of these things as a group and time to connect more with the ninth graders. That

would be my one request. You can read your way through almost anything, but it's the lack of time just to talk that is a real killer.

Several teachers had been given time away from their classes by their school districts to work in teams or with teachers from other schools to write new curriculum units around learning outcomes. They clearly appreciated the investment of time by the district to build some momentum in the difficult task of curriculum writing:

> The four of us went out quite a lot and talked to other schools about integration. In fact, other staff did a presentation at the university. We've done a lot of staff in-servicing for other schools and principals. When Transition Years was first implemented, we went around and talked to principals and teachers. I was very honest and said, "Here's what I'm concerned about." It has been worthwhile. My eighth graders do a buddy system. I always walk around and just take a look, because you can learn so much from a primary classroom.

Another teacher spoke of the importance of time for team building to nurture trusting relationships where ideas about teaching, learning, and curriculum change could be shared freely:

> I would say the most useful staff development has been during professional development days where we have been allotted time as teams to do planning and to try and sift through this information in a more relaxed atmosphere. In terms of comfort level, that's been the easiest, most advantageous way for me to learn.

Once teachers were given time to plan during the school day, they were prepared to extend their time commitments far beyond it:

> We did a lot of collaboration, and we still do a lot outside regular school time and coming in on holidays and that sort of thing. This gives us time in class and to make sure we touch base with each other, the program, and the kids.

> We were able to lock ourselves away in a little room in the back hall for two days to develop our program. That's what it took—just meeting and brainstorming.

Making time available to teachers to work together in the school day helps improve the quality of curriculum, teaching, and learning that teachers can prepare for their students (Hargreaves, 1994). Reductions and restrictions in preparation time hamper teachers' abilities to innovate effectively and limit the quality of what they are able to prepare for their classrooms.

Time and resources taken away from teachers outside the class-room affect the quality of what can be achieved within it. Educational activity and expenditure outside the classroom is not, as politicians sometimes want to portray it, all administrative waste. Some of it is essential support on which the quality and improvement of teaching in a rapidly changing world absolutely depends. This important reality is one that many governments and members of the wider public have yet to confront or understand. Subsequent to the period of this study, for example, Ontario's new Conservative government introduced legislation that, among other measures, reduced the amount of preparation time for high school teachers and cut financial resources for tasks performed outside the classroom. Our analysis indicates that such policies are ultimately counterproductive in terms of teachers' ability to improve their practice in ways that support student learning.

Collaborative planning and cross-curricular planning are difficult. Teachers do not necessarily already know how to do them. Planning to address integrated curriculum, assessment criteria, and learning outcomes and standards requires more than relying on published guidelines. Teachers must be able to identify their criteria or targets, know when each student has achieved them, and ensure that their programs do not minimize or neglect important knowledge and skills. Just as teachers need others to show them how to teach differently, they also need others to help them learn how to plan new kinds of curricula effectively (Panaritis, 1995).

One school district assigned process consultants to groups of schools to work with teachers on planning integrated units around common learning criteria. The skills and support of the process consultants were strongly appreciated by the teachers who worked with them. One teacher said that working with consultants helped her rethink her own approach to and experience of curriculum integration, especially her expectations about the amount of time and energy needed for implementing new units:

I was invited to attend the Integrated Curriculum Institute. It was five or six days put on by consultants and very well run. I went through lots of valleys very early. I thought, "Oh, why can't I get this? This looks so easy. I'm surprised I can't do this because I'm usually successful when I try something new." So it was sitting in that institute for a length of time that was valuable—where we have two days straight, and then we'd come out and try a few things and then we'd go back in for two days.

Another teacher said she was exhausted after an intense and demanding collaborative process of writing many integrated units over several years. Yet she and her team colleagues, with consultant and school district financial support, were then able to inject new life into their planning and writing efforts together:

We met with consultants, and we wrote three units to start off with. Then in grade 6, the first year we were here, we wrote another unit. Then we wrote another one when we were here in grade 7. So the four of us did a lot of unit writing. When we moved up to grade 8, we decided that we were getting a little burned out. We had been busy writing all these integrated units and hadn't had any reflection time at all. We were realizing that there were some things that weren't working. So when we got to the third year of it, we decided we wanted to look at what other people had been doing. One year we applied for a project. They gave us a thousand dollars, and we worked in the summer and wrote a unit. It was nice. They gave us a lot of freedom by that time because they knew we had been fairly responsible.

Particularly when budgets are tight, educational consultants outside the classroom are easily regarded and politically portrayed as an expendable frill, as money wasted "outside the classroom." Yet the testimonies of our teachers suggest that this support can be invaluable in helping teachers adjust and implement new planning practices that make a real difference to the quality of curriculum that they provide in their classrooms.

Complex curriculum change depends for its success on forms of planning and professional learning that are embedded in and not appended to the fundamental work of teaching. This requires time and human support that are part of a redesigned conception of teaching where learning to teach better becomes part of teaching itself (Lieberman, 1995). Providing and protecting this time and support is a responsibility that extends far beyond individual schools—to school districts, governments, and those who elect them. Without this fundamental commitment to external support, deep and successful change in curriculum and assessment will likely be confined to temporary, localized reform projects, and not be generalizable to or sustainable in large groups of schools as a whole.

Professional Discretion

While some things in education can be mandated successfully—courses of study, standardized tests, or the end of corporal punishment, for example—deep and complex changes in teaching and learning need more than mandates to make them succeed. Indeed, policy mandates that are overly detailed and standardized can undermine such changes. Complex changes in curriculum and assessment work best when teachers are granted strong elements of professional discretion to plan them. When students' learning needs are diverse and contextualizing learning so that it is relevant to and engages students is a priority, the planning and development process needs to be able to accommodate student input and build on the collaborative efforts of colleagues who know their students well. As one teacher put it:

> I think the Common Curriculum Policy [described in Chapter One] gives teachers a lot of freedom, and I like that. I love sitting down and writing program and designing curriculum. I find it so exciting—the piggy-backing of ideas. We go with an initial thought, and everything just expands. I just find it so rich for the kids. In my classroom now, compared to what I saw three years ago, I do things so much better.

The teachers who were developing and teaching integrated curriculum units welcomed this professional discretion:

> There is certainly a very strong leadership from our administration. They've allowed us to go through some growing pains, and we did a lot of experimentation. We have a marvelous group of people—very intelligent and dedicated teachers—to make all of this happen, so it's great to bounce ideas off people.

Teachers seemed to thrive intellectually and emotionally in school cultures and within a policy context that encouraged professional discretion, collaboration, and continuing growth. There was real professional exhilaration for teachers in having the freedom to explore new intellectual territory, push beyond traditional ideas of curriculum, form new collaborative relationships, and develop multidisciplinary units that were truly relevant for students and exciting to teach.

In general, it is exactly this professional discretion that has been sacrificed in many contemporary curriculum reform efforts. Professional discretion has been a casualty of centralized and standardized curriculum reform movements where the necessity of ploughing through large quantities of mandated curriculum content and meeting hundreds of prescribed learning standards makes teachers feel as if they are "teaching in a box" (Helsby, 1999). In these ever more common policy contexts, instrumental, utilitarian approaches to teaching are increasingly the norm (Jeffrey & Woods, 1996; McNeil, 2000), not ones that develop the deep kinds of learning that are repeatedly called for in the informational society. Successful change in the curriculum and the classroom depends on teachers' being accorded enough curriculum space to exercise their professional discretion—to engage their intellectual and emotional investments in their work on behalf of and sometimes in collaboration with the students they know best. Curriculum policy must create, not close down, the spaces in which professional discretion can exert these effects on a local basis. It makes no sense at all to improve and deepen the learning of our students by dumbing down teachers.

School Leadership

Significant schoolwide change is impossible without effective school leadership. The educational change literature consistently points to school administrators as vital agents for creating the conditions in which school reform can succeed (Fullan, 1991; Leithwood, Jantzi, & Steinbach, 1999; Hall, 1988). Yet there are many competing demands on a principal's time, and initiating or supporting change is only one of them (Evans, 1997). Indeed, because principals are under constant pressure to maintain stability within their schools, this can easily thwart their own change efforts. Therefore, as Fullan (1991, p. 161) notes, "The role of the principal is not in implementing innovations or even in instructional leadership for specific classrooms. There is a limit to how much time principals can spend in individual classrooms. The larger goal is in transforming the culture of the school."

Most teachers in our study viewed their own principal as the key person who could create a supportive environment for change. Data from principals and teachers alike indicated that most principals did indeed try to create the conditions that would foster and nurture cultures of change in their schools. When school leadership worked in their favor, supporting their efforts, teachers described their school's administration as "very supportive; they like what we are doing, they encourage it," and as people who "encourage change and have done everything they possibly can to help us."

Across our school sites, teachers who felt they were making good progress in changing their curriculum and assessment practices identified three sets of supports that their administrators provided. These were the ability to:

- Be intellectual leaders by interpreting, translating, and articulating policy directions.
- Be cultural and emotional leaders by building cultures of collaboration and risk taking.
- Be strategic leaders by procuring and providing the required material and human resources to facilitate change efforts.

Intellectual Leadership

Teachers discussed how important it was that their administrators showed leadership in and support for the intellectual work of change by taking

> some fairly "airy-fairy" kind of stuff and make it very real for people—getting people to understand that they don't have to throw out everything and start over again but can work within what they've got and it's not such a huge link to a more finished product.

Teachers relied heavily on their principals and vice principals to help them sift and sort through the most bewildering parts of policy documents. Good administrators hooked into existing committee business to get support and advice to teachers through existing channels, or they rearranged the timetable to think and work through the reforms with their teachers as a team.

Administrators sometimes served on committees as curriculum facilitators to model and help teachers understand the changes on which they were focusing. One described the process of taking the staff through the curriculum policy document, "defining what it was, what the objectives were, and how you do indicators, and that was probably the hardest part of the terminology and still is." Another took one member of our research team into an office where two teachers were planning rubrics for curriculum outcomes on a computer and sat alongside them, interacting with them as they did so. This support, the teachers observed, was characteristic of her.

In one or two cases, administrators took their advice and support beyond meetings into the classroom by offering hands-on assistance. One teacher described appreciatively how

> when we plan sections of the unit and each person is going to be responsible for an integral part, it is not just that administration is providing time to do the planning, but they're actually involved in the teaching end of things too.

In all these cases, principals and vice principals took an active role in mediating, interpreting, and helping transform written policies and guidelines as they passed from the ministry and the school district to the classroom teacher. Indeed, in terms of the clarity and accessibility of policy, it was interesting that the teachers in our study viewed administrators outside the school largely as obstacles, whereas principals inside the schools where teachers prospered were mainly seen as supports.

Cultural and Emotional Leadership

School administrators also supported change by building collaborative work cultures among their staffs (Fullan & Hargreaves, 1991; Nias, Southworth, & Yeomans, 1989). They did this, in part, by manipulating the timetable to allow joint planning sessions or even by involving teachers in making structural changes. One teacher commented that "the principal turned the scheduling over to me because the whole staff has been going that way."

Often administrators offered more personal and diffuse kinds of encouragement and support for teachers to show professional initiative, take risks, and not look fearfully over their shoulders. One teacher reflected, "It's been great around here because the administration is very much a moving force and wanting people to try new ideas and be comfortable with what they can teach." Another appreciated the freedom of being able to keep the stereo on during her class at what some people might regard as unacceptable noise levels because the music encouraged activity within the classroom. The administration had not challenged her, but, she noted, "if the wrong type of administration came in, then I would have a hard time dealing with that." Another teacher alluded to the administration's general ease with

> encouraging risk taking, trying out new things without fear of curling up and dying if it doesn't work. We have a lot of leeway to explore, a lot of in-house meetings to get the team back together to talk about how things were going. Our principal is very dynamic.

Encouraging, participating in, and providing time for dialogue were viewed as especially positive forms of administrative support by teachers. Ultimately, though, actions spoke louder than words, particularly when principals "got involved and helped the teachers implement the change." One teacher reflected:

> You're not just left out in the cold, to do it on your own. They are right there, giving suggestions, if you want them. I mean they don't force themselves on you. If you've got a problem and you're not sure, the principal is willing to free up other teachers to help solve the problem.

Such principals were seen as being an integral part of the collaborative process. Administrators themselves echoed the same sentiments. One reflected that "collaboration was the first thing we started to develop with staff." Another tried to model what "I believe, not expecting everyone to be jumping on board with 100 percent enthusiasm." While trying to reculture their schools, however, administrators did not want to be seen as forcing collaboration or particular reform initiatives on teachers, yet their efforts at change and reculturing were still characterized by determination.

One especially telling example involved a principal in a school that one of our research team had studied several years previously. Then the school had been a prime example of what was described as "contrived collegiality" (Hargreaves, 1994), where the staff had been compelled by the principal and vice principal (both nearing retirement) to work in collaborative teams. Teachers resented this imposition. Many left, some were forcibly transferred, and quite a number simply resisted the initiative.

Seven years later, the school's principal had changed. In this district, new principals assigned to schools with "difficult" staffs were often offered the option by district superintendents of nominating two of their most troublesome teachers to be transferred elsewhere. On arriving at her new school, however, this principal reassured every member of staff that she was prepared and wanted to work with all of them, with the strengths and contributions they had to offer. Supportive and encouraging, she was also remorseless in her pursuit of dialogue and deadlines. She talked to staff endlessly, walked miles and miles around the hallways of the school, dropped into classrooms, joined teacher meetings, and interacted extensively with the students. She facilitated and supported teachers, but she also never let up on them. "If she really cares about something," said one of her teachers, "she's like a dog with a bone"; she would not leave it alone.

The results of her supportive efforts could be seen in the warm remarks about her leadership made by teacher interviewees, in the Valentine cards from eighth graders that covered her office door, and, not least, in the changed behavior of two midcareer teachers who had been regarded as being resistant to change by the previous leadership regime but who now came into school on weekends and stayed late in the evenings with parents from the community to build a multimedia laboratory for the students.

We cannot emphasize enough how important the process of leadership succession is in being able to prepare a school to deal effectively with change. Equally, however, when new principals show indifference or discouragement, schools quickly retreat into their shells and withdraw from engaging with change. Thus, when one year after our initial interviews, the principal had been transferred to another school, a trouble spot in need of some dynamic leadership, the school she left (the one we studied) did not cruise on autopilot because its departing leader had set the controls. When the new principal, close to retirement, was drafted in and was perceived by staff as less engaged with their change efforts and less visible in their classrooms, our interviewees reported that the seventh- and eighth-grade innovation committee collapsed, teachers withdrew to their own classrooms again, and students were starting to damage school equipment in ways the staff had never seen before.

In another school, a change of principal signaled a diminished interest in and support for curriculum integration and a shift of innovative focus and support toward implementing the use of computers in classrooms. This new focus was seen as quite separate from and not as an extension of the previous commitments to integration. As a result, one of the teachers we had originally interviewed in this school moved to a position elsewhere, while the other continued her own interest in integration, but within the confines of her own classroom, in isolation from others.

School system administrators often try to stimulate school improvement by moving principals around the schools and assigning the best leaders to the schools that need them most. Research studies on school improvement often concentrate on and celebrate the successes of individual schools that have had dynamic new leaders assigned to them, but rarely are those schools followed through the process of leadership succession to see how they and their cultures fare when their exemplary leaders leave (Fink, 2000). The instances we have described raise the question of whether a policy of rotating principals regularly makes school improvement into a revolving door, where individual schools are "in" one year and "out" the next (Macmillan, 2000). One of the greatest challenges of educational change, in this respect, is how to create and sustain effective leadership across entire school systems, not how to assign it to or move it around between fleetingly "improving" schools.

Strategic Leadership

The majority of teachers in our project commented on how administrators provided them with material and human resources to support their change efforts:

We would like some resources, and we would like some time, and the answer is always, "Yes, yes, yes." Part of that is because of the trust with regard to the direction we are going. The principal can delegate a lot of stuff to us and come directly to us. We make the decision. If we have a new principal who comes in and doesn't like this or says, "No, this is the way we are doing it," we are going to have a hell of a problem, because there is no way that a lot of the staff will go back to being dictated to.

School and district administrators supported their teachers by opening up opportunities for them to engage in professional learning. Teachers described the ease with which they could discuss the need to go to in-service workshops or conferences. A teacher interested in cooperative learning commented on it to the principal, who "right away was looking for everything he could to get me to those conferences." As one teacher noted, "Whatever comes across is posted or the principal is out here walking the halls and saying, 'Come in for an in-service. Are you interested?'" Another observed, "The administration really goes over backward to make sure that they have done their job in making sure people are out there, picking up ideas beyond our own school, if they want to be, and that's important." Yet another teacher said, "Our vice principal has been my major support. She is always finding something neat to read, always finding new ways for you to look at something when you thought it didn't look good at all."

Principals and vice principals, in other words, helped and encouraged teachers to engage in the intellectual labor of educational change by supporting their efforts to undertake in-service courses, letting them know about training and professional learning opportunities, making professional reading available to them, and generally encouraging them to connect with other ideas and practices beyond their own school (Hargreaves & Fullan, 1998). In general, teachers believed that their districts and the four-district consortium within which they worked would provide the resources (such as consultants) and staff development that they needed to become more expert. Moreover, by building stronger professional cultures in their schools, principals were also ensuring that professional learning took place on the job, as an integral part of it, as well as in courses and workshops off-site.

Implications

Learning to teach differently is complex and demanding (McLaughlin & Talbert, 1993). Even the highly committed seventh- and eighth-grade teachers in this study needed many months to learn to plan around standards rather than subject matter, work effectively with colleagues, develop complex assessment strategies, and create integrated curriculum materials. Indispensable forms of support for them included time to plan in the school day, opportunities to work with colleagues, visits to see exemplary practice in other schools, job-embedded approaches to professional learning, on-the-spot coaching from consultants, emotional support from skilled leaders, and a light policy touch that left teachers with professional scope and discretion to design and adjust changes in ways that worked well with the students they knew best. Too often these are the very areas of policy support that are most likely to fade beyond short-term pilot projects and localized initiatives (Darling-Hammond, 1998), threatening the sustainability and generalizability of educational change (Hargreaves & Fink, 2000).

Chapter Eight

Conclusion
Learning to Change

Our book has highlighted a group of teachers who have brought about exciting changes in their classrooms under the banner of curriculum integration, broadly defined learning outcomes, and alternative systems of classroom assessment and reporting. The literature of educational reform is often a catalogue of teachers' failures and shortcomings as they repeatedly fall short of the ever-rising and changing expectations that reformers outside the classroom set for them. Our research has taken a different tack. It has looked closely at the achievements of teachers who have been willing and able to bring about complex and demanding changes in their classrooms and to make a difference in the quality of what takes place there.

The pictures we have painted of improvement-oriented teachers and their work have not been wholly romantic. The achievements of the teachers we studied have not been won easily. They have required intense intellectual work as teachers have struggled to make sense of very broadly defined principles and policy guidelines and to turn them into working realities in their classrooms. Teachers' successes have also required immense amounts of emotional labor. They tried to ensure that the changes they made preserved and strengthened the emotional bonds they valued with their students. They had to develop and work through complex and sometimes difficult relationships with their colleagues, whose views of change did not always agree with theirs. They also struggled to maintain their personal commitments to their families and friends when their commitments to their work and to improving it demanded much of them.

This final chapter draws together the main findings of our study and discusses their implications. First, it outlines what we have learned about curriculum integration, learning outcomes and standards, and alternative classroom assessment and reporting systems from teachers who have been committed to making changes in these areas. These areas of innovation are sometimes portrayed, even pilloried, as wishy-washy, mediocre, and ill thought out. For the teachers we studied, nothing could be further from the truth. Curriculum integration and other innovations were rigorous and sophisticated in their conception and execution. Mediocrity is not intrinsic to interdisciplinary work and associated innovations any more than dull exposition is to more traditional forms of subject teaching. What matters is how these innovations are defined, supported, and used in practice. This book has moved beyond the rhetoric of curriculum and assessment reform to explore some of the realities of reform at its best.

Second, at a time when imposed educational reform shows no signs of abating, this closing chapter highlights what deep change demands of teachers practically, intellectually, and emotionally. Educational change that truly elevates what teachers do and students achieve in the classroom is not secured simply by announcing new standards or issuing fresh mandates, or by a swish of the pen. Policymakers who believe and act otherwise tread a fine line between ignorance and arrogance. Meaningful educational change that leads to more powerful teaching and learning is demanding and difficult, even for the best teachers. This last chapter points to the indispensable forms of support for teachers that are needed if this kind of change is to succeed and be sustained.

Change Substance

Change has substance and form, content and process. This final chapter looks at these interrelated aspects of educational shape in sequence, drawing together the findings of our study and setting out recommendations on the basis of them.

Outcomes and Standards

Whatever curriculum developers and standards reformers officially recommend, our evidence is that teachers rarely followed a linear planning process in which they map backward from outcomes or standards to indicators of achieving those standards and the methods and materials that would get them there. Instead, teachers were more likely to plan integrated units of work or other kinds of classroom learning based on what they knew about their students, what they felt excited and engaged their students, what had worked with similar students in the past, and what they could picture working well in their classes. Rather than being the starting point and the supreme organizer for curriculum planning, the outcomes gave teachers a touchstone for validating their teaching. Teachers began with what they felt and knew and used the outcomes to give the overall program a shape and a language to use with students and parents.

Whether planning from the heart as much as the head is inherent in all effective curriculum and classroom planning, or whether learning standards and outcomes can eventually become so well integrated into teachers' professional thinking and language that teachers use them spontaneously in their planning from the outset, is hard to tell. Only longitudinal study will be decisive on this. But for now, making teachers plan by mapping backward from standards or outcomes may go against the grain of how many good teachers plan in practice.

Despite the peculiarities of the planning process, teachers still found the outcomes very useful, especially for talking with students about their learning and helping them take responsibility for it. Sharing outcomes with students helped them become actively involved in developing the curriculum. Students were encouraged to take the outcomes home and show them to their parents. In this respect, outcomes became a foundation for conversations with parents too. In the process of discussing outcomes with others, teachers became clearer themselves about what they were trying to accomplish.

However, when districts started to specify and break down the outcomes in intricate detail (as many jurisdictions now do with standards), teachers experienced them as cumbersome and overwhelming and did not know where to start in interpreting and using them. Whereas broad frameworks of learning outcomes or standards can help teachers achieve balance and direction in the curriculum and stimulate constructive conversations about learning with students and parents, defining the outcomes or standards in laborious detail returns us to the worst excesses of mastery learning and behavioral objectives. It turns standards into hurdles, replaces conceptual depth with a frenetic compulsion to achieve coverage, and standardizes learning to such an extent that it cannot be easily adapted to a diverse student body, and still less include students directly in how the standards are interpreted and defined. The technical detail of specifying standards or outcomes can all too easily crowd out any opportunity for imagination or emotional engagement in learning.

At the same time, outcomes were sometimes written too vaguely, in the circumlocutory language of "educationese." Teachers complained about this often. Standards and outcomes should therefore remain ambitious, but they should also be expressed with great clarity. This is one of the converse advantages in the more recent standards movement, of defining them more precisely. However, the challenge is not to make learning standards simple but to describe them in simpler terms.

Last but not least, in our findings about outcomes and standards was the dilemma teachers had in deciding whether to try to get all students to meet one set standard (only to find that those with serious learning difficulties would inevitably fall short) or to modify the standard so that all students could meet it (but destroying the very idea of a standard and making it meaningless as a result). Getting around this dilemma by stating that students can achieve particular standards "with support," as is common in many standards frameworks, means that almost everyone can then achieve the standard by definition. Unless policymakers can be clearer and more realistic about who can reach their standards, teachers will be unable to extricate themselves from this dilemma.

Following are the action implications of our findings for those who deal with common learning standards or outcomes:

- Use learning standards and outcomes as a conscience or touchstone as much as a target when planning your teaching.

- Plan for standards and outcomes with your heart as well as your head. Do not let the steps of rational planning occlude your emotional and imaginative engagement in the planning process.
- Plan with your colleagues and not just on your own. Collaborative planning leads to clearer goals and more confident teaching.
- Share standards and outcomes openly with your students (and in policy, define them sufficiently broadly to leave space for student inclusion).
- Communicate standards and outcomes clearly to parents.
- At the policy level, avoid squeezing all the imagination out of teaching by making standards too numerous, too detailed, and too specific. Don't let standards or outcomes get too cumbersome and too standardized.
- Describe learning standards more simply, but don't narrow or simplify them.
- Set ambitious but also realistic standards. Not all children can learn anything and everything. It is important to push more and more children to reach given standards but unrealistic to insist that virtually everyone must achieve all of them.
- Ensure that standards promote curricular breadth by including arts and social studies, and do not reduce the curriculum to a utilitarian preoccupation with literacy and numeracy in isolation from other engaging and important forms of learning and experience.

Assessment

Teachers said that assessment, evaluation, and reporting to parents were the hardest parts of their work. Many admitted that they were uncomfortable with judging students. They viewed student assessment as complex, demanding, time-consuming, and worryingly subjective. If teachers fake the confidence and certainty with which their judgments are made in unadorned numbers and letter grades, they are condemned to feel like assessment impostors and to become defensive when others scrutinize those judgments. The emergence of more complex and sophisticated assessment techniques further undermined teachers' abilities to trust and use their own tacit knowledge when evaluating students.

Despite all this, many teachers' commitments to their students and to parents of those students led them to develop new assessment practices and more open reporting systems that demystified the assessment process. Paradoxically, this approach added to rather than undermined teachers' professional judgments by bringing students and parents in on the secret of how these judgments were made.

Reporting to parents is one of the most challenging and also most anxiety-provoking parts of teachers' work. Teachers are all too aware that their students are precious to their parents and that parents want good information about their children's progress. When this strong parental need is coupled with teachers' insecurities about assessment, the consequences are potentially explosive, leading teachers and parents to argue with or avoid each other.

The strides these teachers were making in involving parents and students in the assessment process were significant. The teachers in our study had developed many innovative ways to increase their contacts with parents and provide them with much more information than a written report card. They wrote newsletters, made telephone calls, and held student-led parent conferences, for example.

It is clear that teachers are technically capable of significantly expanding their assessment repertoire and developing their assessment expertise. They are also often culturally sensitive and politically committed to involving students and parents in the hitherto secret activities of assessment practice. Teachers' willingness and ability to become more creative and proficient in classroom assessment, however, seems to depend on their readiness to put students' needs, and the bonds of understanding and involvement they build with students and their parents, before their own anxieties and insecurities about assessment. Indeed, openness about assessment may be one of the strongest antidotes to insecurity. If this openness is to reduce, not heighten, teachers' assessment anxieties, however, teachers must spend more time talking about assessment practices together and agreeing on reasonably clear and specific assessment criteria with their colleagues. This kind of shared agreement about assessment can alleviate teachers' debilitating senses of uncertainty. To be open about assessment with parents is honorable. To be open, alone, and unsure when facing their questions is folly.

These intrinsic anxieties about assessment are rarely alleviated by government policy. The schizophrenic nature of assessment policy assails teachers with conflicting demands and virtually impossible challenges. Policymakers want assessment practices that involve students and motivate them. They also want assessment practices to diagnose students' difficulties so that teachers can help them in their learning. At the same time, they want assessment practices to rate, rank, sort, and select students and schools, leading students to hide their weaknesses and teachers to teach to the test. Teachers in our study (as in many places elsewhere) were left to deal with the consequences of these broader policy contradictions. The ongoing evaluations they tried to make of their students' progress were, for example, interrupted by large-scale assessment demands, which necessitated detailed documentation as well as suspension of other parts of the curriculum.

Another face of the assessment contradiction is found in what parents want from assessment. Thus, with lower-achieving students, teachers produced modified assessments that evaluated students against their own prior progress, whereas parents might want students to be measured against each other or against a single standard that should apply to everyone. It is unlikely that these contradictions will ease in the near future. What teachers can hope to achieve, though, is greater expertise and diversity in their assessment practices, opening up the mysteries of assessment to students and their parents, developing shared confidence in assessment criteria by talking them through with their colleagues, and speaking out from the newly acquired wisdom of their practice against assessment policies that may be politically attractive but hold few benefits for students.

Following are the action implications of our findings on teachers' approaches to alternative forms of assessment:

- Develop a broad repertoire of assessment practices to capture the full range and different forms of your students' achievements.
- Make your assessment criteria specific and clear to students.
- Involve students in some of their own assessment through strategies like peer evaluation, self-assessment, and sharing targets with your classes.
- If all students can learn, so can all parents. Do not pander to parents' existing recollections and preconceptions about what

"real" report cards and assessment schemes look like. Work with parents to deepen understanding of assessment issues together.

- Extend your dialogue with parents beyond written report cards—for example, by using portfolios that students take home and undertaking three-way interviews between teacher, parent, and child.
- Be careful when assessing students' affective characteristics. Do not assess only behaviors that are really synonyms for compliance. Recognize behaviors like initiative and assertiveness that will make it easier for students to have worthwhile lives when they become adults even if it may make them harder to teach now.
- Discuss with your colleagues assessment criteria and how you would assess particular pieces of student work. Take the mystery out of marking.
- Address the schizophrenia of assessment policy so that school assessment practices support rather than interfere with each other.

Curriculum Integration

These seventh- and eighth-grade teachers were extremely willing to experiment with curriculum integration, because they believed it would make learning more relevant and beneficial for their students. The integrated units they described were almost always connected with real issues in students' lives, the world around them, or social questions. Teachers believed that relevance was essential if students were to engage fully with their learning. This relevance manifested itself not so much in the overall themes that defined integrated units as in the ideas and content that made up the details of them. For some teachers, this relevance was virtually guaranteed by involving students in planning and brainstorming ideas for the integrated units.

Teachers were proud about the integrated units they had developed and enthusiastic about showing them to us. The most thorough ones had benefited from thoughtful and extensive preparation with other teachers at their grade level from elsewhere in the system. This kind of planning (some of it during school time) was especially welcomed by teachers as providing essential support for curriculum integration. They regarded it as valuable job-embedded professional development and praised the district consultants who had sometimes been allocated to work with their planning teams. Integration was less successful where this team approach was missing or where teams had been imposed by the principal as a form of contrived collegiality rather than being constituted with the support of teachers themselves.

Planning integrated units was exhausting but exhilarating work for teachers. By the time teachers got into creating ideas and materials for the third unit or beyond, the joy of curriculum integration started to wear thin. Schools and teachers therefore need to search for an optimum balance between inventing new integrated units themselves (as a stimulus for professional learning) and taking other units off the shelf that their colleagues have developed elsewhere in the system as a way to husband their energies.

In almost all schools, efforts at integration are in tension with existing systems of subject specialization. This was somewhat true even for our sample of seventh- and eighth-grade teachers, whose subject attachments are often weaker than those of their high school colleagues. Sometimes these tensions resulted from teachers' ingrained subject identities and attachments, which they found hard to abandon. Sometimes they resulted from integration being inserted into a system whose other components remained subject based, as in report cards that were organized according to subject categories. At other times, however, the tensions stemmed from teachers' genuine concerns that curriculum integration required them to teach subject matter about which they were not confident and where their knowledge of it was insufficiently deep.

Integration works best not when every individual teacher is expected to have a deep understanding of many subjects and disciplines, but when teachers pool their complementary subject expertise to teach (and not just plan) together in ways that meet the goals of integration and students' learning needs. Curriculum integration works best not when it ideologically eliminates school subjects but when it draws these subjects and their teachers together in pursuit of higher educational principles that transcend them.

Following are the action implications of our findings on curriculum integration:

- Use integration to make sure that learning is relevant to and contextualized in students' needs, interests, and lives.
- Extend this notion of relevance beyond workplace relevance, to family, community, and sociopolitical relevance.
- Plan integrated units as a team.
- Find the optimum point in writing new integrated units where excitement is still sustained and exhaustion has not yet taken over. Write new units, but make wise use of old ones as well.
- Provide advice and support for team planning.
- Provide scheduled time for curriculum writing.
- Do not make integration the enemy of all specialization. Integration works best when it is a judicious, not a promiscuous, feature of the curriculum.
- Beware of specifying standards in such an exclusively subject-based way that they reduce or remove opportunities for teachers to contextualize curriculum and learning in students' culturally diverse lives.

Change Process

The educational changes that the seventh- and eighth-grade teachers tried to implement presented them with formidable intellectual and emotional challenges: connecting the changes with their values, decoding what exactly they meant, trying to work out how to make them effective in practice, and so on. The kinds of supports that helped teachers work through these challenges were described in the previous chapter and are well documented throughout the change literature:

- Scheduled time for teachers to plan and think through the new practices they were implementing in ways that made sense to them and their students
- Hands-on assistance of district consultants to help teachers figure out the intricacies of the planning process
- A team approach to change that was supported by teachers themselves and not imposed on them as contrived collegiality without their consent
- Leadership from principals that did not just support the ideas behind the curriculum and assessment changes but that also

involved principals' becoming engaged in some of the practicalities of curriculum planning and change themselves.

Alongside these familiar issues of how to support teachers who were working their way through complex changes, our study also generated greater insights into the emotional dimensions of teaching and their importance for the educational change process. Teaching was not just a technical exercise but a deeply emotional experience for the teachers we studied. It was part of a wider educational and social mission that gave meaning to their work. These teachers valued the emotional bonds they had with students and cared a great deal for the students they taught. They saw themselves not just as preparing learners and future workers but as developing citizens too. Cultivating students' emotional development or emotional intelligence was one of the central parts of their work. It affected how they taught and related to all students, including students with special needs and from diverse cultural backgrounds. The strength of teachers' emotional concern for and connection to students influenced everything they did. Whenever any change was contemplated, their first questions were, "How will this affect my students?" and "What will it look like in my classes?" The educational change literature and the standards-based reform movement are largely silent on the emotional aspects of teaching and educational change. The qualitative nature of our investigation drew these emotions to our attention. They stared out from the page at us. Our teachers were passionate teachers, and understanding this yielded important and surprising insights.

For example, teachers liked core programs and other flexible time structures embedded in the Transition Years reforms because they allowed them to follow the intellectual and emotional flow of their teaching and to establish stronger emotional bonds with and closer understanding of their students so that they could plan and adjust the learning for them more effectively. In addition, teachers were not dogmatic about any one best approach to teaching but used a formidable array of methods to make things interesting and effective for their students. They used a variety of both traditional and innovative teaching approaches. Teachers in our study portrayed themselves as vivid and vital presences in their classrooms, who sometimes facilitated learning but sometimes taught very directly and inspirationally as well. The ways teachers chose to teach were also shaped by their own emotional needs to be involved in classroom activities that ignited their own interests and passions.

Teachers planned integrated units and planned around outcomes in ways that were emotional as well as rational. "Emotional planning" might strike many people as an oxymoron, but for the teachers in our study, it was essential to their being engaged in the planning process effectively. In this area of curriculum, however, teachers' emotional goals for students and the emotional needs that teachers had for themselves were not synchronized with each other so easily. On the one hand, teachers often identified with students' needs to see the connections in what they studied. At the same time, many teachers were anxious about abandoning their own subject attachments even if they acknowledged the argument that doing so might be better for students. Synchronizing teachers' emotional goals for students, and their own needs for emotional security or engagement, is a major challenge of school reform.

Following are the action implications of our findings on how teachers experienced and dealt with the process of educational change:

- Redesign your timetable so that it is aligned with your curriculum purposes instead of squeezing those purposes into existing time frames.
- Provide time, lots of it, for teachers to think their way through reforms together, to try them out in their own classrooms, and to reflect on them and refine them with their colleagues. Time, on an ongoing basis, within as well as outside of the school day, is indispensable to successful school change. Make time for teachers to work their way through change. Do not treat it as an expendable luxury or, worse, trim it for cost reasons.
- Make professional development time for teachers to plan, talk about, and review the changes they are undertaking together a higher priority than short, sharp in-service training sessions.
- Successful integration calls for good teamwork. Build teams carefully; do not just throw them together administratively. Teams without trust rarely succeed.

- As a principal or lead teacher, do not just orchestrate how other people should change, but get involved alongside your colleagues in the personal and practical messiness of change yourself.
- Within a district, try to ensure consistency of leadership when sustaining change is a priority. Developing the leadership of a whole system is, in this respect, better than rotating a few exceptional leaders from school to school within the system.
- Accord high priority to the emotional as well as intellectual goals you have for your students and the emotional bonds you have with them.
- Create school structures that strengthen the emotional bonds that you and your colleagues have with your students.
- Develop a broad teaching repertoire. Include traditional and inspirational teaching within it. Teachers need to know how to facilitate learning and also how to inspire it directly.

The Demands of Change

This book and the research on which it is based have portrayed what it is possible to achieve on the leading edge of educational change among teachers who are excited about teaching, open to change, and committed to students. It has shown that making learning relevant to students' lives in the broadest sense can lead to learning experiences of great rigor and sophistication that are appropriate to the complex, diverse, and turbulent environments in which students now live and in which they will take up careers and responsibilities as adults.

Designing education around what standards students should achieve and not what teachers have been used to teaching is essential if we are going to prepare young people effectively for the demands and opportunities of the informational society. Setting demanding standards that will draw out the deep learning that is needed to participate in such a society is far preferable to restricting standards to the narrowest concepts of basic skills and technical competence or to the more utilitarian areas of literacy and numeracy, instead of or in isolation from areas like the arts and social studies, which can provide powerful sources of engagement for many poor and minority students. Broader outcomes and curriculum integration, we have seen, carry the potential, among some of our best teachers, to reach the standards and levels of sophistication and need not subject students to a mishmash of ill-conceived themes and topics.

Working with dedication, imagination, and passion to connect the curriculum to young people's prior understandings, when they come to their learning from many different cultures and back-grounds, is exceptionally difficult work, even for the best teachers. Learning to change, in ways that will help them serve their students well in our complex world, stretches teachers to the limit. New cur-ricula; new ways of defining, setting, and reaching standards; and new approaches to teaching and learning are not grasped by read-ing printed guidelines, attending a few isolated workshops, or front-loading all the thinking and preparation time ahead of the practice (in vacation time, for example). It is in the details of the practice, in and around the classroom itself, where the difficulties and com-plications are first encountered, and that is where teachers most need support.

Learning to change is intellectually demanding, and teachers need lots of time, inside and outside of the school day, to think through complex curriculum changes individually and with their colleagues. They need advice and support from skilled principals and other support persons to steer them through the process of making sense of new approaches. And they need emotional sup-port from colleagues, leaders, administrators, and parents as they try to realign their teaching to deliver the kinds of learning that students really need. Trying to cut corners, save costs, and reduce the need for support by writing all standards centrally, in great de-tail, in a "teacher-proof" way that is locked in to associated texts and assessment systems pushes teachers and teaching along the path of deprofessionalization. This path leads teachers toward a job that has less discretion, less judgment, and less likelihood that curriculum and learning will meet the needs of the particular and diverse group of students that each teacher knows best. You do not raise standards for students in the informational society by dumb-ing down their teachers with inflexible systems of standardization.

Most teachers today are having to learn to teach in ways in which they have not been taught themselves. This is intellectually and emotionally demanding. Standards with flexibility rather than standardization with force can provide teachers with an excellent framework to help them move forward. Time, advice, support, and encouragement are the most precious commodities for helping them to do this. Yet these qualities are often considered to be the most easily expendable commodities of educational spending. Those who believe that teaching can and should get better as the world their students enter demands more and more of their skills should care deeply that these essential supports that will help teachers improve are not only preserved but increased. With these supports, high standards and sustained improvements in the kinds of learning that really matter for all students and that the practices of teachers in this book represent will no longer be frustratingly beyond reach.

References

Acker, S. (1999). Realities of teaching. London: Cassell.

Adelman, N. E., & Walking-Eagle, K. P. (1997). Teachers, time and school reform. In A. Hargreaves (Ed.), *Rethinking educational change with heart and mind: The 1997 ASCD Yearbook.* Alexandria, VA: Association for Supervision and Curriculum Development.

Aronowitz, S., & Giroux, H. (1991). *Postmodern education: Politics, culture and social criticism.* Minneapolis: University of Minnesota Press.

Ashforth, B. E., & Humphrey, R. H. (1993). Emotional labor in service roles: The influence of identity. *Academy of Management Journal, 18*(1), 88–115.

Ashton, P., & Webb, R. (1986). *Making a difference: Teacher's sense of efficacy and student achievement.* New York: Longman.

Ball, D. L. (1990, Fall). Reflections and deflections of policy: The case of Carol Turner. *Educational Evaluation and Policy Analysis, 12*(3), 263–275.

Bandura, A. (1986). *Social foundations of thought and action.* Englewood Cliffs, NJ: Prentice Hall.

Barlow, M., & Robertson, H-J. (1994). *Class warfare: The assault on Canada's schools.* Toronto: Key Porter Books.

Bascia, N., & Hargreaves, A. (Eds.). (2000). *The sharp edge of educational change.* Bristol, PA: Falmer Press.

Beane, J. (1991). The middle school: The natural home of integrated curriculum. *Educational Leadership, 49*(2), 9–13.

Beane, J. A. (1995). Curriculum integration and the disciplines of knowledge. *Phi Delta Kappan, 76*(8), 616–622.

Bernstein, B. (1971). On the classification and framing of educational knowledge. In M.F.D. Young (Ed.), *Knowledge and control.* London: Collier-Macmillan.

Black, P. (1998). *Testing: Friend or foe? The theory and practice of assessment and testing.* Bristol, PA: Falmer Press, 1998.

Blackmore, J. (1996). Doing "emotional labour" in the education market place: Stories from the field of women in management. *Discourse: Studies in the Cultural Politics of Education, 17*(3), 337–349.

199

Boler, M. (1999). *Feeling power: Emotions and education.* New York: Routledge.

Brady, L. (1996). Outcome-based education: A critique. *Curriculum Journal, 7*(1), 5–16.

Broadfoot, P. (1996). *Education, assessment and society.* Bristol, PA: Open University Press.

Case, R. (1991). *The anatomy of curricular integration.* Forum on Curriculum Integration. Tri-University Integration Project, Occasional Paper 2. Burnaby, BC: Simon Fraser University.

Case, R. (1994). Our crude handling of educational reforms: The case of curricular integration. *Canadian Journal of Education, 19*(1), 80–93.

Castells, M. (1996). *The rise of the network society.* Oxford, England: Blackwell.

Castells, M. (1997). *The power of identity.* Oxford, England: Blackwell.

Castells, M. (1998). *The end of millennium.* Oxford, England: Blackwell.

Cochran-Smith, M., & Lytle, S. L. (1992). Communities for teacher research: Fringe or forefront? *American Journal of Education, 100*(3), 298–324.

Cohen, D. (1995). What is the system in systemic reform? *Educational Researcher, 24*(9), 11–17, 31.

Cox, C., & Scruton, R. (1984). *Peace studies: A critical survey.* Occasional paper no. 7. Institute for European Defence and Strategic Studies. London: Alliance.

Csikzentmihalyi, M. (1990). *Flow: The problem of optimal experience.* New York: HarperCollins.

Cumming, J. (1996). *From alienation to engagement: Opportunities for reform in the middle years of schooling.* Australia: Australian Curriculum Studies Association.

Cummins, J. (1998). Language issues and educational change. In A. Hargreaves, A. Lieberman, M. Fullan, & D. Hopkins (Eds.), *International handbook of educational change.* Norwell, MA: Kluwer Press.

Cunningham, G. (1998). *Assessment in the classroom: Constructing and interpreting tests.* Bristol, PA: Falmer Press.

Dadds, M. (forthcoming). The politics of pedagogy. *Teachers and Teaching.*

Darling-Hammond, L. (1992, Nov.). Reframing the school reform agenda. *School Administrator: Journal of the American Association of School Administrators,* pp. 22–27.

Darling-Hammond, L. (1997). *Doing what matters most: Investing in quality teaching.* New York: National Commission on Teaching and America's Future.

Darling-Hammond, L. (1998). Policy and change: Getting beyond bureaucracy. In A. Hargreaves, A. Lieberman, M. Fullan, & D. Hopkins (Eds.), *International handbook of educational change.* Norwell, MA: Kluwer.

Datnow, A., & Castellano, M. (1999, Apr.). *An "inside look" at the implementation of Success for All: Teachers' responses to the reform.* Paper presented to the American Educational Research Association annual meeting, Montreal, Canada.

Dauber, S. L., & Epstein, J. L. (1993). Parents' attitudes and practices of involvement in inner-city elementary and middle schools. In N. Feyl Chavkin (Ed.), *Families and schools in a pluralistic society* (pp. 53–72). Albany, NY: State University of New York Press.

Davis, J. (1992). *Cultures and subcultures in secondary schools.* Paper presented to the annual meeting of the American Educational Research Association, San Francisco.

Day, C. (1998). *Developing teachers: The challenges of lifelong learning?* Bristol, PA: Falmer Press.

Deal, T., & Kennedy, A. (1982). *Corporate cultures.* Reading, MA: Addison-Wesley.

Dean, C. (2000). Anxiety mounts over staff shortage. *Times Educational Supplement,* June 30.

Denzin, N. (1984). *On understanding emotion.* San Francisco: Jossey-Bass.

Dewey, J. (1938). *Experience and education.* New York: Touchstone Press.

Donofrio, H., & Davis, K. (1997, Apr. 2–6). *Oral communication across disciplines: Adding value to academic pursuit and marketability.* Paper presented at the annual meeting of the Southern States Communication Association, Savannah, GA.

Drake, S. (1991, Oct.). How our team dissolved the boundaries. *Educational Leadership, 49*(2), 20–22.

Drake, S. M. (1998). *Creating integrated curriculum.* Thousand Oaks, CA: Corwin Press.

Earl, L., & Cousins, J. B. (1995). *Classroom assessment: Changing the face; Facing the change.* Ontario: Ontario Public Service Teachers' Federation.

Earl, L., & Katz, S. (2000). Changing classroom assessment: Teachers' struggles. In N. Bascia & A. Hargreaves (Eds.), *The sharp edge of educational change.* Bristol, PA: Falmer Press.

Earl, L., & Lee, L. (1998). *Evaluation of the Manitoba School Improvement Program.* Toronto: Walter and Duncan Gordon Foundation.

Earl, L. M., & Lee, L. L. (1996). *Evaluation of the Manitoba School Improvement Program.* Toronto: International Centre for Educational Change at OISE/UT.

Earl, L., & LeMahieu, P. G. (1997). Rethinking assessment and accountability. In A. Hargreaves (Ed.), *Rethinking educational change with heart and mind: The 1997 ASCD yearbook.* Alexandria, VA: Association for Supervision and Curriculum Development.

Edmonds, R. R. (1979). Effective schools for the urban poor. *Educational Leadership, 37,* 15–24.

Eisner, E. W. (1992). The federal reform of schools: Looking for the silver bullet. *Phi Delta Kappan, 73*(9), 722–723.

Eisner, E. W. (1995, June). Standards for American schools: Help or hindrance. *Phi Delta Kappan, 76*(10), 758–760, 762.

Elkind, D. (1989). *The hurried child: Growing up too fast too soon.* Cambridge, Mass.: Perseus Publishing.

Elkind, D. (1997). Schooling in the postmodern world. In A. Hargreaves (Ed.), *Rethinking educational change with heart and mind: The 1997 ASCD Yearbook.* Alexandria, VA: Association for Supervision and Curriculum Development.

Elmore, R. (1995). Getting to scale with good educational practice. *Harvard Educational Review, 66*(1), 1–26.

Entwistle, H. (1979). *Conservative schooling for radical politics.* New York: Routledge.

Epstein, J. L. (1988). *Schools in the center: Schools, family, peer and community, connections for more effective middle grade schools and students.* Baltimore, MD: John Hopkins University Center for Research on Elementary and Middle Schools.

Evans, R. (1997). *The human side of school change: Reform, resistance, and the real-life problems of innovations.* San Francisco: Jossey-Bass.

Eyers, V. (1992). *The report of the junior-secondary review: The education of young adolescents in South Australian government schools.* Adelaide: Department of Education of South Australia.

Farson, R. (1996). *Management of the absurd: Paradoxes in leadership.* New York: Simon & Schuster.

Fielding, M. (1999). Radical collegiality: Affirming teaching as an inclusive professional practice. *Australian Educational Researcher, 26*(2), 1–34.

Fink, D. (2000). *Good schools/real schools: Why school reform doesn't last.* New York: Teachers College Press.

Firestone, W. A., Mayrowetz, D., & Fairman, J. (1998). Performance-based assessment and instructional change: The effects of testing in Maine and Maryland. *Educational Evaluation and Policy Analysis, 20*(2), 95–113.

Fogerty, R. (1991). Ten ways to integrate curriculum. *Educational Leadership, 49*(2), 61–65.

Ford, M. (1992). *Motivating humans: Goals, emotions and personal agency beliefs.* Thousand Oaks, CA: Sage.

Foucault, M. (1977). *Discipline and punish: The birth of the prison.* New York: Pantheon.

Fried, R. (1995). *The passionate teacher.* Boston: Bacon Press.

Fullan, M. (1991). *The new meaning of educational change.* New York: Teachers College Press.

Fullan, M. (1993). *Change forces: Probing the depths of educational reform.* Bristol, PA: Falmer Press.

Fullan, M. (1999). *Change forces: The sequel.* Bristol, PA: Falmer Press.

Fullan, M. (2000). The return of large-scale reform. *Journal of Educational Change, 1*(1), 5–28.

Fullan, M., & Hargreaves, A. (1991). *What's worth fighting for? working together for your schoool.* Andover, MA: The Regional Laboratory for Educational Improvement of the Northeast & Islands.

Fullan, M., & Hargreaves, A. (Eds.). (1992). *Teacher development and educational change.* Bristol, PA: Falmer Press.

Fullan, M., & Hargreaves, A. (1996). *What's worth fighting for in your school (2nd ed.).* New York: Teachers College Press.

Fullan, M., with Stiegelbauer, S. (1991). *The new meaning of educational change.* New York: Teachers College Press.

Garbarino, J. (1995). *Raising children in a socially toxic environment.* San Francisco: Jossey-Bass.

Gedge, J. (1991). The hegemonic curriculum and school dropout: The Newfoundland case. *Journal of Education Policy, 6*(2), 215–224.

Gehrke, N. (1991). Explorations of teacher development of integrated curriculums. *Journal of Curriculum and Supervision, 6*(2), 107–117.

Giddens, A. (1991). *Modernity and self-identity.* Cambridge: Polity Press.

Giles, C. (1997). *Improving school development planning: Theoretical and practical perspectives.* Unpublished doctoral dissertation, University of Nottingham.

Gilligan, C. (1982). *In a different voice: Psychological theory and women's development.* Cambridge, MA: Harvard University Press.

Gipps, C. V. (1994). *Quality assurance in teachers' assessment.* Paper presented at the annual meetings of the American Educational Research Association (New Orleans, LA, April 4–8) and the British Educational Research Association.

Goleman, D. (1995). *Emotional intelligence.* New York: Bantam Books.

Goleman, D. (1998). *Working with emotional intelligence.* New York: Bantam Books.

Goodlad, J. I. (1984). *A place called school: Prospects for the future.* New York: McGraw-Hill.

Goodson, I. F. (1988). *The making of curriculum.* Bristol, PA: Falmer Press.

Goodson, I. F. (1999). The educational researcher as public intellectual. *British Educational Research Journal, 25*(3), 277–297.

Goodson, I. F., & Ball, S. (Eds.). (1985). *Defining the curriculum.* Bristol, PA: Falmer Press.

Gramsci, A. (1971). *Selections from the prison notebooks.* London: Lawrence & Wishart.

Green, B., & Bigum, C. (1993). Aliens in the classroom. *Australian Journal of Education, 37*(2), 119–141.

Grundy, S., & Bonser, S. (1997). Choosing to change: Teachers working with student outcome statements. *Curriculum Perspectives, 17*(1), 1–12.

Guskey, T. R. (1986). Staff development and the process of teacher change. *Educational Researcher, 15*(5), 5–12.

Gutierrez, C. (2000). Teaching and learning are complex and evolutionary but market forces can collide with quality practice [Review of *Change forces: The sequel*]. *Journal of Educational Change, 1*(2).

Habermas, J. (1972). *Knowledge and human interests.* Boston: Beacon Press.

Hall, G. (1988). The principal as leader of the change facilitating team. *Journal of Research and Development in Education, 22*(1), 49–59.

Hall, G. E., & Loucks, S. (1977). A developmental model for determining whether the treatment is actually implemented. *American Educational Research Journal, 14*(3), 263–276.

Hamilton, D. (1989). *Towards a theory of schooling.* Bristol, PA: Falmer Press.

Hansberry, L. (1959). *Raisin in the sun.* London: Samuel French.

Hargreaves, A. (1986). *Two cultures of schooling: The case of middle schools.* Bristol, PA: Falmer Press.

Hargreaves, A. (1989). *Curriculum and assessment reform.* Buckingham: Open University Press.

Hargreaves, A. (1994). *Changing teachers, changing times: Teachers' work and culture in the postmodern age.* New York: Teachers College Press.

Hargreaves, A. (1995). Towards a social geography of teacher education. In N. K. Shimahara & I. Z. Holowinsky (Eds.), *Teacher education in industrialized nations.* New York: Garland.

Hargreaves, A. (1996, Jan.–Feb.). Revisiting voice. *Educational Researcher,* pp. 1–8.

Hargreaves, A. (1997a). New ways to think about teachers and time. In N. E. Adelman, K. P. Walking-Eagle, & A. Hargreaves (Eds.), *Racing with the clock: Making time for teaching and learning in school reform* (pp. 79–88). New York: Teachers College Press.

Hargreaves, A. (1997b). Rethinking educational change: Going deeper and wider in the quest for success. In A. Hargreaves (Ed.), *Rethinking educational change with heart and mind: The 1997 ASCD yearbook.* Alexandria, VA: Association for Supervision and Curriculum Development.

Hargreaves, A. (1998a). Teachers' role in renewal. *Orbit, 29*(1), 10–13.

Hargreaves, A. (1998b). The emotions of teaching and educational change. In A. Hargreaves, M. Fullan, A. Lieberman, & D. Hopkins (Eds.), *The international handbook of educational change.* Norwell, MA: Kluwer.

Hargreaves, A. (1998c). The emotional politics of teaching and teacher development: With implications for educational leadership. *International Journal of Leadership in Education, 1*(4), 315–336.

Hargreaves, A. (1999). The psychic rewards (and annoyances) of classroom teaching. In M. Hammersley (Ed.), *Researching school experience: Ethnographic studies of teaching and learning* (pp. 87–106). Bristol, PA: Falmer Press.

Hargreaves, A. (2000). Four ages of professionalism and professional learning. *Teachers and Teaching: Theory and Practice, 6*(20), 151–182

Hargreaves, A. (forthcoming). Beyond anxiety and nostalgia: Building a social movement for educational change. *Phi Delta Kappan.*

Hargreaves, A. (forthcoming). Mixed emotions: Teachers' perceptions of their interactions with students. *Teaching and Teacher Education.*

Hargreaves, A., Baglin, E., Henderson, P., Leeson, P., & Tossell, T. (1988). *Personal and social education: Choices and challenges.* Oxford, England: Basil Blackwell.

Hargreaves, A., Beatty, B., Lasky, S., Schmidt, M., & Wilson, S. (forthcoming). *The emotions of teaching.* San Francisco: Jossey-Bass.

Hargreaves, A., Earl, L., & Ryan, J. (1996). *Schooling for change: Reinventing education for early adolescents.* Bristol, PA: Falmer Press.

Hargreaves, A., & Evans, R. (Eds.) (1997). *Beyond educational reform.* Buckingham: Open University Press.

Hargreaves, A., & Fink, D. (2000). Three dimensions of educational reform. *Educational Leadership, 57*(7), 30–34.

Hargreaves, A., & Fullan, M. (1998). *What's worth fighting for out there? Breaking down the walls of schooling.* New York: Teachers College Press.

Hargreaves, A., Leithwood, K., Gérin-Lajoie, D., Cousins, B. L., & Thiessen, D. (1993). *Years of transition: Times for change.* Final report of a project funded by the Ontario Ministry of Education. Toronto: Queen's Printer.

Hargreaves, A., Lieberman, A., Fullan, M., & Hopkins, D. (Eds.). (1998). *The international handbook of educational change.* Norwell, MA: Kluwer.

Hargreaves, A., & Moore, S. (2000). Educational outcomes, modern and postmodern interpretations: Response to Smyth and Dow. *British Journal of Sociology of Education, 21*(1), 27–42.

Hargreaves, D. (1982). *The challenge for the comprehensive school: Culture, curriculum and community.* New York: Routledge.

Haynes, N. (Ed.). (1998, Apr.). Changing schools for changing times: The Comer School development program. *A Special Issue of the Journal of Education for Students Placed at Risk.*

Helsby, G. (1999). *Changing teachers' work.* Bristol, PA: Open University Press.

Helsby, G., & Saunders, M. (1993). Taylorism, Tylerism, and performance indicators: Defending the indefensible? *Educational Studies, 19*(1), 55–77.

Hill, P. W., & Crévola, C. A. (1999). The role of standards in educational reform in the 21st century. In *Preparing our schools for the 21st century: The 1999 ASCD yearbook* (pp. 117–142). Alexandria, VA: Association for Supervision and Curriculum Development.

Hochschild, A. R. (1983). *The managed heart: Commercialization of human feeling.* Berkeley: University of California Press.

Hopfl, H., & Linstead, S. (1993). Passion and performance: Suffering and the carrying of organizational roles. In S. Fineman (Ed.), *Emotion in organizations.* Thousand Oaks, CA: Sage.

House, E. (1981). Three perspectives on innovation: Technological, political and cultural. In R. Lehming & M. Kane (1981), *Improving schools: Using what we know.* Thousand Oaks, CA: Sage.

Huberman, M. (1993). *The lives of teachers.* London: Cassell and New York: Teachers College Press.

Huberman, M., & Miles, M. (1984). *Innovation up close.* New York: Plenum.

Jeffrey, B., & Woods, P. (1996). Feeling deprofessionalized: The social construction of emotions during an OFSTED inspection. *Cambridge Journal of Education, 126*(3), 235–343.

Joyce, B., & Showers, B. (1988). *Student achievement through staff development.* White Plains, NY: Longman.

Kain, D. (1996). Recipes or dialogue? A middle school team conceptualizes "curricular integration." *Journal of Curriculum and Supervision, 11*(2), 163–187.

Khattri, N. (1995). How performance assessments affect teaching and learning. *Educational Leadership, 53*(3), 80–83.

King, J., & Evans, K. (1991, Oct.). Can we achieve outcome-based education? *Educational Leadership, 49*(2), 73–75.

Lave, J., & Wenger, E. (1991). *Situated learning: Legitimate peripheral participation.* Cambridge: Cambridge University Press.

Lawton, D. (1975). *Class, culture and curriculum.* New York: Routledge.

Leinhardt, G. (1992). What research on learning tells us about teaching. *Educational Leadership, 49*(7), 20–25.

Leithwood, K. A., Jantzi, D., & Steinbach, R. (1999). *Changing leadership for changing times.* Bristol, PA: Open University Press.

Lieberman, A. (1995). Restructuring schools: The dynamics of changing practice, structure and culture. In A. Lieberman (Ed.), *The work of restructuring schools: Building from the ground up.* New York: Teachers College Press.

Lieberman, A., & McLaughlin, M. (2000). Professional development in the United States: Policies and practices. *Prospects in Education.*

Lima, J. de (2000). Forgetting about friendship: Using conflict in teacher communities as a catalyst for school change. *Journal of Educational Change, 1*(3).

Linn, R., Baker, & Dunbar (1991). Complex performance-based assessment: Expectations and validation criteria. *Educational Researcher,* *20*(3), 15–21.

Little, J. W. (1990). The persistence of privacy: Autonomy and initiative in teachers' professional relations. *Teachers College Record, 91*(4), 509–536.

Little, J. W. (1993). Teachers' professional development in a climate of educational reform. *Educational Evaluation and Policy Analysis, 15*(2), 129–51.

Livingstone, D., Hart, D., & Davie, L. (1998). *Public attitudes toward education in Ontario, 1998: The twelfth OISE/UT survey.* Toronto: OISE/UT.

Lortie, D. (1975). *Schoolteacher: A sociological study.* Chicago: University of Chicago Press.

Macmillan, R. (2000). Leadership succession, culture of teaching, and educational change. In N. Bascia & A. Hargreaves (Eds.), *The sharp edge of educational change.* Bristol, PA: Falmer Press.

Manning, S., Freeman, S., & Earl, L. (1991). *Charting the voyage of planned educational change: Year one—The Scarborough Transition Years pilot projects.* Scarborough, Ontario: Scarborough Board of Education.

Marsh, M. (1999). Life inside a school: Implications for reform in the 21st century. In *Preparing our schools for the 21st century: The 1999 ASCD yearbook* (pp. 185–202). Alexandria, VA: Association for Supervision and Curriculum Development.

Marzano, R. J., Pickering, D., & McTighe, J. (1993). *Assessing student outcomes: Performance assessment using the dimensions of a learning model.* Alexandria, VA: Association for Supervision and Curriculum Development.

Maurer, R. (1996). *Beyond the wall of resistance.* Austin, TX: Bard Books.

McAdoo, M. (1998). Buying school reform: The Annenberg grant. *Phi Delta Kappan, 79*(5), 364–69.

McGilp, E. J., & Michael, M. (1994, July 3–6). *The home-school connection: Empowering the professional.* Paper presented at the 24th annual meeting of the Australian Teacher Education Association, Brisbane, Queensland, Australia.

McLaughlin, M. W. (1989). The RAND change agent study ten years later: Macro perspectives and micro realities. Paper based on address given at the annual meeting of the American Educational Research Association (San Francisco, CA, March 27).

McLaughlin, M., & Talbert, J. (1993). *Contexts that matter for teaching and learning.* Stanford University, CA: Center for Research on the Context of Secondary School Teachers.

McNeil, L. (2000). *Contradictions of reform.* New York: Routledge.

McTaggart, R. (1989). Bureaucratic rationality and the self-educating profession: The problem of teacher privatism. *Journal of Curriculum Studies, 21*(4), 345–361.

Meier, D. (1998). Authenticity and educational change. In A. Hargreaves, A. Lieberman, M. Fullan, & D. Hopkins (Eds.), *International handbook of educational change* (pp. 596–615). Norwell, MA: Kluwer.

Mestrovic, S. G. (1997). *Postemotional society.* London: Sage.

Metz, M. (1991). Real school: A universal drama amid disparate experience. In D. Mitchell & M. Gnesta (Eds.), *Education politics for the new century: The twentieth anniversary yearbook of the Politics of Education Association.* Bristol, PA: Falmer Press.

Mintzberg, H. (1994). *The rise and fall of strategic planning.* New York: Free Press.

Muller, C., & Kerbow, D. (1993). Parent involvement in the home, school and the community. In B. Schneider & J. S. Coleman (Eds.), *Parents, their children and schools* (pp. 13–42). Boulder, CO: Westview Press.

Muncey, D., & McQuillan, P. (1996). *Reform and resistance in schools and classrooms: A view of the Coalition of Essential Schools.* New Haven, CT: Yale University Press.

Murphy, R., & Broadfoot, P. (1995). *Effective assessment and the improvement of education: A tribute to Desmond Nuttall.* Bristol, PA: Falmer Press.

National Commission on Time and Learning. (1994). *Prisoners of time.* Washington, D.C.: U.S. Department of Education.

Newmann, F., & Wehlage, G. (1995). *Successful school restructuring.* Madison, WI: Center on Organization and Restructuring Schools.

Newmann, F., & Wehlage, G. (1996). *Authentic achievement: Restructuring schools for intellectual quality.* San Francisco: Jossey Bass.

Nias, J. (1989). *Primary teachers talking.* New York: Routledge.

Nias, J. (1991). Changing times, changing identities: Grieving for a lost self. In R. G. Burgess (Ed.), *Educational research and evaluation: For policy and practice.* Bristol, PA: Falmer Press.

Nias, J., Southworth, G., & Yeomans, A. (1989). *Staff relationships in the primary school.* London: Cassell.

Nieto, S. (1998). Cultural difference and educational change. In A. Hargreaves, M. Fullan, A. Lieberman, & D. Hopkins (Eds.), *International handbook of educational change.* Norwell, MA: Kluwer.

Nikiforuk, A. (1993). *School's out: The catastrophe in public education and what we can do about it.* Toronto: Macfarlane, Walter and Ross.

Noddings, N. (1992). *The challenge to care in schools.* New York: Teachers College Press.

Norton, R. (1988). Similarities between history-social science framework and English-language arts framework: What it means for elementary teachers. *Social Studies Review, 28*(1), 48–52.

Nuttall, D. (1994). Choosing indicators. In K. Riley & D. Nuttall (Eds.), *Measuring quality: Educational indicators, the United Kingdom and international perspectives.* Bristol, PA: Falmer Press.

Oakes, J., & Lipton, M. (1998). *Teaching to change the world*. New York: McGraw-Hill.

Oakes, J., Wells, A., Yonezawa, S., & Ray, K. (1997). Equity issues from detracking schools. In A. Hargreaves (Ed.), *Rethinking educational change with heart and mind: The 1997 ASCD yearbook*. Alexandria, VA: Association for Supervision and Curriculum Development.

Oatley, K. (1991). *Best laid schemes: The psychology of emotions*. Cambridge: Cambridge University Press.

O'Day, J., Goertz, M., & Floden, R. (1995). *Building capacity for educational reform*. Policy brief. Consortium for Policy Research in Education, Carriage House at the Eagleton Institute of Politics, Rutgers University.

Ontario Ministry of Education and Training. (1995). *The common curriculum: Policies and outcomes, Grades 1–9*. Toronto: Queen's Printer.

Ontario Ministry of Education and Training. (1997). *Ontario secondary schools: Discussion document*. Toronto: Queen's Printer.

Panaritis, P. (1995). Beyond brainstorming: Planning a successful interdisciplinary program. *Phi Delta Kappan, 76*(8), 623–628.

Pirsig, R. (1991). *Lila*. New York: Bantam Books.

Pliska, A., & McQuaide, J. (1994, Mar.). Pennsylvania's battle for student learning outcomes. *Educational Leadership,* 16–21.

Pollard, A., Broadfoot, P., Croll, P., Osborn, M., & Abbott, D. (1994). *Changing English primary schools: The impact of the Education Reform Act at key stage one*. London: Cassell.

Postman, N. (1995). *The end of education: Redefining the value of school*. New York: Vintage Books.

Rasinski, T., & Padak, N. (1995). *Curriculum integration in even start programs*. Occasional paper 5. (ERIC Document Reproduction Service No. ED 388 948.)

Ritzer, G. (1999). Enchanting a disenchanted world: Revolutionizing the means of consumption. Thousand Oaks, CA: Pin Forge Press.

Rosenholtz, S. (1989). *Teachers' workplace*. New York: Longman.

Rowan, B. (1994). Comparing teachers' work with work in other occupations: Notes on the professional status of teaching. *Educational Researcher, 23*(6), 4–17.

Rudduck, J. (1991). *Innovation and change: Developing involvement and understanding*. Philadelphia: Open University Press.

Rudduck, J., Day, J., & Wallace, G. (1997). Students' perspectives on school improvement. In A. Hargreaves (Ed.), *Rethinking educational change with heart and mind: The 1997 ASCD yearbook*. Alexandria, VA: Association for Supervision and Curriculum Development.

Ryan, J. (1995, June). *Organizing for teaching and learning in a culturally diverse school setting*. Paper prepared for the Annual Conference of the Canadian Society of the Study of Education.

Sabar, N., & Silberstein, M. (1998). Toward a more balanced curriculum: Multi-oriented curriculum structure in Israeli primary schools. *Journal of Curriculum and Supervision, 14*(1), 43–67.

Said, E. W. (1994). *Representations of the intellectual.* London: Vintage Books.

Sarason, S. (1971). *The culture of school and the problem of change.* Needham Heights, MA: Allyn & Bacon.

Sarason, S. (1990). *The predictable failure of educational reform.* San Francisco: Jossey-Bass.

Schlechty, P. (1990). *Schools for the twenty-first century: Leadership imperatives for educational reform.* San Francisco: Jossey-Bass.

Scruton, R., Ellis-Jones, A., & O'Keefe, D. (1985). *Education and indoctrination?* London: Sherwood Press.

Sergiovanni, T. J. (1990). *Moral leadership: Getting to the heart of school improvement.* San Francisco: Jossey-Bass.

Sergiovanni, T. J. (2000). *The lifeworld of leadership.* San Francisco: Jossey-Bass.

Shave, D. (1979). *Psychodynamics of the emotionally uncomfortable.* St. Louis, MO: Warren H. Green.

Sheppard, L. (1991). Psychometricians' beliefs about learning. *Educational Researcher, 20*(7), 2–16.

Shimahara, K., & Sakai, A. (1995). *Learning to teach in two cultures: Japan and the United States.* New York: Garland.

Shmerling, L. (1996). *Communication in the workplace.* Victoria, Australia: Macmillan Education.

Sikes, P. (1985). The life cycle of the teacher. In S. Ball & I. Goodson (Eds.), *Teachers' lives and careers.* Bristol, PA: Falmer Press.

Siskin, L. (1994). *Realms of knowledge.* Bristol, PA: Falmer Press.

Siskin, L. S. (1995). Subject divisions. In L. S. Siskin & J. W. Little (Eds.), *The subjects in question: Departmental organization and the high school* (pp. 23–47). New York: Teachers College Press.

Siskin, L. S., & Little, J. W. (Eds.). (1995). *The subjects in question: Departmental organization and the high school.* New York: Teachers College Press.

Smith, L. M., Dwyer, D. C., Prunty, J. J., & Kleine, P. F. (1987). *The fate of an innovative school.* Bristol, PA: Falmer Press.

Smith, W. J., Donahue, H., & Vibert, A. B. (1998). Student engagement in learning and school life: Case reports from project schools. In A. Vibert, J. Portelli, C. Shields, & L. LaRoque (Eds.), *Curriculum practice in elementary schools: Curriculum of life, voice and community.* Montreal, Quebec: Office of Research on Educational Policy, McGill University.

Smyth, J., & Dow, A. (1998). What's wrong with outcomes? Spotter planes, action plans, and steerage of the educational workplace. *British Journal of Sociology in Education, 19*(3), 291–303.

Sockett, H. (1989). *The moral base for teacher professionalism.* New York: Teachers College Press.

Spady, W. (1994). *Outcomes based education: Critical issues and answers.* Arlington, VA: American Association of School Administrators.

Spady, W., & Marshall, K. (1991). Beyond traditional outcomes-based education. *Educational Leadership, 49*(2), 67–72.

Spies, P. (1996). High school learning teams: Engaging and empowering students and teachers through interpersonal and interdisciplinary connections. *New Schools, New Communities, 12*(2), 45–51.

Stanl, S. A., & Miller, P. D. (1989). Whole language experience approaches for beginning reading: A quantitative research synthesis. *Review of Educational Research, 59*(1), 87–116.

Stiggins, R. (1991, Mar.). Assessment literacy. *Phi Delta Kappan, 72*(7), 534–539.

Stiggins, R. J. (1995). Assessment literacy for the 21st century. *Phi Delta Kappan, 77*(3), 238–245.

Stiggins, R. J. (1996). *Student centered classroom assessment.* Englewood Cliffs, NJ: Prentice Hall.

Stiggins, R. J., & Bridgeford, N. J. (1985). Ecology of classroom assessment. *Journal of Educational Measurement, 22*(4), 271–286.

Stoddart, T. (1999, Apr. 19–23). *Integrating science learning and language development.* Paper submitted in a symposium at the annual conference of the American Educational Research Association, Montreal, Canada.

Stodolsky, S. S. (1988). *The subject matters: Classroom activity in math and social studies.* Chicago: University of Chicago Press.

Stoll, L. (1999, Jan.). *Realizing our potential building capacity for lasting improvement.* Keynote presentation to the Twelfth International Congress for School Effectiveness and Improvement, San Antonio, TX.

Tharp, R., Dalton, S., & Yamauchi, L. (1994). Principles for culturally compatible Native American education. *Journal of American Education, 11*(3), 33–39.

Thomson, P. (1999). *Doing justice: Stories of everyday life in disadvantaged schools and neighbourhoods.* Unpublished doctoral dissertation, Deakin University, Australia.

Tom, A. (1983). *Teaching as a moral craft.* White Plains, NY: Longman.

Torrance, H. (1995). Investigating teacher assessment in infant classrooms: Methodological problems and emerging issues. *Assessment in Education, 2*(3), 305–320.

Torrance, H., & Pryor, J. (1998). *Investigating formative assessment: Teaching, learning and assessment in the classroom.* Bristol, PA: Falmer Press.

Troman, G., & Woods, P. (2000). Careers under stress: Teachers' adaptations at a time of intensive reform. *Journal of Educational Change, 1*(3).

Tucker, M. S., & Codding, J. B. (1998). *Standards for our schools: How to set them, measure them, and reach them.* San Francisco: Jossey-Bass.

Tucker, M. S., & Codding, J. B. (1999). Education and the demands of democracy in the next millennium. In D. D. Marsh (Ed.), *Preparing our schools for the 21st century: The 1999 ASCD yearbook* (pp. 25–44). Alexandria, VA: Association for Supervision and Curriculum Development.

Tunstall, P., & Gipps, C. (1996). Teacher feedback to young children in formative assessment: A typology. *British Educational Research Journal, 22*(4), 389–404.

Tyack, D., & Tobin, W. (1994). The grammar of schooling: Why has it been so hard to change? *American Educational Research Journal, 31*(3), 453–480.

Tye, B. (1985). Multiple realities: A study of 13 American high schools. Lanham, MD,: University Press of America.

Vincent, C. (1996). *Parents and teachers: Power and participation.* Bristol, PA: Falmer Press.

Wallace, M. (1991). Flexible planning: A key to the management of multiple innovations. *Educational Management and Administration, 19*(3), 180–192.

Wang, M., Haertel, G., & Walberg, H. (1998). *Achieving student success: A handbook of widely implemented research-based educational reform models.* Philadelphia: Temple University Center for Research in Human Development and Education.

Webb, R., & Vulliamy, G. (1993). A deluge of directives: Conflict between collegiality and managerialism in the post-ERA primary school. *British Education Research Journal, 22*(4), 441–458.

Werner, W. (1988). Program implementation and experienced time. *Alberta Journal of Educational Research, 34*(2), 90–108.

Whitford, B. L. (2000). Commitment and compliance: High stakes consequences in Kentucky. *Journal of Educational Change, 1*(1), 107–112.

Whitty, G., Power, S., & Halpin, D. (1998). *Devolution and choice in education: The school, the state and the market.* Melbourne, Australia: Open University Press.

Wideen, M., Mayer-Smith, J., & Moon, B. (1996). Knowledge, teacher development and change. In I. Goodson & A. Hargreaves (Eds.), *Teachers' professional lives.* Bristol, PA: Falmer Press.

Wiggins, G., & McTighe, J. (1998). *Understanding by design.* Alexandria, VA: Association for Supervision and Curriculum.

Wilson, R. (1990). Classroom processes in evaluating student achievement. *Alberta Journal of Educational Research, 36*(1), 4–17.

Woloszyk, C. (1996). *Vocational education's linkages with the business community of Michigan.* East Lansing: Michigan Center for Career and Technical Education.

Woodhead, C. (1995). *Education—the elusive engagement and continuing frustration.* Times Educational Supplement: First Annual Lecture to Her Majesty's Chief Inspectors.

Woods, P. (1993). *Critical events in teaching and learning.* Bristol, PA: Falmer Press.

Woods, P., Jeffrey, B., Troman, G., & Boyle, M. (1997). *Restructuring schools, reconstructing teachers.* Bristol, PA: Open University Press.

Wraga, W. (1997). Patterns of interdisciplinary curriculum organization and professional knowledge of the curriculum field. *Journal of Curriculum and Supervision, 12*(2), 98–117.

Wylie, C. (1997). *Self-managing schools seven years on: What have we learnt?* Wellington: New Zealand Council for Educational Research.

Wyn, J. (1994). Continuing inequalities into new times, in J. Kenway (Ed.), *Schooling what future? Balancing the education agenda* (pp. 101–112). Deakin, Australia: Deakin Centre for Education and Change, Deaking University.

Zlatos, B. (1993, Sept.). Outcomes-based outrage. *Executive Educator, 15*(9), 12–16.

Index

Professional community culture, 165–169
Professional development. *See* Teacher professional development
Professional discretion, 174–175
Prunty, J. J., 159
Pryor, J., 54, 55

R

A Raisin in the Sun (film), 95
Rasinski, T., 111
Ray, K., 129
"The Real Game" unit of study, 90, 92
Ritzer, G., 59
Robertson, H.-J., 88
Rosenholtz, S., 165, 166
Rubrics orthodoxy, 2
Rudduck, J., 4, 5, 39, 165
Ryan, J., 4, 57, 58

S

Sabar, N., 86
Said, E., 102
Sakai, A., 144
Sarason, S., 115, 164
Saunders, M., 46
Schlechty, P., 1, 87
School architecture, 162–163
Schooling for Change (Hargreaves), 168
School leadership: cultural and emotional, 177–180; intellectual, 176–177; role in educational change by, 175–176; strategic, 180–181. *See also* Administration
School structures: cultures of collaboration and, 166–169; educational change0 support by, 160–165; emotional work and, 144–147
Scruton, R., 83
Sergiovanni, T. J., 5, 9, 21, 124
Shave, D., 123
Sheppard, L., 54
Shimahara, N. K., 144
Shmerling, L., 89
Showers, B., 170

Sikes, P., 152
Silberstein, M., 86
Simulations curriculum, 101
Siskin, L., 103, 104, 159
Smith, L. M., 159
Smith, W. J., 85
Smyth, J., 23, 46
Sockett, H., 124
Southworth, G., 38
Space structure (school), 162–163
Spady, W., 17
Special needs students. *See* Learning-disabled students
Spies, P., 84
Standards-based curriculum: contradictory contexts of, 7–8; criticisms of, 20–24; current practices of, 4–5; deprofessionalism and, 6–7; difficulties with integration of, 21–22; focus of, 17–18; learning-disabled students and, 49; moving beyond, 9–11; teacher confronting contradictions in, 63–65
Standards/outcomes agenda: beliefs basic to, 19–20; as challenge to traditional approach, 18–19; content and performance standards of, 20–21; curriculum defined by, 17–18; of educational change, 185–187; focus of, 17; traditional vs., 19. *See also* Learning outcomes
Steinbach, R., 132
Stiggins, R. J., 50, 52, 53, 55, 82
Stoddart, T., 5
Stodolsky, S. S., 103
Stoll, L., 159
Strategic leadership, 180–181
Students: assessing and reporting of outcomes by, 60–63; assessment and relations of teachers with, 70–74; authentic assessment role by, 54; curriculum and personal development/relationships of, 92–97; emotional relationships between teachers and, 139–144;

involved in planning outcomes, 39–41; political perspective of assessment and, 55–56; postmodern perspective of assessment and, 58–60; teacher-parent communication on, 65–70. *See also* Learning-disabled students; Learning outcomes

T

Talbert, J., 103, 165, 182
Teacher culture, 165–169
Teacher discretion, 19
Teacher professional development: change support through, 169–174; educational change and, 131–134
Teachers: advantages of curriculum integration for, 84; affective assessment challenges for, 75–77; assessing and reporting of outcomes by, 60–61; assessment and relationship between parents and, 65–70; assessment and relations of students with, 70–74; authentic assessment role by, 54; challenges of technical assessment for, 53; confronting curriculum contradictions, 63–65; on cumbersome outcomes, 28–29; curriculum reform study focus on, 11–14; using curriculum relevant to work, 87–92; developing assessment repertoire by, 74–80; educational reform thinking by, 124–134; emotional resonance vs. rationality of planning outcomes by, 35–36, 46–47; emotional work of, 136–156; enhancing student personal development by, 92–97; impact of standard-based curriculum on, 23–24; intellectual functions of, 121; involving parents in planning outcomes, 41–44, 47–48; involving students in planning outcomes, 39–41; on measuring

outcomes, 29–30; on modifying learning outcomes, 30–32; of Ontario educational system, 11; planning collaboration between, 36–39; on planning outcomes, 33–44; political perspective of assessment and, 55–57; public underestimation of, 48; questioning of assessment by, 77–80; reaction to National Curriculum by, 6, 46; reform difficulties faced by, 134; response to standards-based curriculum by, 6–7; role in implementing curriculum integration, 103–106; on vague learning outcomes, 25–28
Teaching: change support and culture of, 165–169; emotional work of planning, 153–155; emotional work and structure of, 144–147; emotions and pedagogy strategies used in, 147–153; implications of emotional work for, 155–156
Technical perspective: of assessment, 51–53; of educational change, 116–117
Tharp, R., 5, 85
Thomson, P., 8
Time resources, 170–171
Times Educational Supplement (England), 8
Tobin, W., 115, 145, 159, 164
Tom, A., 124
Torrance, H., 52, 54, 55
Troman, G., 6
Tucker, M. S., 1, 4, 5, 19
Tuck Everlasting, 94
Tunstall, P., 50
Tyack, D., 115, 145, 159, 164
Tye, B., 147

U

University of Toronto, 11

V

Vague learning outcomes, 25–28, 45–46

Verisimilitude principle, 101
Vibert, A. B., 85
Vincent, C., 43, 65
Vulliamy, G., 128

W

Wahlberg, H., 84
Walking-Eagle, K. P., 164
Wallace, G., 4
Wallace, M., 46
Wang, M., 84
"War and Peace," 96
Webb, R., 128, 165
Wehlage, G., 162, 165
Wells, A., 129
Wenger, E., 5
Werner, W., 125
Whitford, B. L., 8, 158
Whitty, G., 8

Wideen, M., 170
Wiggins, G., 51, 53, 54
Wilson, R., 65
Wolf et al., 50
Woloszyk, C., 89
Woodhead, C., 148
Woods, P., 6, 101, 128, 129, 158, 166, 175
Wraga, W., 85
Wylie, C., 8, 20
Wyn, J., 88, 92

Y

Yamauchi, L., 5, 85
Yeomans, A., 38
Yonezawa, S., 129

Z

Zlatos, B., 18, 24, 36